Secularism and Biblical Studies

*BibleWorld*
*Series Editor:* Philip R. Davies and James G. Crossley, University of Sheffield

*BibleWorld* shares the fruits of modern (and postmodern) biblical scholarship not only among practitioners and students, but also with anyone interested in what academic study of the Bible means in the twenty-first century. It explores our ever-increasing knowledge and understanding of the social world that produced the biblical texts, but also analyses aspects of the Bible's role in the history of our civilization and the many perspectives – not just religious and theological, but also cultural, political and aesthetic – which drive modern biblical scholarship.

# SECULARISM AND BIBLICAL STUDIES

Edited by

Roland Boer

LONDON   OAKVILLE

Published by Equinox Publishing Ltd.
UK: 1 Chelsea Manor Studios, Flood Street, London, SW3 5SR
USA: DBBC, 28 Main Street, Oakville, CT 06779

www.equinoxpub.com

First published 2010

British Library Cataloguing-in-Publication Data

A catalogue record for this book is available from the British Library.

ISBN-13  978 1 84553 374 8  (hardback)
         978 1 84553 375 5  (paperback)

Library of Congress Cataloging-in-Publication Data
Secularism and biblical studies / edited by Roland Boer.
    p. cm. — (BibleWorld)
  Includes bibliographical references and index.
   ISBN 978-1-84553-374-8 (hb) — ISBN 978-1-84553-375-5 (pb) 1.
Secularization (Theology) 2.  Secularism. 3.  Bible—Criticism,
interpretation, etc.  I. Boer, Roland, 1961-
BT83.7.S44 2008
220.601—dc22
                              2007037245

Typeset by S.J.I. Services, New Delhi
Printed and bound in Great Britain by Lightning Source UK Ltd, Milton Keynes

# CONTENTS

# LIST OF CONTRIBUTORS

*Yairah Amit*, Tel Aviv University, Israel

*Hector Avalos*, Iowa State University, Ames, Iowa, USA

*Jacques Berlinerblau*, Georgetown University, Washington DC, USA

*Ward Blanton*, University of Glasgow, Scotland

*Roland Boer*, University of Newcastle, Australia

*Athalya Brenner*, University of Amsterdam, the Netherlands

*Mark G. Brett*, Whitley College, Melbourne, Australia

*Philip Chia*, Chinese University of Hong Kong, Hong Kong

*Edgar W. Conrad*, University of Queensland, Australia

*Philip Davies*, University of Sheffield, England

*Michael V. Fox*, University of Wisconsin-Madison, Madison, USA

*Niels Peter Lemche*, University of Copenhagen, Denmark

*Joseph A. Marchal*, Ball State University, Muncie, Indiana, USA

*Heike Omerzu*, University of Copenhagen, Denmark

*Todd Penner*, Austin College, Sherman, Texas, USA

*Hanna Stenström*, Svenska Kyrkans Forskningsenhet (Research Unit of the Church of Sweden), Stockholm, Sweden

# INTRODUCTION: SECULARISM AND THE BIBLE

*Roland Boer\**

What is secular biblical criticism? Each of the essays gathered in this collection seeks to answer this disarmingly simple question. Rather than take up a position (which I do in my manifesto a little later), in this introduction I seek to map out some of the issues at stake. The issues fall into two groups: those that swirl around the terms secularism and secularization, and then those that explore the nature of biblical criticism.

## Varieties of Secularism

Secularism, as many will know, is contested ground. The essays here take various positions on what secularism might mean. Now, while I loathe to judge those different takes one way or another, it is worthwhile doing a little etymological legwork. "Secularism" comes from the Latin *saeculum* (adjective, *saecularis*), and it designates an age or era, or the spirit of an age. As far as the English term is concerned, it was first coined by a certain George Holyoake in the middle of the nineteenth century after a stint in prison for blasphemy (yes, there once was a time when many of the views expressed in this volume would have landed the author a short, sharp burst in gaol). Drawing up the Latin sense of the word *saeculum*, secularism means *a system of thought and a way of living that draws its terms purely from this age and from this world*. Note that it is a positive term, and not, as so many seem to think, a negative one. It does, of course, have an implied negative: secularism does not draw its ultimate reference point from what is beyond this world, whether that is a god or the gods above, or a time in the future, or indeed a text like the Bible that spends a good deal of time talking about both.[1]

If secularism designates a certain perspective on the world, indeed a worldview, then secularization designates the way in which secularism takes place. In other words, secularization is usually understood as the long and winding road along which we have gradually replaced our ultimate reference points on the world beyond with our present world. One after another, our cultural and social assumptions – all the way from the black cat that crosses our path to the purpose of sex – have gradually moved away from a transcendent reference. Despite the odd hurdle and ditch, secularization is generally taken as an inevitable process, at least since the Enlightenment.

I suggest that these senses are basic to understanding secularism and secularization. Immediately, someone may object: what about the anti-religious element of secularism? What about the separation of church and state? And what about the nature of intellectual inquiry? Each of these – secularism as an anti-religious programme, the separation of church and state, and intellectual inquiry – are secondary or derivative features of the senses of secularism and secularization I have just outlined. Elsewhere I have argued that each of these secondary features of secularism are riven with paradoxes, so much so that the programme of secularism as we know it is deeply flawed. But that is another argument.[2]

Let me take each of these secondary senses of secularism in turn. The assumption that secularism is by definition separate from religion has become widespread, so much so that it has crept into some dictionary definitions. Thus, as Philip Davies points out in his essay, *The Chambers Dictionary* defines secularism as "the belief that the state, morals, education, etc. should be independent of religion".[3] For many, secularism is taken to be opposed to religion, or at least religious commitment. Now, this is one negative outcome of the basic sense that I outlined above. At times, this position moves on to argue that atheism and secularism go hand in hand. This anti-religious position may follow from secularism, it may even be an implication of it, but then we come up against the problem of religious secularists who see no contradiction in holding both religion and secularism together. Mark Brett's essay in this volume takes such a position, arguing that secularism is in fact the basis for religious tolerance. According to this position, secularism actually arose as an effort to deal with the religious conflict between Roman Catholics and Protestants in Europe. No one religion should lord it over another, and the only way to ensure such tolerance is to insist on a secular society that favours none. But what has really happened with this argument for religious secularism is that it slips in another secondary feature of secularism, namely the separation of church and state, to which I now turn.

Although they obviously overlap in some respects, the independence from religion and the separation of church and state are separate issues. Among the most well-known version of the separation of church and state is the First Amendment of the Constitution of the United States. The relevant section reads: "Congress shall make no law respecting an establishment of religion, or prohibiting the free exercise thereof". While it may initially have been a response after the American War of Independence to the established Church of England, it has been subsequently interpreted as any act by the Congress and the legislature that should be seen to foster one religion at the expense of another. The issue has come up again and again in the area of state-funded education: the Bible should not be taught, prayer is not appropriate and one cannot teach religious doctrines in state schools. Nothing shows up the tension more than the battle to have "intelligent design" taught as a scientific alternative to evolutionary theory. While the advocates of intelligent design argue that the theory is scientific and not religious theory, the courts keep deciding otherwise, persistently keeping the theory of intelligent design out of public schools.

The catch is that in the United States we come up against a paradox: the more strictly the courts apply the First Amendment, the more religion pervades public life. Looking in from the outside, I cannot help but notice that religion saturates public life in the USA, from the founding biblical myth of the escape from oppression to a land of freedom to the sharp polarization over religion in the Bible Belt where one is either passionately Christian or passionately atheist. Both are, of course, religious positions. A different but comparable paradox shows up in France, especially over the issue of *hijab* (literally "modesty"), a covering or veil, by Muslim women. On the one hand, the French doctrine of *Laïcité* – according to which the government must not support any religious position, including atheism[4] – led to the law of 15 March 2004 that bans overtly religious dress and signs in public or state-run schools. While the law does not state what items of clothing or signs are to be banned – it may well be Sikh turbans, Christian crosses or Jewish skullcaps – the issue that sparked the law was the *hijab* for Muslim women, or more specifically the *khimer* or headscarf. This is where the paradox shows up: allowing the *hijab* is an exercise of religious toleration and freedom; banning the *hijab* asserts the non-religious nature of French public institutions. Both positions are consistent with the separation of church and state, and yet both cannot exist together.

What has all this got to do with biblical studies? As an intellectual discipline, biblical criticism is intimately involved in the third derivative category of secularism: intellectual inquiry should operate in a secular manner. Quite simply, the claim that biblical criticism should be "scientific" is a claim that it should be a secular discipline like any other. A discipline is "scientific" if it makes use of evidence and develops its hypotheses and theories on the basis of such evidence, not on any divine revelation. Biblical criticism is thus concerned with the hard data of textual manuscripts, history, archaeological artefacts and other pieces of empirical evidence. Divine forces or influences, indeed matters of faith, are not viable categories of scientific inquiry. In fact, for some proponents of this position, such theological matters act as a hindrance to proper inquiry. There is a history behind such a secular biblical criticism. In one sense it is quite old. Did not "higher criticism" in the nineteenth century claim to be scientific and secular? Was this not part of its scandal? Even more, secular biblical criticism was a late arrival in the club of secular intellectual disciplines.

As more than one scholar has pointed out, all of the disciplines we now practice grew from the seedbed of theology and biblical studies. One by one, from anthropology to literary criticism, they peeled off from theology and biblical studies to gain their independence. For example, anthropology struggled for a long time to throw off the shackles of biblical models. For this reason, Lewis Henry Morgan's *Ancient Society* was such a revolutionary text, since it broke with the biblical narrative of the development of family and society.[5] Morgan has a good deal to say about the Bible, but mostly in order to undermine the dominant assumptions of anthropology. Modern biblical criticism followed suit, although it was more of a case of self-surgery than something like anthropology. In seeking to become a secular discipline, biblical studies sought to free itself from itself. Or rather, it tried to break away from the control of theological categories and assumptions.

The catch with such an attempt to create a secular biblical criticism is that it is by no means complete, as more than one contributor to this volume points out. Indeed, biblical criticism faces a paradox (which I would argue is part of the paradox of secularism). A substantial number, if not most biblical scholars, live double lives: while they undertake their secular "scientific" research by excluding matters of religious commitment, they simultaneously attend a church or synagogue on the weekend. Even more, many of the students they teach, whether in secular universities or in theological colleges, often train for some form of ministry in church or synagogue. Of course, the way such a paradox manifests itself varies from place to place: the situation in Serbia is different from China, as is that in Scandinavia from Australia.

In order to overcome this paradox, many of the contributors to this volume argue that the full secularization of biblical criticism is yet to be achieved. Their challenge takes various forms, such as pointing to the paradox I have just outlined, or arguing that what appears to be a secular biblical criticism has been domesticated by the church, or that biblical criticism as we know it is not yet truly secular, or that what was a secular biblical criticism has been eroded by biblical scholars who allow their religious faith to affect their work.

Why, then, has this debate over secular biblical studies erupted once again? Is it because biblical criticism as a whole has shuffled towards a more conservative position (although it has always been quite conservative)? Has the religious right, especially in the USA with regard to the Society of Biblical Literature, decided to storm this citadel as well? Is it because the old programme of secularism is itself flawed and riven with paradoxes, as I have argued elsewhere? Or is one reason for the re-emergence of this debate due to something else?

## Post-Secularism

The last question is somewhat rhetorical, for the debate is both a response to and a sign of what has come to be known, for better or worse, as post-secularism. As for post-secularism, two features are worth noting: first, post-secularism is a wholesale critique and re-assessment of secularism; second, it is the flowering of a multitude of spiritualities and, in the last few years, of religion itself.[6] That is to say, the "post" of post-secularism has both critical and historical dimensions. If the critical element has highlighted the paradoxes of the old programme of secularism, the historical element traces the way our intellectual landscape has changed.

In the historical narrative of post-secularism we can mark out two phases: the earlier one is the sprouting like mushrooms after rain of myriad private spiritualities, and the more recent one is the forceful return of religion on the public and global stage. Each one is a distinct moment. As for the various spiritualities – ranging all the way from crystals and pyramids to humming the sacred syllable while meditating – we can look back to the 1960s and 70s when hippie culture and the alternative lifestyle movement sought out alternative religious practices that had been buried for so long under a dominant Christian culture. Here we find the stirrings of interest in indigenous religions, astrology, various forms of Buddhism, the Tao and

Hinduism and so on, all adapted and moulded for newer purposes. Before we rush in to blame the 60s for our problems, it is worth pointing out that the spiritualities we have now are really a betrayal of the counter-cultural wave. For what happened is that all too soon these spiritualities were absorbed into capitalism in its perpetual search for what is new and different: the spiritualities became big business. So they shifted their focus to the private individual and the inner life. That strange inner peace became a distinctly private affair. Soon we found all manner of spiritual entrepreneurs, selling insights into one's past life or the future, offering massages that aligned one's inner poles, reading the stars and Tarot over a latte, or offering a bewildering range of items at the local incense-laden shop.

By the 1990s one could be spiritual in all sorts of ways, which came to mean that you could pick and choose from supposed ancient practices or from whatever new type of spirituality that happened to appear. Eclectic, private, free from political as well as institutional connections, these spiritualities both battered secularism like a storm in a gale and yet adhered to one of its fundamental features. Their rise was and is a challenge to secularism, and yet at a deep level they respect secularism. What I mean here is that they maintained the idea that any spiritual or religious belief should be a private affair and should not be broadcast over the airwaves or influence one's exercise of public office. All the same, these spiritualities constituted the first major signal of what came to be called post-secularism, for they both built upon and reacted to secularism.

The private nature of spirituality came to an abrupt halt when a couple of planes happened to bump into the World Trade Centre in New York on 11 September, 2001. Less a cause of change than a signal of a change that was already underway, what the attack indicated in a stark and clear fashion was that religion itself and not merely spirituality was back on the public, political and global agenda. In the last decade or so religion has appeared in all manner of ways, from rhetoric of the "axis of evil" and the "evil empire" invoked by President George W. Bush of the United States in order to designate various enemies, through vilification of Muslims by politicians in places like Australia or Denmark in what has become the new version of anti-Semitism, to the rediscovery by thoroughly secular states of their Christian heritage by people who haven't seen the inside of a church since cousin Johnny was baptised. This last point is endlessly fascinating (and a little frightening). Even in the most secularized societies, there has been a sharp recovery of the idea that "Western" society is based on biblical and Christian values, that the Bible is its founding document, if you will. Of course, this recovery has much to do with the perceived threat of Islam. For example, confident, robust and open societies across Western Europe once brought in workers from the Middle East, most of them Muslims, to do the jobs that no-one else wanted to do. These people settled, brought their families, and had children. Yet today the countries that first actively encouraged these immigrants have become afraid. I have little sympathy with the politics of fear, the touting of a so-called "terrorist" attack, since I have about as much chance of drowning in my bath as I have of dying in a bomb attack. The threat may be largely a fiction, but the fear is real – even if it is the manifestation of a host of other fears such as climate change or economic collapse. So in response to that fear we find assertions of the essentially Christian nature of the West by people who barely know who Abraham was (or was not).

With the return of religion, we find a move from the eminently private affair of spirituality to the public and political nature of religion. In the midst of these changes, the Bible has made a spectacular return to the public arena. All the straws in the wind point to a revival, in all manner of senses, of interest in the Bible. At the level of global politics, tensions between the "religions of the book" have reached levels not seen for a good many years, if not centuries. The Bible is once again gunpowder on a geopolitical scale, as politicians scramble to ease the tensions between Christian, Muslim and Jewish majority states. At a more local level, there is talk of religious revival, especially in the United States, with the Third or Fourth (depending on your method of counting) Great Awakening. And this revival is of a distinctly conservative, "Bible-believing" type with all the usual paraphernalia of "family values".

In other countries that do not have that curious history of the United States, the Bible is creeping back as a founding document. Biblical scholars, as they peer up from their texts in Hebrew, Greek, Latin, Aramaic and so on, blink in the spotlights suddenly thrown on them as they are called upon to answer questions of global significance. What role has the Bible played in the current global struggles? Is it a violent text, or is it the foundation of "family values"? Is it the basis of what is called Western culture and "democracy"? Do you need to believe in God to be able to understand it? What was once a quaint and esoteric discipline (all those languages!) has now become a skill in demand in order to understand a time of troubles, as the Russians like to call it. For there is a suspicion, among sundry politicians, commentators, policy makers and newspaper editors, that the Bible may well have some role to play in our current situation of global fear. There are, then, two features of post-secularism, one a critical perspective on secularism (especially its paradoxes) and the other a historical shift to spiritualities and religion itself. This, I would suggest, is the context for the various positions debated and taken in this collection (as it is the context of the related and very public debate over atheism and religion that crowds the bookstores, newspapers and airwaves and which is carried on by the likes of Richard Dawkins and all manner of imitators). Is biblical criticism a secular discipline? Does the programme of secular biblical studies need to be reasserted or reclaimed? Or do we permit all manner of spiritual, religious and political readings? It should not be at all surprising that these issues are at the forefront today.

## Biblical Studies

There are more than enough efforts to map biblical studies, so I won't spend an inordinate amount of time doing it yet again. If I stand on my mythical scholarly height, then I can espy a number of fields of debate and conflict. On one side the die-hard historical critical scholars are under pressure from the literary (or "postmodern") scholars. Depending upon whom you happen to ask, the conflict may be between critical scholarship and dilettantes, or between serious and cute biblical studies, or even between what is well-tried over against flimsy and whimsical work. Then again, another might describe these debates of the last three decades as a struggle between tired and worn-out historical criticism and the innovative questions opened by literary criticism, or even between historical and non-historical scholarships. Yet another may speak of the insular and parochial versus the broad-minded nature of newer approaches.

Shifting my gaze to another part of the field, the contest seems to be quite different. Here we find a vigorous effort by a smallish group of "minimalists" to overturn the positions of the "maximalists". The struggle here is over the Hebrew Bible, how reliable it is for historical reconstruction (hardly at all for the minimalists and quite a bit for the maximalists), when it might have been written (very late for the minimalists and a good deal earlier for the maximalists), and how to read archaeological evidence. An observer on the hill can't help notice that the sceptical minimalists have mostly European accents while the maximalists tend to speak with the strange nasal drawl of North Americans. Depending upon whom you ask, we have here a debate between non-scholarship and real scholarship, or between critical Europeans and those all too conservative Americans. A comparable struggle in New Testament studies is the notorious Jesus Seminar. Based in the USA, the seminar still causes waves with its effort to identify the genuine sayings of Jesus and publish them in red-letter text.

The result: 16 percent of the sayings in the Gospels are genuine. In the USA, the Jesus Seminar looks for all the world like the New Testament version of the minimalists. There scholars and churches still cry out, "so little". Not so in Europe, where the response was, "so much!" For many Europeans, the seminar seemed like a version of the maximalists.

In another part of the field there are all sorts of confused and confusing skirmishes. A tight knot of Marxists take on the large and docile mob of bourgeois biblical critics, the feminists encircle the men who have shaped and continue to dominate the discipline, the queer lobby takes on the hetero-normatives, and the postcolonials rail at the use of Bible at the hands of the faded British Empire, bankrupt Eurocentrism and the stumbling American Empire. For their part the cultural critics are busy looking for a bottle of wine and a cinema to see what the hell Mel Gibson is up to with his latest film, while the theory heads are trying to decide what Lacan or Žižek or Kristeva or Irigaray or Agamben might have to say about all of this.

Needless to say, the view from my hill is more complex than this, for the occasional Marxist may be a historical critic; so may the odd feminist or postcolonial critic. One or two might switch sides, responding to a Damascus-road experience and taking up a minimalist position, or perhaps a queer approach after years of historical critical study. Or one of the postmodern bunch may simply tire of all that new stuff and go back to the old friend of historical critical study.

But then, in a corner of the field that has been hidden from view for quite some time, there appears a new debate. Or rather, it is an old debate that has gained new life. And that is the one between secular and anti-secular biblical critics. This struggle may take various forms as well. For some, it is a debate between those who have a religious faith and those who do not, between those motivated to study the Bible due to religious convictions and those who do so for literary, historical and cultural reasons. For others, it is a struggle between those who rely on a transcendent category in order to interpret the Bible and those who draw their terms purely from this world. And yet for others, it is a question of which worldview is appropriate. When it becomes heated, all manner of charges fly about – pseudo-scholarship, non-scholarship, the abandonment of reason, confusion and so on.

This secular debate also cuts across the other debates in biblical studies. Among those arguing for some form of secular biblical studies, we find a motley coalition. Some are primarily historical critics, others literary or "postmodern" critics. Some may be minimalists (there are no overt maximalists in this collection), others may have dabbled in Marxist, queer, feminist or postcolonial biblical criticism. In their work they may focus primarily on historical questions (Niels Peter Lemche, Philip Davies) with only a passing interest in theory, or they may have produced deeply literary readings of biblical texts (Michael V. Fox, Edgar Conrad). Then again, they may seek out the role of a public intellectual in very different contexts, whether in the USA (Jacques Berlinerblau) or in China (Philip Chia), or they may have made contributions in feminist criticism (Athalya Brenner, Hanna Stenström and Joseph Marchal). After an immersion in critical theory they may have embraced postcolonial criticism (Mark Brett), or perhaps moved from historical criticism to take up something like reader-response approaches (Edgar Conrad). Others may seek to work from within to challenge and reshape historical critical assumptions in light of more recent theoretical concerns (Todd Penner and Heike Omerzu). Still others may take up questions of ethnicity, race and disability studies to challenge the way both historical reconstruction and reception of the Bible are understood (Hector Avalos). However, they all agree that the problem of secularism and biblical studies is an urgent and important one. The way they deal with the problem varies, sometimes considerably, and the answers offered cover a wide range.

In these myriad overlays, I have decided to structure the collection as follows. The essays and positions gathered here represent the confluence of four streams. The first stream comes from a debate that first flared on the Society of Biblical Literature Forum (www.sbl-site.org). Michael V. Fox and Jacques Berlinerblau set a bomb under the Forum, which is still having repercussions as I write. Revised versions of those earlier contributions to the Forum appear here. Hector Avalos also threw himself into the fray, but I have placed his essay in another section, "The End of Biblical Studies" (see below). The second tributary was a session at the International Meeting of the Society of Biblical Literature in Edinburgh in 2006. Under the expert eyes of Caroline van der Stichele and Todd Penner papers were presented at a session that went under the banner of my "Manifesto for Biblical Studies". In this event Hanna Stenström, Mark Brett, Todd Penner and Niels Peter Lemche engaged in a lively and critical response to the manifesto, pulling it to pieces and reassembling some of it. Revised versions of the original manifesto and their responses appear here.

Our third stream was another session in Edinburgh, again under the auspices of Caroline van der Stichele and Todd Penner, this time with the title "The End of Biblical Studies?" Here Hector Avalos presented a version of the essay that appears in this volume (an earlier version appeared on the

SBL Forum). Joining the fray were Heike Omerzu, Philip Chia and Joseph Marshall. Heike Omerzu and Joseph Marchal's papers appeared, albeit in shorter versions than here, after the Edinburgh conference on the SBL Forum.

Finally, the fourth rivulet is comprised of four pieces commissioned for this collection – those by Ward Blanton, Edgar Conrad, Athalya Brenner, Yairah Amit and Philip Davies. All five have been interested in the question of a secular biblical criticism for some time. The essays by Conrad, Brenner and Amit are really case studies, one a look back to his place of birth in the USA and what has happened to the Bible there, and the other two dealing with the contemporary situation in Israel where Bible and state come into contact with one another. Last, but by no means least, Philip Davies' essay has its own agenda, which is to argue for a secularism deeply embedded within the Bible. Reminiscent of Ernst Bloch's *Atheism in Christianity*, Davies tracks this secular current within the Bible to overturn the argument that a secular program of scholarship is foreign to the Bible. Not at all, he argues. Rather, one based on religious commitment is the intruder. Philip Davies has, of course, published earlier work on these matters, most notably and controversially his *Whose Bible Is It Anyway?* (1995), and his essay here is in many respects an addendum to that earlier work.[7] I mention Davies for another reason too: he was the one who commissioned this collection in the first place, so thanks are due to him (yet again). The reader will find no uniform position on secularism and biblical studies in these pages – an approach that was first mooted as a way to approach this collection. In the end, it seemed to me far better to let the various voices speak, to take up differing positions and questions for debate. Yet all of us agree that the issue is an important one, since it has a direct bearing on the way we understand and undertake our work as biblical scholars. Finally, I owe a deep debt to Mark Crees for his careful work on this collection. Without his assistance it would not have seen the light of day.

## Endnotes

[*] Roland Boer is Research Professor in Humanities and Social Science at the University of Newcastle, Australia.

1. Note that the influential works of Hans Blumenberg and Karl Löwith postulate a secularism that eschews any reference to a better future, whether eschatological, utopian or whatever. See Hans Blumenberg, *The Legitimacy of the Modern Age* (trans. R.M. Wallace; Cambridge, MA: MIT, 1966), and Karl Löwith, *Meaning in History: Theological Implications of the Philosophy of History* (Chicago, IL: University of Chicago Press, 1949).

2. Roland Boer, *Rescuing the Bible, Blackwell Manifestos* (Oxford: Blackwell, 2007), pp. 6–32.
3. Chambers, *The Chambers Dictionary* (Edinburgh: Chambers Harrap, 2003), p. 1371.
4. The First Article of the French Constitution reads: "La France est une République, unie, indivisible, laïque et sociale".
5. Lewis Henry Morgan, *Ancient Society, or, Researches in the Lines of Human Progress from Savagery through Barbarianism to Civilization* (Chicago, IL: C.H. Kerr, 1877).
6. London Metropolitan University's "Centre for Postsecular Studies" defines post-secularism in a slightly different fashion: "A postsecular society is one with a renewed interest in the spiritual life. It is postsecular rather than presecular because it renews the inquiry into the spiritual life by building on the hard-won rights and democratic freedoms of expression in the secular world" (see www.jnani.org/postsecular/index.htm). Obviously there is agreement with my point concerning spiritualities, but I find it strange to associate "rights and democratic freedoms" with secularism.
7. Philip Davies, *Whose Bible Is It Anyway?* (Sheffield: Sheffield Academic Press, 1995).

# Part A

## INITIAL ENGAGEMENT AT THE FORUM

# Scholarship and Faith in Bible Study[*]

## Michael V. Fox[**]

Recently, claims have been made for the legitimacy of faith-based academic scholarship. In my view, faith-based study has no role in academic scholarship, whether the object of study is the Bible, the Book of Mormon, or Homer. Faith-based study is a different realm of intellectual activity that can legitimately draw on Bible scholarship for its own purposes but cannot contribute to it. I distinguish faith-based Bible study from the scholarship of persons who hold a personal faith. In our field, there are many religious individuals whose scholarship is secular and who do not impose their faith on the premises of their argumentation, although they may separately speak from a stance of faith in a denominational forum.

Faith-based study of the Bible certainly has its place – in synagogues, churches, and religious schools, where whatever religious texts one gives allegiance to serve as a normative basis of moral inspiration or spiritual guidance. This kind of study is not scholarship – by which I mean *Wissenschaft*, a term lacking in English that can apply to the humanities as well as the hard sciences, even if the modes and possibilities of verification in each are very different. (It would be strange, I think, to speak of a "faith-based *Wissenschaft*".)

Any discipline that deliberately imports extraneous, inviolable axioms into its work belongs to the realm of homiletics, spiritual enlightenment, moral guidance, or whatnot, but not scholarship, whatever academic degrees its practitioners may hold. Scholarship rests on evidence. Faith, by definition, is belief when evidence is absent. "There can...be no faith concerning matters which are objects of rational knowledge, for knowledge excludes faith" (thus Aquinas, as paraphrased by the *Encyclopedia of Philosophy* 3.165). Evidence must be accessible and meaningful apart from the unexaminable axioms, and it must not be merely generated by its own premises. (It is not evidence in favor of the Quran's divine origin, for example, that millions of people believe it deeply, nor is it evidence of its inerrancy that it proclaims itself to be "the Scripture whereof there is no doubt".) To be sure, everyone has presuppositions and premises, but these are not inviolable. Indeed, it is the role of education to teach students how to recognize and test their premises and, when necessary, to reject them.

Faith-based Bible study is not in the realm of scholarship even if some of its contentions turn out to be true. If scholarship should one day prove the existence of a Davidic Empire, for example, faith-based Bible study will have made no contribution to the discovery because it starts with the conclusions it wishes to reach. Some of the epigraphers, archaeologists, and historians who achieve this discovery may hold religious beliefs, but this is a matter of biography, not scholarship. Their scholarly assumptions, methods and arguments, if effective, will be distinct from their faith and not dependent on it. There is an atmosphere abroad in academia, one loosely associated with postmodernism, that tolerates and even encourages ideology in scholarship and advocacy in instruction. Some conservative religionists have picked this up. I have heard students – and read authors – who justify their biases by the rhetoric of postmodern self-indulgence. Since no one is viewpoint-neutral and everyone has presuppositions, it reasons, why exclude Christian presuppositions? Why allow the premise of errancy but exclude inerrancy? Why allow evolution but not creationism? Such sophistry can be picked apart, but the climate does favor it.[1] The claim of faith-based Bible study to a place at the academic table – with the jobs and grants associated with it – takes a toll on the entire field of Bible scholarship. The reader or student of Bible scholarship is likely to suspect (or hope) that the author or teacher is moving toward a predetermined conclusion. Those who choose a faith-based approach should realize that they cannot expect to be taken seriously by those who don't share their postulates. The reverse is not true. Scholars who are personally religious constantly draw on work by scholars who take a secular approach, who bracket out their own beliefs from their scholarly work. One of the great achievements of modern Bible scholarship is that it communicates across religious borders so easily that we usually do not know the beliefs of its practitioners. Trained scholars quickly learn to recognize which authors and publications are governed by faith and tend to set them aside, not out of prejudice but out of an awareness that they are irrelevant to the scholarly enterprise. Perhaps it would be worthwhile to go through faith-driven publications and pick out the wheat from the chaff, but time is limited. The best thing for Bible appreciation is a secular, academic, religiously-neutral hermeneutic. (I share Jacques Berlinerblau's affirmation of the secular hermeneutic though not his ideas about what it constitutes or where it leads.)[2] Secular scholarship allows the Bible to be seen as a rich and vibrant mixture of texts from an ancient people in search of God and moral culture. Its humanness – and primitiveness – can allow us both to recognize and make allowances for some of its uglier moments (Lev. 18:22, for example or Deut. 20:10–20, or much of Joshua). These things would (in my view) be abhorrent coming from the Godhead, but tolerable when viewed (and dismissed) as products of human imperfection and imagination in an ancient historical context. For those of us who teach in state-sponsored universities, secularity in the classroom is essential to professional integrity – and effectiveness. In that setting, presuppositions of faith stifle honest communication, and rational analysis gives way to pronouncements and preachments, often of an angry sort. We should not speak about faith-based Bible scholarship in a vacuum. If faith-generated axioms are valid in Bible study, they should be valid everywhere, including Sanskritology, Classics, linguistics, law, and (as some have indeed insisted) biology. Or is our field to receive a special dispensation, along with the condescension that attends such concessions? We are in a time when pseudo-scientific claims are demanding a place as equals in the science curriculum, and cosmologists, biologists and zoologists cannot afford to ignore them. Similar voices wish to insert themselves into academic Bible scholarship, and serious adherents of *Bibelwissenschaft* should likewise offer opposition.

### Excursus on the Debate

My *SBL Forum* article provoked a lively debate. Responses to my article are at http://www.sbl-site.org/Article.aspx?ArticleId=502 and my reply is at http://www.sbl-site.org/Article.aspx?ArticleId=521; parts of the present essay are based on the reply.

Several editorials appeared in blogs in response to my essay. For a heated denunciation of my views, see "Dr Mohler's Blog" at http://www.albertmohler.com/commentary_read.php?cdate=2006-07-31. It should be clear from the present essay – and my entire body of publications – that I by no means think that "Jewish scholars who would wish to publish academic research on the Old Testament are simply to be discounted because they may well believe in the existence of deity and may see the Old Testament writings as sacred"; nor do I think that "Christians are to be discounted wholesale, and Christians who engage in biblical scholarship are to be denied the status of scholars, regardless of which testament is their focus of study" (see Dr Mohler's Blog). Dr Mohler, it should be noted, assumes that he can divine my personal religious beliefs from my statements about their role in scholarship. For a more considered critique see Dave Beldman (http://beldmandave.blogspot.com/2006_02_01_archive.html). A sophisticated argument for the faith-based approach is C.G. Bartholomew's *Reading Ecclesiastes*[3] I critiqued his reasoning in a review in *Interpretation*.[4] But what I found most puzzling is that when he went to demonstrate his own "Christian hermeneutic" in a study of the book of Qohelet, he uses philological and literary arguments accessible to all, without building on Christian premises. Why then insist on a logic of faith accessible only to the faithful?

The foremost proponent of the traditional Christian perspective in university education is George Marsden, especially in his history of the secularization of American academia, *The Soul of the American University*.[5]

Marsden laments the dislodging of this perspective under pressures from liberal Protestantism and calls for its reintroduction. He claims that "there is little reason to exclude a priori all religiously based claims on the grounds that they are unscientific" (Marsden 1994: 430), since science too is not "neutral objective"[6] But the premises of science are open to critique and falsification; faith is inviolable by experiential criteria. Marsden advocates the legitimacy of religiously oriented universities as institutions of higher learning, and this, I think, is undeniable. No one would say otherwise about Notre Dame and Yeshiva University. But institutions, whatever their sponsorship, that base their scholarship on premises of faith and require conclusions consonant with those premises are not joining in the shared academic enterprise in good faith *for the affected subjects*. In any case, advocacy theology and any disciplines promoting religious doctrines of any sort would be open to legal challenge in publicly funded institutions in the United States.

## Endnotes

*   An earlier version of this essay first appeared on the SBL Forum 2006 (http://www.sbl-site.org/Article.aspx?ArticleId=490). Mary Bader had earlier raised the pedagogical issue of bringing students to an academic approach to Bible studies on SBL Forum 2005: 'Strategies for Moving Students from Faith-based to Academic Biblical Studies' at http://www.sbl-site.org/Article.aspx?ArticleId=467. The present essay was part of a discussion that grew out of her essay and the responses to it; see http://www.sbl-site.org/Article.aspx?ArticleId=473.

**       Michael V. Fox is the Halls-Bascom Professor of Hebrew in the Department of Hebrew and Semitic Studies at the University of Wisconsin, USA.

1.   Inerrancy and errancy are not comparable doctrines. The antithesis of inerrancy would be total-errancy, the assumption (held by no one) that *everything* in the Bible is false. The stance of biblical errancy is an openness to the possibility of claims, stories, and assumptions in the Bible being factually wrong – or right, or non-adjudicable and therefore irrelevant to scholarship.

2.   See Jacques Berlinerblau, *The Secular Bible* (Cambridge: Cambridge University Press, 2005). My unpublished review of his book, presented in an SBL panel, is available at http://palimpsest.lss.wisc.edu/~mfox/publications/Secular_Bible.htm

3.   C.G. Bartholomew, *Reading Ecclesiastes*, Analecta Biblica 139 (Rome: Pontifical Biblical Institute, 1998).

4.   Michael V. Fox, "C.G. Bartholomew, *Reading Ecclesiastes* (1998)", *Interpretation* 54 (2000), pp. 195–98.

5.   George Marsden, *The Soul of the American University* (Oxford: Oxford University Press, 1994).

6.   Marsden, *The Soul*, p. 430.

# The Unspeakable in Biblical Scholarship

*Jacques Berlinerblau**

I read Professor Michael Fox's recent contribution to the *SBL Forum* – "Biblical Scholarship and Faith-based Study: My View" – with appreciation and glee. Appreciation, because the piece evinces his characteristically level-headed, sober, albeit provocative, style. Glee, because Professor Fox has called attention to a topic that is virtually taboo in biblical scholarship. I disagree strongly with some parts of his analysis. Yet I sense that his remarks may be a cause and an effect of a significant change. We are, after all, conducting this dialogue on the web page of the Society for Biblical Literature – an organization that has traditionally shown itself to be somewhat impervious to the charms of both self-reflexive scrutiny and secularism.

The unspeakable that I allude to in my title concerns what we might label the demographic peculiarities of the academic discipline of biblical scholarship. Addressing this very issue thirty years ago, M.H. Goshen-Gottstein observed: "However we try to ignore it – practically all of us are in it because we are either Christians or Jews".[1] In the intervening decades, very little has changed. Biblicists continue to be professing (or once-professing) Christians and Jews. They continue to ignore the fact that the relation between their own religious commitments and their scholarly subject matter is wont to generate every imaginable conflict of intellectual interest. What's more, they still seem oblivious to how strange this state of affairs strikes their colleagues in the humanities and social sciences.

Be that as it may, we Biblicists – perhaps I should say *you* Biblicists – are a fascinating and sometimes laudably heretical lot. How many times have exegetes inadvertently come to conclusions that imperilled the dogmas of the religious groups to which they belonged? In *The Secular Bible: Why Nonbelievers Must Take Religion Seriously*, I ascribed a heroic function to biblical scholars, depicting them as (unwitting) agents of secular modernity.[2] I would note that Julius Wellhausen and William Robertson Smith were most decidedly *not* Voltaire and Marx. They were not cultured despisers of religion, but profoundly pious individuals. It is a world-historical irony that their heresies played a role in the continuing secularization of the Occident. Subsequent generations of Biblicists have followed suit, and by dint of their efforts they have legitimated and routinized the right of an individual to criticize the sacred.[3] As recent current events indicate, this is no mere cartoon heroism.

All honour, then, is due to believing critics past and present. This is why, incidentally, I deplore the current secular chic of denigrating all forms of religious thought. Indeed, the tendency of today's Celebrities of Nonbelief to depict theistic thinkers as dupes and imbeciles actually exemplifies the cultural impoverishment (and desperation) of today's free thinking movements. Secular intellectual culture is moored in the 90s, and by this I mean the 1890s. A more serious engagement with religious thought would serve it well. But this does not mean that all is well with modern biblical research. For believing criticism should not be the most extreme form of religious criticism. In order to expand upon this point, let me return to Fox's piece. In his article he drew a distinction between faith-based Bible study and the "secular, academic, religiously neutral hermeneutic". We would both agree that faith-based Bible study has every right to take place in seminaries and religiously chartered institutions. I am a bit concerned, as I imagine he might be, by the degree to which explicitly confessional researchers sit on editorial boards of major journals, steering committees, search committees, and the hierarchy of the Society of Biblical Literature. To their credit, however, faith-based scholars are often cognizant that they are engaged in a confessional enterprise. It is another category of Biblicist that, to my mind, is far more problematic. It is comprised of researchers who in every facet of their private lives are practicing Jews or Christians, but who – somehow – deny that this may influence their professional scholarly work (which just happens to concern those documents that are the fount of Judaism and Christianity!). This category extends to researchers in ancient Near Eastern Studies, who, anecdotally, are often very conservative in their religious views. It also applies, with some sectarian modifications, to many members of the American Academy of Religion. I am always amused to hear how some higher-ups in the latter society complain about the religious conservatism of the SBL – as if the AAR embodies the blasphemous spirit of Jean-Paul Sartre, Chairman Mao, and the Oakland Raiders of the 70s. But I am digressing. When Fox speaks of a "secular academic, religiously-neutral hermeneutic", I can only wonder from where this hermeneutic is supposed to emerge. In this discipline, there is no organic sociological base from which such an approach can develop. And this is because nearly every single one of my colleagues has entered this discipline *qua* Christian or Jew. (True, they sometimes exit as something else, but that's another story altogether.) What results is a situation in which biblical scholarship's "secular" wing is more like a reformed religious or liberal religious wing. If one of the classic definitions of secularism centres on the holding of agnostic or atheistic beliefs, then biblical scholarship (and religious studies in general) is "secular" in a way that no other discipline in the Academy is secular. Does this invalidate the findings of biblical scholarship? Absolutely not. It does, however, point to a collective ideational drift in the field, one that makes it difficult to think or speak about Scripture in certain ways. Now we can better identify what is not well with biblical scholarship. Composed almost entirely of faith-based researchers on one extreme and "secularists" on the other, the field itself is structurally preconditioned to make heretical insight difficult to generate and secular research nearly impossible. To the non-believing undergraduate who tells me that he or she wants to go into biblical studies, I respond (with Dante and Weber) *lasciate ogni speranza*. This is not so much because they will encounter discrimination. They might, but if my experiences are representative, they will more frequently be the beneficiaries of the kindness of pious strangers. There is a much more mundane reason for prospective non-theist Biblicists to abandon hope: there are no jobs for them. Assume for a moment that you are an atheist exegete. Now please follow my instructions. Peruse the listings in *Openings*. Understand that your unique skills and talents are of no interest to those institutions listed there with the words "Saint" and "Holy" and "Theological" and "Seminary" in their names. This leaves, per year, about two or three advertised posts in biblical studies at religiously un-chartered institutions of higher learning. Apply for those jobs. Get rejected. A few months later learn – preferably while consuming doughnuts with a colleague – that the position was filled by a graduate of a theological seminary. Realize that those on the search committee who made this choice all graduated from seminaries themselves. Curse the gods. Before this response begins to sound like the prelude to a class-action suit, permit me to observe that the type of discrimination encountered by secularists in biblical studies *is precisely what believers working in the humanities and social sciences have endured for decades.* The secular bent and bias of the American research university is well known. It is undeniable that many of its workers are prejudiced against sociologists,

English professors, and art historians who are "too" religious. I do not know what the solution is, but I do know that two major neglected questions in our profession concern how religious belief interacts with scholarly research and how secular universities manage the study of religion. In closing, let me mention that in recent years I have increasingly noted the presence in both societies of a small, but growing cadre of non-believers, heretics, and malcontents. Whether we have anything of substance to offer our disciplines remains to be seen. Of course, this begs the question of whether our colleagues will ever consent to listen to us.

### Endnotes

\* Jacques Berlinerblau is Director and Associate Professor of Jewish Civilization at Georgetown University in Washington DC, USA.

1. M.H. Goshen-Gottstein, Christianity, Judaism, and Modern Bible Study, *Supplements to Vetus Testamentum* 28 (1975), pp. 68–88, see especially p. 83.

2. Jacques Berlinerblau, *The Secular Bible: Why Nonbelievers Must Take Religion Seriously* (Cambridge: Cambridge University Press, 2005).

3. These arguments are elaborated upon in Jacques Berlinerblau, "'Poor Bird, Not Knowing Which Way to Fly': Biblical Scholarship's Marginality, Secular Humanism, and the Laudable Occident", *Biblical Interpretation* 10 (2002), pp. 267–304; and Berlinerblau, *The Secular Bible*, pp. 70–73, 116–29.

# Part B

## THE MANIFESTO DEBATE

# A Manifesto for Biblical Studies

*Roland Boer**

For too long has the Bible been colonized, dominated and (ab)used by church and state, especially the religious and political right. The recent quickening of such (ab)use, from Washington to Baghdad, is but the latest chapter in a much longer history. And biblical scholars have readily let these institutions off the hook, turning a blind eye to exploitation and oppression carried out in the name of the Bible.

What, then, is to be done? – as Lenin asked, quoting Chernishevsy, in a somewhat different situation. First, as far as the *institutional* situation of biblical studies is concerned, we need to assert that an unruly Bible (let alone biblical studies) has been colonized, kidnapped and made respectable by church, theology and theological programmes. Then, in terms of the *discipline* of biblical studies, we must seek a strategy for removing biblical studies from its tutelage to theology, to gain some crucial perspective in order to hold the church to account for its abuse of the Bible. *Politically* we have to recognize that the institutions of religion are sites of crucial ideological and political battles, that a marginalized religious left needs all the help it can get, and that the Bible has become a central player in contemporary global politics. To act politically in this environment we must seek alliances, offer sustained and informed criticism of the way the Bible has been used and abused, and hold both church and state to account for such misuse.

Before I proceed, let me say a word on what I mean by "abuse" of the Bible. I mean not merely the twisting of biblical texts away from their supposed original meaning, but especially the *use* of those texts that openly support oppression and exploitation – whether in terms of economics, politics, religion, gender, race and so on. It involves, in other words, the *use of abusive texts* from the Bible.

## Institutions: Colonization and Suspicion

Three pervasive opinions dominate biblical studies. First, the majority of those both outside and within biblical studies somehow assume that one would want to study the Bible only on the basis of religious commitment. This assumption would have to be one of the strangest making the rounds today. It is shared by apparatchiks of the church as well as people with no religious commitment whatsoever, much to the chagrin of an increasing number of biblical scholars. Yet, we don't expect an art critic to be an artist, a literary critic to be a novelist or a poet, a student of classical Greece to be a believer in Apollo or Venus, or a lecturer in French to be a French national. Why then, must a biblical critic have a religious commitment?

Second, and following on from this first opinion, biblical studies continues to be regarded as a subset of theology. As far as theology is concerned, the Bible remains the source and inspiration for theology, for which it then becomes the dutiful servant. Despite a relatively long history of struggles to remove biblical studies from such a tutelage, especially in the name of "scientific" and "secular"[1] approaches to the Bible that claim not to take theological matters into consideration, it seems to me that the overwhelming assumption remains that biblical studies, even "scientific" biblical scholarship, is a part of theology.

Third, the way such an assumption shows up most sharply is in the disciplinary home of biblical studies, which is largely within a theological programme, whether that is the theological college or the theology faculty within a university. If the theological college is more characteristic of countries such as Australia, the USA or France, where there is a strong tradition of the separation of church and state, or indeed those countries with a communist heritage such as Bulgaria or China, the theology faculty is a dominant feature of countries, mostly European, with their own traditions of the established church.

Now, one may introduce a series of qualifications of such a statement. I restrict myself to two. In Australia, there has been a move over the last decade for universities to offer theology degrees. This has been done through deals with theological colleges, which now become de facto theology departments in some universities. This qualification merely reinforces my point, namely that the assumption remains that the proper place for biblical studies is within a theology programme. Further, in Europe the universities have for a long time been secular institutions and their theology faculties are not beholden to the agendas of the churches. Even more, the move to disestablish the church has gained momentum in recent years. And yet, if one wishes to study for the ministry or the priesthood, then it is to the theology faculty that one goes, there to take up biblical studies as part of the programme.

While these dirty little relationships between biblical studies, religious commitment, theology and theological programmes might be read as recognition of the institutional history of biblical studies, it is a category mistake. It gives ground far too readily. For the underlying assumption is that the Bible belongs to the church. Not only is the church the purveyor of the Christian tradition, of a belief system to which one should commit for the sake one's very life, but it also claims theology as its own, and the long arm of the church continues to hover over theology programmes. Even in the most secular of theology faculties, the majority of teaching staff professes religious commitment and involvement in the church.

What then of the Bible? In a wonderful phrase, Ernst Bloch points to the nub of the problem: "The Bible has always been the church's bad conscience".[2] Indeed, the church has colonized and domesticated a collection of texts that by no means sits easily in that situation. Not only was the Hebrew Bible, which forms that vast bulk of the Christian Bible, allegorized and typologized into a text that would conform with Christian theology, rendering Hebrew Bible scholars explorers and colonizers of foreign soil, but the New Testament in its various canons was selected and shaped to suit theological concerns. Such a process of selection, adaptation and appropriation of a set of writings from a larger mass signals the *effort to suppress and bring to order an unruly and fractious mob of literature.* The remainder was consigned to the refuse pile outside the gates. And the usual tactics were applied: division into rival groups, exclusion of undesirables, containment and ideological control of the remainder. Due to the fractiousness of the biblical texts, their resistance to control and domination, we contest at every step the assumption that the proper "home" for the Bible is the church or synagogue, that biblical studies is a subset of theology, and that the natural habitat of biblical studies is the theological college or theology faculty. In fact, an increasing number of biblical scholars carry out their work without religious commitment, let alone being tied to a theological college or theology faculty.[3]

What would biblical studies look like if it was not tied to religious commitment, theology or theological institutions? Such a remodelled biblical studies, I suggest, requires a moment of theological suspicion, especially in light of the curious "dialectic of enlightenment" in which the banishment of superstition leads to yet more superstition.[4] Witch hunts are notorious for producing yet more witches. Simply banishing theology, let alone religion, from our work is in many respects a futile task, for theology has a knack of sneaking in through the back gate. Indeed, many "scientific" or "critical" biblical scholars have tried to do so time and again, while still holding religious commitments and being based within theological programmes, even in the most secular institutions. So I suggest that theological suspicion is crucial not only for biblical studies but for theology itself. It is not just a case of treating the Bible as one text, albeit a major text, in the Western canon, subject to all of the methodological concerns of any other literary text. Rather, what we need is an approach that accounts, in the very process of interpretation, for the theological effects of the text. This is partly due to the context in which this text has been passed down, but also due to its content. In other words, we are looking for an approach that not only interprets the Bible without the imposition of theological issues but one that also takes into account and enables a critique of precisely the theological underpinnings of biblical criticism. Similarly, we need a mode of holding the church itself responsible for its domination and (ab)use of the Bible, for its tactics of conversion and missionary work, for its continued rejection in many quarters of people due to gender, sexuality, race and class. We must not, as Jione Havea points out, let the church off the hook.[5] What we need to maintain, then, as a necessary element of biblical criticism is a suspicion of its use and appropriation by the church, along with a continuing suspicion of the theological tendencies of the texts themselves and the act of biblical interpretation.

In his own dialectical fashion, Theodor Adorno provides a model for systematically and necessarily countering the theological claims and assumptions that for so long have ridden with the text and are enabled by the text itself. In what may be called "theological suspicion", drawn particularly from his work on Kierkegaard, Adorno cautions against the implications of basing any system on theological categories.[6] He is thinking here of philosophy, but the same applies to biblical studies. This means that it is not merely the understanding of the religious material of the texts as so many forms of ideology, but that the ideological force of the texts must be accounted for, criticized and where necessary resisted as part of the process of interpretation itself. For, as Adorno also argues, it is too easy to dispense with theology in a secularizing drive that in fact allows theological categories to carry on a powerful half-life in which the secular categories themselves gain theological authority.

## Disciplines

Let us now move away from situations where, for historical reasons, theology and the church have been regarded as the natural homes for study of the Bible. We can delineate two such zones: the first is where neither church nor Bible has had any influence; and the second is where we find interest in the Bible but no church to speak of. The latter is the most interesting for our purposes.

Let us pose the question this way: if we are to hold the church to account, precisely from the perspective of biblical studies, then how can we gain some distance, how can we step back from a situation in which Bible and church are inextricably intertwined in an unholy embrace? Perhaps we can learn something from the Chinese, where missions failed miserably, where the church has never been strong. Currently the Chinese government is sending students and scholars to seminaries and universities in Hong Kong and elsewhere in order to study the Bible. Not, however, for the sake of training religious professionals, not for spiritual development or the deepening of one's religious commitment, but for the purpose of teaching about the Bible as a major aspect of Western culture in China.[7] Even more, much to the chagrin of the churches themselves, the Chinese government has commissioned a translation of the Bible that is to be done by scholars trained in biblical languages but not tied to any theological or ecclesiastical institution.

It is a perspective that has been lost to us, if we ever had it – those of us in societies and cultures where the Bible is overwhelmingly assumed to be the "sacred scriptures" of church and synagogue. For we find ourselves too close, too enmeshed with those institutional structures. But let me return to our question: in what way might something comparable take place in a situation in which all and sundry assume that the Bible belongs in church or synagogue? One strategy, and the one I will explore here on an institutional level, is that *biblical studies needs to reshape itself as a discipline in interaction with literary, cultural, philosophical, legal, historical and social scientific studies.* For it is *the* canon on which these discourses are based. Another strategy is to move outside the traditional institutional location of biblical studies, to seek the insights of "common readers", as Ernesto Cardenal did in Nicaragua and Gerald West does in South Africa. We leave that for those best able to outline what the implications of common readers might be for biblical studies. People often point out that biblical studies is not a hermetically sealed discipline: it is in fact the intersection of a number of disciplines such as literary criticism, languages, linguistics, historical inquiry, the social sciences and so on. We fully agree! So why not reconstitute biblical studies in this light, rather than perpetuate theology or the church's claim to ownership?

It is one thing merely to make such an assertion, but quite another to find a much deeper theoretical reason why biblical studies must be seen as a discipline at the intersection of so many others. In order to locate that reason, I turn to Michel de Certeau. My focus is his suggestion concerning the beginnings of the various disciplines of Western scholarship (and in this respect de Certeau is not alone). This may best take its designation from a volume of de Certeau's *Le christianisme éclaté*, the dispersal or shattering of Christianity.[8] De Certeau argues that Christian theology – his theological works remain largely untranslated – is the original discipline that produced the "secular" disciplines that hived off after the Enlightenment, when Christianity is both abandoned and unveiled. Historiography, sociology, psychology, anthropology, philosophical ethics, and so on, all fall under this same logic.[9] Although de Certeau is not the only one to argue this position, it is an extremely important thesis, with its own curious contradiction:

> In every study devoted to it since the eighteenth century, religion has always presented this ambiguity of its object: for example, its past is by turns explained through the very sociology it has nonetheless organized, and offered as the explanation for this sociology which has replaced it. More generally, every society born and issued forth from a religious matrix (are there any other kinds of society?) must affront the relation that it keeps with its archeology. This problem is inscribed within contemporary culture by dint of the fact that religious structures have been peeled away from religious contents in organising rational forms of behavior. In this respect, the study of religion is tantamount to reflecting on what its contents have become in our societies (that is, 'religious phenomena'), in the name of what its formalities have also become in our scientific practice.[10]

De Certeau's naming of the contradiction – that religion may now be studied by the tools it first made itself – is not to be read as a lament, as a desire for a lost Christendom. Rather, it is a subtle historicising of Western scientific disciplines. And just in case anyone should wish to claim that all these secular disciplines are really theological at their core (as John Milbank tries to do), de Certeau points out that it is no longer possible to think of these methods and forms of thinking as theological, "since they have precisely ceased to be such".[11] The forms have been re-employed; their theological flavour has been entirely lost. As non-religious disciplines that once began in theology, it is now possible to use these disciplines to study religion and theology as though from "outside". Thus, sociology analyses a form of religion or theology through its organization, the nature of its hierarchy, its doctrinal themes and so on, as a type of society; individual religious affirmations become representations of psychological categories, and so on. In short, religious claims are understood as symptoms of something else, whether social, historical or psychological, rather than truth claims relating to belief.[12]

De Certeau's focus is on theology. However, it also applies to biblical studies. Pursuing the logic of de Certeau's argument beyond his own text I want to ask: do not contemporary methods of literary criticism derive ultimately from biblical interpretation? As with religion, whose content is now studied with the methods that originated in theology, so also is the Bible's content now studied with methods that are no longer biblical but have their beginnings in biblical studies. That is, the host of approaches that go under various inadequate labels such as the "literary turn" or "postmodern" approaches, from Marxism to postcolonialism and queer studies, let alone the old and weary staples of historical criticism and social scientific methods – are those which derive from biblical criticism, although their content is anything but biblical. But we can go further: do not even the most fundamental issues of meaning and sense, the interplay of grammar, syntax and interpretation, translation, commentary and the trail of commentators, the conflict of multiple interpretations, (in)determinacy and so on rely on the enabling possibilities of biblical studies? If we grant this position, then any new discipline, any new approach to the Bible owes its ultimate logic to biblical studies.

Yet, the question of origin is but a small part of de Certeau's discussion: what interests him far more is the curious dialectic whereby the very disciplines that began in theology (and, we would add, biblical studies) have now become anything but theological and biblical. Not only does this raise the suggestion that the theological "content" was but a moment in a much longer history, but it also suggests that only when such approaches have shed their theological trappings may they be applied to theology and the Bible from "outside". I would go further: all of these approaches and more should be applied to theology and the Bible, precisely because they are no longer religious, let alone theological. Once the various dimensions of literary studies owed their very possibility to biblical studies; now, the possibility of biblical studies relies on precisely those disciplines. Biblical studies has for too long hidden from the consequences of the methods it unwittingly unleashed.

Many straws in the wind indicate that the time is right, a *kairos* if you will, for a complete rethink of biblical studies in the university. The increasing interest in the Bible (let alone theology) from within critical theory and philosophy indicates the urgent need for biblical studies in the context of literary studies, if not philosophy and political science. We refer to but one current: the explosion in interest in the political thought of Paul (Alain Badiou, Slavoj Žižek, Giorgio Agamben, Jacob Taubes, Alberto Moreiras and so on). That such engagement is not tied to religious commitment, not to theology or theological programmes, not even the church, goes without saying.

## Politics

The church, however, is not monolithic, however much different sections might claim to hold the only truth. Nor indeed are theological colleges or faculties monolithic. I have given them all a hard time until now, so let me now come around another way and read the situation in a different light. The reason for doing so is that I now wish to speak of politics, and politics is, of course, the art of compromise. In this section I suggest a new context for a political reading of the Bible. There are three points: institutions like the church are sites of profound conflict; since the religious left is in retreat and marginalized, it needs all the help it can get; in criticizing the sustained abuse of the Bible by church and state, a crucial leverage may be obtained from biblical studies outside church and theology.

To begin with, institutions that claim the Bible are unstable and conflictual sites. Or, to use a term Louis Althusser first championed, they are Ideological State Apparatuses.[13] In the midst of a much longer argument, Althusser argues that Ideological State Apparatuses are *sites of struggle*, especially ideological struggle. This applies as much to other Apparatuses, such as education, family, judiciary, politics, communications, culture and so on. Unlike the police, the control of these Apparatuses is never certain and so various groups wage constant struggles over who will set the agenda. We have only to think of the struggles within the churches over gay clergy, over the ordination of women (in some churches at least), over indigenous rights, over environmental concerns and so on – all of them turning on one way or another of reading the Bible. In other Apparatuses we can witness the debates over media representation (is it biased or balanced?), education (public versus private, and the drive to render universities subject to the vagaries of the market), religious institutions (orthodoxy versus social justice), culture (funding for the arts), the continued attacks on trade unions as part of a neo-liberal agenda and so on.

Within religious institutions, the struggles often fall into the opposition between what may loosely be called the religious right and the religious left. In this landscape the religious left is on the run before the religious right. A cursory look provides the following picture. Everywhere, reactionary and fundamentalist, or so-called "Bible-based" religion seems to triumph. In Rome, one right-wing pope is followed by another. The Roman Catholic hierarchy watches its educational wing closely in order to ensure a narrow orthodoxy among its teachers. On a range of moral issues, it rails against contraception, abortion and stem-cell research. It systematically weeds out its radical clergy and scholars. In the USA, Bible-brandishing fundamentalist Protestant Christianity is so deeply entrenched, especially in the southern states, that the primary question for teenagers is not, "have you had sex yet?" but "have you accepted Jesus yet?" Climate change, peak oil, the disaster in Iraq, even the election of Democrat Barack Obama in the US presidential elections are all signs of the imminent end of the world, the Rapture, Armageddon and then the return of Jesus (one may even find a "Rapture Index" at http://www.raptureready.com/rap2.html, which is described as "prophetic speedometer of end-time activity"). In Australia, vast conglomerates, such as the Hillsong Enterprise in northern Sydney, spread their mega-churches further and further a-field. In verses such as "A rich man's wealth is his strong city; the poverty of the poor is their ruin" (Prov. 10:15) and "The blessing of the Lord makes rich" (Prov. 10:22), they tout a "wealth gospel": God will bless you with wealth if you believe and are faithful, but will curse you with poverty if you are not faithful and sin just a little too much. Others, such as the Planetshakers in Melbourne, attract swathes of teens and 20-somethings to their mix of Christian rock and evangelical Christianity, urging young people to devote their lives to Jesus. In parts of the Roman Catholic Church of Australia where the conservative thug, Cardinal George Pell, holds sway there is a systematic effort to return to a pre-Vatican II agenda, especially in theology, education and sexual morality, and Islam has become the great enemy. Even politicians are noticing, celebrating what they perceive as the return to conservative religion and biblical values. In each case, the religious right bases itself on the Bible. In each case, they have driven the religious left underground. In each case, right-wing religious belief and practice by and large is wedded to right-wing politics.

The religious left has responded by focusing on identity politics – championing the causes of women's ordination, of indigenous rights, of gay and lesbian clergy, of environmental good practice, and so on. In each case, the Bible becomes the site of struggle, the focus of differing opinions and struggles, and texts are thrown at one's opponents with increasing ferocity. However, let me make the following point here: the religious left has made a serious mistake in diverting its energy into such identity politics. On the one hand, it is vitally important that those who espouse justice on a range of fronts, from sexuality to indigenous politics, should gain the upper hand. The possibility of just societies depends on it. On the other hand, the move into identity politics as the key ground of struggle in these religious institutions is also a great problem. Why? The religious right has been able to designate these matters as "issues" peripheral to the main message, if not waywardness from the straight and narrow path. Texts such as "You shall not lie with a male as with a woman" (Lev. 18:22) and "I permit no woman to teach or to have authority over men" (1 Tim. 2:12) add ammunition to a religious right that takes the Bible as God's infallible word. In short, the religious right has been able to claim the Bible for itself while the religious left, as it takes on the various causes of identity politics, has surrendered the Bible and the very definition of what it means to be a "believer" into the right's hands.

For this reason too the religious left has become a minority voice and is in desperate need of alliances with those outside church and synagogue. While I recognize the vital work done by the religious left within religious institutions, inspired as they are by the Bible, they are beleaguered and under attack from all angles by conservatives who seek to marginalize them in the name of orthodoxy. What the religious left needs, then, are alliances with progressive movements outside those religious institutions, with those individuals and movements who can assist in the long and difficult ideological and political battles, especially those who work tirelessly for equal distribution of resources, against hunger, poverty and exploitation. What such an alliance would show is that the various causes pursued by the religious left are actually parts of a deeper common political agenda.

The lifelines to a beleaguered religious left may come from a resurgent secular left, which has also found in the Bible motivation for their programmes. It may also come from biblical scholars who are outside the complex allegiances to church and theology that I explored earlier. Indeed, those who practice biblical criticism outside such allegiances – and their number continues to grow – provide a crucial perspective on the political abuse of the Bible by both religious institutions and the state. For that abuse is so systematic and so ingrained that those within can sometimes not see the wood for the trees, and may in fact be unwittingly complicit with such abuse.

This context is the one in which a distinctly political reading of the Bible may take place. What kind of readings of the Bible might they be? To begin with, they would condemn abuses of the Bible, especially those readings that use biblical texts to abuse others. I think here of the way fundamentalist Christians who assume erroneously that the Bible is inerrant have access to the halls of power, and thereby a disproportionate influence on domestic and foreign policy. Even more, in the USA we find a sustained effort to slip into the Bible as a superpower, one whose task is to protect an Israel that really becomes an extension of itself. In Australia, conservative Christians form a powerful lobby group (the Lyons Forum), within parliament touting the ridiculous agenda of "family values" and "biblical values". Meanwhile, conservative politicians construct a myth of a comfortable Christian Australia, untroubled by those annoying interest groups such as feminists, gays and lesbians, indigenous activists, greenies and, of course, Muslims. In Israel, ultra-conservative Jews generate *the* major tension in Israeli society between religious and secular Jews, pushing for a raft of measures that includes the dispossession of Palestinians. And before the perceived threat of Islam, we find one "Western" nation after another recovering a sense of being a "Christian" nation based on the Bible, especially by people that hardly know what that collection of texts contains. These are all abuses of the Bible.

Further, the readings of the Bible by the secular and the religious left would affirm the tradition of revolutionary inspiration that comes from the Bible. Despite all of its ambiguity, despite the fact that it is not always folly to the rich,[14] the Bible is in the end the church's bad conscience. Liberation and political theologies saw something of this,[15] as did Gerard Winstanley and the Diggers, as did Thomas Müntzer and the peasants in Germany, as did Ernst Bloch and the peasants who fought for the communist revolutions in Eastern Europe, as did the fight against slavery and then, with Martin Luther King Jr, the battle against segregation in North America, as did the anti-colonial struggles the world over, as did the anti-apartheid struggle in South Africa.

However, my urging of an alliance of convenience may raise the suspicion that I am a closet advocate of religious institutions such as synagogue or church, so let me be perfectly clear: I do not harbour any hope that they can become progressive institutions as a whole. You simply have to be kidding if you think they can on their own become prophetic bodies, offer possibilities of improving society, or make the world a better place. They are inherently conservative, patriarchal, stuffy and often brutal institutions. Yet there are elements within them, elements I have called the religious left, that continue to struggle despite the odds, and their struggle is worth all the support it can get.

## *Theses for Biblical Studies*

1. Since an unruly and fractious Bible has been colonized by church, theology and theological programmes, teaching and research in biblical studies must free itself from such connections.
2. In light of its history and current practice in many areas, biblical studies must proceed with a healthy theological suspicion. The Bible and its use must be held accountable for its myriad justifications of oppression and exploitation, past and present.
3. Biblical studies needs to reshape itself as a discipline in interaction with literary, cultural, philosophical, legal, historical and social scientific studies.
4. Since they have been marginalized, the religious left needs allegiances with those who are outside church, theology and theological programmes.
5. There is an urgent need for the development and encouragement of a sustained criticism of the abuse of the Bible by church and state, as well as a recovery of the revolutionary readings of the Bible.

## *Endnotes*

\* Roland Boer is Research Professor in Humanities and Social Science at the University of Newcastle, Australia.
1. In light of this and other contradictions, I have argued elsewhere that the old programme of secularism has by and large collapsed, and that what we need is a new secularism. See Roland Boer, *Rescuing the Bible* (Oxford: Blackwell, 2007).
2. Ernst Bloch, *Atheism in Christianity: The Religion of the Exodus and the Kingdom* (trans. J.T. Swann; New York: Herder and Herder, 1972), p. 21.
3. As a sample, see: R.S. Sugirtharajah *The Bible and the Third World: Precolonial, Colonial and Postcolonial Encounters* (Cambridge: Cambridge University Press, 2001); Sugirtharajah, *Postcolonial Criticism and Biblical Studies* (Oxford: Oxford University Press, 2002). Erin Runions, *How Hysterical: Identity and Resistance in the Bible and Film* (New York: Palgrave Macmillan, 2003); Stephen Moore, *God's Gym: Divine Male Bodies of the Bible* (New York: Routledge, 1996); Moore, *God's Beauty Parlour: And Other Queer Spaces in and Around the Bible* (Stanford, CA: Stanford University Press, 2001). George Aichele, *The Control of Biblical Meaning: Canon as a Semiotic Mechanism* (Lewisburg, PA: Trinity Press International, 2001); Edgar Conrad, *Reading the Latter Prophets: Toward a*

*New Canonical Criticism* (London: T. & T. Clark, 2003). See also Philip Davies, *Whose Bible Is It Anyway?* (Sheffield: Sheffield Academic Press, 1995); and Roland Boer, *Marxist Criticism of the Bible* (London: T. & T. Clark Publishers, 2003).

4.  See Max Horkheimer and Theodor Adorno, *Dialectic of Enlightenment* (London: Continuum, 1999).

5.  In a discussion at the first airing of the manifesto at the Bible and Critical Theory Seminar, held at the Ramsgate Hotel, Adelaide, 28–29 June 2003.

6.  Theodor Adorno, *Kierkegaard: Construction of the Aesthetic* (Minneapolis, MN: University of Minnesota Press, 1989).

7.  These comments are based on conversations with Philip Chia and Douglas Knight.

8.  Michel de Certeau and Jean-Marie Domenach, *Le Christianisme éclaté* (Paris: Seuil, 1974).

9.  John Milbank's *Theology and Social Theory: Beyond Secular Reason* (Oxford: Blackwell, 1993), has explored the theological roots of modern social theory at great extent, but he does not go as far as de Certeau's dialectical argument on which we rely here. Milbank contents himself with finding the theological core of a range of contemporary approaches and then showing how that theology is inadequate, thereby rendering the social theory inadequate.

10.  Michel de Certeau, *The Writing of History* (trans. Tom Conley; New York: Columbia University Press, 1988), p. 176.

11.  de Certeau, *The Writing of History*, p. 175.

12.  Michel de Certeau, Luce Giard (ed.), *La Faiblesse de Croire* (Paris: Seuil, 1987), p. 192.

13.  Louis Althusser, *Lenin and Philosophy and Other Essays* (trans. Ben Brewster; London: New Left Books, 1971), pp. 121–73.

14.  Bloch, *Atheism in Christianity*.

15.  We would do well to recognize the deadly insight of the International Monetary Fund, Ronald Reagan's Administration in the United States and the tyranny of the recently deceased Pope John Paul II. Reagan and the IMF listed liberation theology as a threat to "security", thereby unleashing a bloodbath of oppression that saw hundreds of thousands of those involved in the movement of liberation theology executed. Meanwhile, the pope, with Cardinal Ratzinger at the helm of the successor to the Inquisition, bawled out one liberation theologian after another while Reagan's forces did the dirty work for them.

BOER'S *MANIFESTO*: PART OF THE SOLUTION OR PART OF THE
PROBLEM? SOME REFLECTIONS FROM A SWEDISH PERSPECTIVE

*Hanna Stenström\**

### *Introductory Reflections*

When I gave my response to an earlier version of Roland Boer's *Manifesto*
at the SBL International Conference in Edinburgh 2006, I began by telling
the audience that my first reaction to this manifesto was "Yes, indeed, I
agree". From a Swedish perspective, it is not controversial to argue for a
"secular" biblical scholarship, that is, a biblical scholarship located at non-
confessional state universities, a scholarship that can be practised by
members of different religious faiths or no faith at all. Until recently, exegesis
and other disciplines in the field of religious studies and theology were
always located at non-confessional state universities, and academic theology
was understood as another word for "religious studies". At that time, my
problem was that I couldn't come all the way from Sweden to a panel at a
conference just to say "I agree", so I had to find some objections to make and
some questions to ask, through which I hope to contribute to this
conversation. Finally, through a lot of work, I succeeded.

When I now prepare this revised version of my contribution to the
discussion after reading the revised version of the *Manifesto*, I realize that
I must have succeeded to the degree that some of the critical remarks I
made are no longer relevant, or at least not as relevant. The basic issues are
the same in the revised *Manifesto*, but it seems to me that the description
of reality which I had some problems with – since it universalized what are
in fact contextual circumstances – is now more nuanced and written in
awareness of the differences between the conditions for biblical scholarship
in, for example, the Scandinavian countries and the US.

There is also more room in the present version for those of us who are Christians but not fundamentalists, and who find it invaluable that there is a biblical scholarship which is not tied to churches and denominations, and which is thus free to fulfil a critical task. Therefore, an article that really does justice to Boer's *Manifesto* in its present form must be different from my original contribution in a number of respects, since a version with just some minor corrections runs the risk of being unfair and partly irrelevant. At the same time, a complete and comprehensive discussion of the *Manifesto* is not possible in the limited space of this essay. Therefore, I have chosen to do what has been possible for me within the space and the time I have, namely a revised version of my response to the *Manifesto* that keeps my main points. As I will show below, I will retain my main points even in some cases when the *Manifesto* has been changed and my criticism may therefore appear somewhat unfair or beside the point. I do this because the positions I criticize are positions still taken in debates over the tasks and identity (or rather identities) of biblical scholarship, even if those positions are no longer part of a modified *Manifesto*.

I will begin with a short presentation of my own presuppositions, followed by a passage on the dangers inherent in manifestos, which in content corresponds to my response in Edinburgh, but is somewhat different in its form. Finally, I have added some reflections on the issues discussed in the manifesto, with my own context as my point of reference.

### My Own Pre-suppositions

To begin with my own context and work, I am a Swede, with a Swedish education which led to my dissertation in New Testament in Uppsala 1999. In other words, I am educated as a biblical scholar at a secular state university,[1] and I have been teaching at such universities until recently. It may be assumed, thus, that I have lived my life as a student and biblical scholar in such milieus that Boer expresses a longing for in his *Manifesto*.

Furthermore, in my own work as a feminist biblical scholar, I have criticized the strongly theological tradition of feminist biblical scholarship that we connect with, for example, Elisabeth Schüssler Fiorenza. In my own way, I have argued for a "secular biblical scholarship" in a specific sub-field, trying to show, against Schüssler Fiorenza, that a feminist biblical scholarship that proclaims no intention of creating new models of biblical interpretation for the churches will not lose its *political* edge and power.[2]

## *The Problems Inherent in Manifestos*

As I understand Boer's *Manifesto,* it is written from a basic political stance that I am willing to make my own as a *basic* stance (I cannot know whether I am willing to take the same consequences as Boer in all specific cases).

I understand this basic political stance as a position where resistance against all structures of domination is central and a concern for the contextual is basic. Biblical scholarship is not seen in isolation from its social, historical and political contexts, but is understood as formed by its contexts. It is not the work of free, great minds searching for objective truths. Therefore, it is considered important that biblical scholars analyse their own role in their contexts, and take responsibility towards the contexts and real human beings living there.

On the basis of this shared political stance, I found some problems in the earlier version of the *Manifesto,* namely that it was at risk of being in tension with its own political stance, and that this risk may still be present in international discussions of the tasks and identity/ies of biblical scholarship. It is therefore necessary to mention them again, to keep them on the agenda.

My first point is the risk that the reality of some is treated as if it was *the* universal reality of biblical scholars. My second is that I doubt that the problems are always due to the fact that biblical scholarship is connected to a church. My third is that manifestos and panels run the risk of reinforcing structures of domination, at the same time as they try to dismantle those structures.

To begin with the first point, it is related to Boer's call for a transformation of biblical scholarship from a church-affiliated, theological, discipline into a secular one. Since I have lived most of my life as a student, teacher and scholar in secular universities, my basic problem with the version of the *Manifesto* I responded to in Edinburgh (the current version makes explicit that there is a secular biblical scholarship in some parts of the world) was that it presupposes a reality different from my own, but argued as if the reality it presupposes was *the* universal reality of biblical scholarship. Isn't this a false universalism, i.e. one of the many ways through which the dominating can uphold their domination over the dominated?

From my Swedish perspective, I also want to remind you of the fact that a secular biblical scholarship is not the solution; it is the presupposition for a, or many, solutions to the problems Boer pre-supposes. It may, in fact, become another version of the problem. Since biblical studies in my context went secular in the heyday of historical-critical scholarship, it became a historical discipline. This secular exegesis is, however, more often than not carried out by Christians, who teach students studying in order to be ordained. Therefore, there is much to tell from a Swedish horizon about the tensions between theory and practice, between the priorities of scholarship and the Church's demands for an education that is useful, between open and hidden agendas – as is also shown in the current version of the *Manifesto*. Furthermore, resistance against the kind of deliberately political biblical scholarship described in the *Manifesto* can still be motivated by a view of exegesis as, ideally, a non-confessional, objective scholarship.

So, a short piece of advice based on our Swedish historical experiences: work for secular biblical studies, but never forget that when you have them, that may be the time when the critical work *really* begins. In such an exegesis values can – under certain circumstances – go underground, and be more difficult to handle since they are not allowed out in the open, not made visible.

Although contemporary Swedish biblical scholarship has developed into much more than a purely historical discipline, this is no guarantee that its practitioners take on the necessary political tasks that the *Manifesto* mentions. Work with the uses of the Bible in culture may still be indifferent to issues of power – while a theological work may be integrated in a radical political agenda.

To be fair to my colleagues, it must be mentioned that the last years have seen a number of publications on "difficult texts", on the uses of the Bible for abusive ends and the responsibilities of biblical scholars in relation to such texts. To mention examples, the article "Som Åke Green läser Bibeln" ["As Åke Green reads the Bible']³ by the Old Testament scholar Inger Ljung[4] was published in one of the biggest Swedish newspapers and shows clearly the absurdities of Åke Green's homophobic interpretation of the Bible. (See also Magnus Zetterholm's article in the same newspaper on a Bible-based Christian resistance against same-sex relationships as ethically unacceptable and intellectually inferior.[5]) In 2006, Jesper Svartvik published *Bibeltolkningens bakgator*, a book on how biblical texts concerning Jews, slavery and homosexuals have been interpreted throughout history. Svartvik's explicit aim is to expose abusive interpretations.[6]

As in the international context, work with difficult and abusive biblical texts and interpretations in Sweden can be based on a general ethics, which does not make issues of power and other political dimensions of texts and interpretations visible,[7] but it can also have a political perspective with issues of power in the centre, be they connected to gender or colonialism.[8]

So, to my second point. In the earlier version of the *Manifesto*, one of the examples used to argue for the necessity of a secular biblical scholarship was the story of a university professor who had been dismissed for his "radical research". Those of you who know about such examples will, I think, still find them important arguments for a secular biblical scholarship, so I'll keep this part of my response.

My question to this example was: is this possible in Sweden? Although I am not really sure that it isn't, I do not think it is. This is not because we do not have theologically conservative people in Swedish theological faculties, or people who are simply afraid when someone becomes too radical. We certainly have this in the midst of secularism. The reason is actually very secular: it is difficult to fire people in Sweden, and there are very strict rules for dismissal. The rules make dismissal possible in certain cases, and it is possible to get rid of persons who bosses find difficult to handle, although this reason is never openly cited. Still, changes in labour legislation are seen as unacceptable by many people, since the labour movement, including the Social Democratic Party, has been the dominant political force in my country for most of the last century.

Furthermore, there is another reason that I doubt whether this could happen in Sweden, and that is also secular: all institutions that are accredited for academic education are monitored by the government's agencies. Of course, you are free to start and run a fundamentalist Bible school if you wish, but if you want an education accredited as equal to a university education it must uphold academic standards – and that is assessed, time and again.

My point is this: Is the example mentioned, that someone is fired for being too radical, solely and precisely about institutional forms for exegesis, or is it also about something else? Isn't it also an issue about what political forces – ISAs – have been dominant in society? Is not the example actually a symptom of a specific social system which has been produced through historical processes different from those in my country? Why is the secularization of biblical studies *the* Solution, removed from other social and political forces? What about trying to write laws that give employees better protection from casual dismissal?

So, to the third point: If we are faithful to the political stance of the *Manifesto*, writing manifestos to be discussed in international contexts such as the SBL becomes paradoxical. On the one hand, we do need those discussions, and we need to think through the tasks and identity/ies of biblical scholarship in a world where the Bible is used and abused for various destructive ends. We need to think together in international contexts since so many problems are global. Biblical scholars do belong to an international community. At the same time, we are a markedly heterogeneous crowd, shaped by local as well as regional and global histories. So, when writing such manifestos, we always run the risk of making the realities, problems and possible solutions of one or some internationally dominant countries and groups into everyone's realities, problems, and possible solutions, thus re-creating structures of domination when trying to dismantle the same structures.

To remind us of our different realities and pre-suppositions, I said in my original response that if we were having this kind of discussion in Sweden among Swedes, I could have spoken very briefly: only combining phrases meaning, if translated, "the task of biblical scholars today" or "to understand the role of the Bible in the contemporary world" with the words 'Knutby'[9] or "Åke Green", would have sufficed to start a long and lively discussion. I suspect that if I had said that in an international context like a panel at an SBL conference, the conversation would have died before it began.

I think all of us know local examples that are highly relevant for the topics we are discussing today, but some of you have local examples – Washington, to name one – that have such consequences for humankind that we must all learn them, while my examples, like the events in Knutby, do not. Some participants in the discussion can take for granted that their realities are known to the rest of us, while others cannot. Isn't this a kind of domination? And how can we create forms for work that counteract the dominance of those who speak a dominant language?

Thus, participating in this discussion as a Swedish scholar is a paradoxical experience. I grew up in a certain time in a small country where solidarity with the so-called Third World was important. I learned that I belong to the upper class of the world: being white, affluent, privileged in all senses,[10] part of the Christian, capitalist, Western civilization. But is it that simple? Can you be white and privileged and at the same time marginalized in a certain context, such as this one, where you cannot use your own language and where your context and the specific development of biblical scholarship in your country in relation to the churches and society at large are not really included in the description of reality that sets the agenda?

## Concluding Reflections

Finally, back to the question: "What can be done?" In many respects, I cannot do much more than agree with the five theses at the end of the *Manifesto*. I share the conviction that we need a new kind of "secular biblical scholarship", which can also form alliances with – for example – members of religious communities, or (not to forget!) a secular biblical scholarship which can even be practiced by those of us who belong to religious communities but find critical approaches to the Bible necessary in a world where there is so much abusive use of the Bible, and where use and interpretation of the Bible is no longer only made in the churches.

I will therefore not say much more about this, just to reiterate my advice that we must not have too much faith in the "secularization" of biblical scholarship. "Secularization" may be a necessary step towards the kind of biblical scholarship that is envisioned in the *Manifesto*, but a secular biblical scholarship may also be, for example, a scholarship that upholds the values that politics and research shall be kept strictly apart. I know that this may be understood as just stating the obvious, but the intense focus on "secularization" as the key to a different (better!) biblical scholarship in the *Manifesto* makes me a little worried that this fact has been forgotten.

So, what else can be done? As can be seen above, one of my problems with the *Manifesto*, a problem that may be inherent in all manifestos, is its relation to the concrete, the actual. On the one hand, it is a strong plea for a biblical scholarship that is concerned, in words and deeds, with concrete abuses of real people, with forming alliances to resist concrete forms of oppression and participate in the work for a better world. On the other hand, it tends to take the realities in some parts of the world as everybody's reality.

Perhaps it is inevitable that manifestos have those tendencies: their very reason for existence is that they make broad and general statements, showing directions for the movement forward but leaving the working out of contextually relevant details to others. Since I agree that we sometimes need manifestos which call us to rethink what we are doing, I can live with this inherent problem, although I still would have liked to see more of a reflection on the inherent paradoxes and problems with manifestos in Boer's *Manifesto*.

Therefore, after reading the *Manifesto*, I started longing for other kinds of texts. Texts which allow for differences between biblical scholarship in various contexts. Texts that may help us work out the details of new kinds of biblical scholarship on the basis of a deeper understanding of how we got where we are. There must be more to do in this respect.

Mainly, I started dreaming about works on the history of research, which do not dwell solely on the internal development of the discipline but discuss the discipline in specific countries in relation to complex social changes in society at large. There are certainly already a number of studies on biblical scholarship as part of the social structures of the society where it is practised, in, for example, feminist and postcolonial exegesis. Still, I think it might be possible to do even more detailed, cross disciplinary, studies of how specific biblical scholars and traditions of scholarship can be understood in relation to the socio-historical development in their own countries and contexts: in relation to secularization, to society's movement in the direction of gender equality, to laws regulating the university systems, the various struggles in various ISAs in different societies.

Such work with the history of biblical research might include studies of how biblical scholarship has been received by persons outside the guild of biblical scholars, for example, to find arguments for the ordination of women, or to resist literalist and fundamentalist interpretations of the Bible concerning sexuality and gender, as well as how others in the churches have refused even to try to integrate the findings of biblical scholarship in a Christian faith. This would also add to our knowledge about biblical scholarship as an actor in society, in both past and present, and maybe help us to find new ways of working in the future.

But if this is the dream, there is also the reality. What must not be forgotten when we write manifestos and envision how we can struggle along with others against abuses are the working conditions for university teachers. At least in Sweden – let others tell their stories – the time for research may differ between 10 percent of full time (4 hours a week) and 33 percent (about 13 hours), and the standard is 20 percent (8 hours). All manifestos for a different scholarship must be put in relation to such very concrete circumstances. Working in a secular state university certainly gives you a freedom to do critical research and a freedom of speech that may be missing in some church controlled universities. But what is the use of freedom of research when your schedule is in fact free from time for research? What is the use of freedom of speech when you are too exhausted to talk?

So, when the manifestos are read and accepted, work begins. Perhaps the proper place to start is with the struggle for different working conditions, not with the relation between biblical scholarship and theology. At least, this is as an important place to start in some contexts.

Finally, I will reflect on Church-related biblical scholarship, which might seem odd in view of the opinions expressed above. However, in fact the secularization of academic biblical scholarship also means that a church that wants to integrate the findings of biblical scholarship in its theology and praxis cannot ask the universities to put the Church's concerns on its agenda. This church must have its own scholars, with an agenda of their own. The *Manifesto* has a tendency to equate a Church-affiliated exegesis with a conservative Christian agenda, and a secular one with a politically progressive agenda which may support the Christian left. As we all know, exegesis carried out by the Christian left has often taken the form of an exegesis that, when critique has been voiced of both text and interpreters, reclaims the text for women or other oppressed groups, and thus runs the risk of loosing its critical edge.[11] But is this the only possible order of things? Why not an exegesis practised by members of the Christian left that sees its main tasks as exposing abusive texts and interpretations?

So, finally, in my historical circumstances, it would be interesting to see what exegetical research and teaching in a Church-related context could be, if it was developed under our historical conditions, as a political act of resistance against fundamentalism. I have started exploring this in my work at the Church of Sweden Research Department. Nevertheless, I see this as *one* of many still not sufficiently explored possibilities and contexts of biblical scholarship, *along with* and *not instead of* the thoroughly secular biblical studies for which the *Manifesto* pleads.

I agree that the need for new kinds of secular biblical scholarship is urgent. To discuss how both secular and church related biblical scholarship can be developed, with resistance to fundamentalism and to abuses of the Bible as a common agenda, would be interesting but that is another essay, another manifesto.

## Endnotes

* Hanna Stenström is a Research Fellow in the Svenska Kyrkans Forskningsenhet (Research Unit of the Church of Sweden), Uppsala, Sweden.

1. Due to political changes in the 1990s, it is today possible also for churches in Sweden to run academic institutions – in practice mainly university colleges – with theological education. A complex of political changes has led to the establishing of a number of new universities, university colleges and other institutions for education on an academic level, run by the state or by a number of other organizations and institutions. All institutions accredited for academic education are monitored by the government and its agencies. To be accredited, the institutions must uphold academic standards.

2. This is not an original opinion today: feminist biblical scholarship is in fact – and has been for about ten years or more – no longer dominated by the theological kind of works, but is a heterogeneous field, with room for both secular and theological works. See Hanna Stenström, "Is a Liberating Feminist Exegesis Possible without Liberation Theology?", *Lectio Difficilior* 1/2002, www.lectio.unibe.ch

3. Åke Green is a Swedish Pentacostalist pastor, who in July 2003 gave a sermon entitled, if translated into English, "Is homosexuality a congenital urge or evil powers playing with human beings?", where he, to take some examples, claimed,

invoking the authority of the Bible, that homosexuality is a cancer on the body of society, that the Lord knows that such perversions will end up with humans raping animals etc. He had invited representatives of the media, who did not turn up, although the sermon was summarized and partly published in some newspapers. Green was prosecuted and sentenced in June 2004 to one month imprisonment for breaking laws against the use of hate-speech and racial agitation, laws which also explicitly protect homosexual persons. Green appealed to a higher court and was acquitted in February 2005. When the case finally reached the Supreme Court, Green was acquitted once again, on the grounds that he had just made explicit the intention and message of the Bible. This case gave rise to a heated discussion in the public realm and the Åke Green-case became an example often referred to in discussions of interpretations of the Bible among biblical scholars and theologians. It is reported in Swedish media that a fundamentalist preacher in the US has declared on his website that the death of many Swedish children in the Tsunami in East Asia December 2004 was God's punishment for the sentence against Åke Green. For Swedish articles where the Åke Green-case is a point of reference for discussions of biblical interpretation and/or the tasks and responsibilities of biblical scholars see, e.g. Karin Johannesson, "Anything goes" – utom det politiskt inkorrekta? In Lars Hartman (ed.); *När religiösa texter blir besvärliga. Hermeneutiska frågor inför religiösa texter. Föredrag vid ett symposium i Vitterhetsakademien 15–16 maj 2006.* Kungl. Vitterhets Historie och Antikvitets Akademien Konferenser 64 (2007), pp. 87–98. See also Mattias Martinson, Text, tolkning och social tolkningskod. In Hartman (ed.); *När religiösa texter blir besvärliga*, pp. 114–28.

4. Inger Ljung, Som Åke Green läser Bibeln. *SvD*, 23 November, 2005. See also Inger Ljung "...att redogöra för Bibelns syn på homosexualitet" Några reflektioner i anslutning till ett rättsfall om kränkning. In Lars Hartman (ed.) *När religiösa texter blir besvärliga*, pp. 99–113.

5. Magnus Zetterholm, Bibelns fördömanden är moraliskt orimliga. *SvD*. 26 January 2005.

6. Jesper Svartvik, *Bibeltolkningens bakgator. Synen på judar, slavar och homosexuella i historia och nutid* (Stockholm:Verbum, 2006).

7. See, e.g., Svartvik, *Bibeltolkningens bakgator*.

8. Hanna Stenström, *The Book of Revelation: A Vision of the Ultimate Liberation and the Ultimate Backlash? A Study in 20ᵗʰ Century Interpretations of Rev. 14:1–5, with Special Emphasis on Feminist Exegesis.* Unpublished PhD Dissertation, Uppsala University, 1999. See also Stenström's, Is a Liberating Feminist Exegesis Possible without Liberation Theology? and Mikael Sjöberg, *Wrestling with Textual Violence. The Jephtah Narrative in Antiquity and Modernity.* The Bible in the Modern World 4 (Sheffield: Sheffield Phoenix Press, 2006); and Anna Runesson, *Exegesis in the Making: The Theoretical Location and Contribution of Postcolonial New Testament Studies.* Unpublished Licentiate Thesis, Lund University, 2007.

9. Knutby is a village close to Uppsala. In January 2004, the wife of a pastor in a charismatic Christian community in Knutby was shot to death, and her neighbour, a man, was wounded by another shot. The killer was a young woman and member of the community who had for a while lived with the pastor's family and helped his wife with taking care of the home and the children. The pastor himself was

found guilty of instigating the murder. The community in Knutby became a serial story in Swedish media, since the events leading to the murder included the still unsolved mystery of the death of the pastor's first wife, the pastor's sexual affairs (including an affair with the young woman he finally used to kill his wife), a female pastor known as the Bride of Christ, SMS messages from God, abuse of power and, of course, a lot of charismatic religiosity. As far as can be judged, the pastor used a mentally unstable young woman who was totally in his power to commit murder for him. For an example of how Knutby can be used as a point of reference in discussions of biblical interpretation see Anders Jeffner, Abraham-trons hjälte, in Lars Hartman (ed.), *När religiösa texter blir besvärliga*, an article on different interpretations of the story of Abraham and Isaac in Gen. 22:1–9. To connect the events in Knutby with Gen. 22:1–9 is relevant, since, as the story is told, the young woman understood the commandment to kill as a test of her faith, the same kind of test that Abraham was once subjected to. If you are Abraham, the biblical story says that God will intervene at the last moment, when you have shown that you are ready to do His will, even if it is an extreme act. But in Knutby, God did not intervene.

10. I grew up in a time and a social context where we even believed that men and women are equals in modern society, and that it was possible for us women to refuse adjusting ourselves to old-fashioned rules and norms of behaviour.

11. See for e.g., Stenström, Is a Liberating Feminist Exegesis Possible without Liberation Theology?

# "Guns Do Not Kill, People Do!"*

*Niels Peter Lemche***

The late André Malraux, former Minister of Culture in France in the days of Charles de Gaulle, a famous author and participant in the Spanish civil war, is supposed to have said that if we have a twenty-first century, it will be religious. Malraux died in 1976, and it was in his time definitely not a certain fact that there would ever be a twenty-first century.

However, looking over the status of religion in the world of today, at the beginning of the twenty-first century, Malraux seems to be right. We have an ongoing war (possibly the 3rd or 4th World War) between various religious groups – Christians, Muslims, Jews – and there seems no limit to the atrocities committed in the name of religion. We, the Christians, are defending Western values against Eastern barbarism (have we perhaps heard that before?). And Islamists are attacking godless America – we may think: Maybe they are wrong: too much of God in "God's own country". We are really back to Tom Lehrer's wonderful National Brotherhood Song: "Oh, the Protestants hate the Catholics and the Catholics hate the Protestants, and the Hindus hate the Muslims, and ev'rybody hates the Jews".

The last time it happened, during the wars of religion following the Reformation in Europe, the fighting lasted for almost two hundred years. Unbelievable cruelty was normal, and millions were killed (Germany lost about a third of its population). We can only hope that the present war will be shorter and perhaps less bloody, although so far this hope finds little support.

The thesis might be: When religion gets in, reason has to leave. We are a far cry from Anselm's *credo, ut intelligam*. He couldn't be more wrong. Religion is definitely anti-intellectual and will always be that in spite of the objections of many religious people. Placing religion and reason together is simply a *contradictio in adjectu*. They will never meet. Theology has a problem in the modern world, and the ironic fact is that at the same time as religion in its many forms tries to govern the world, its anti-intellectualism is of no help to theological faculties trying to sustain an academic level of discourse. On the contrary, we see not only in the United States but also in Europe and elsewhere, so-called "free" theological schools turning up next to the traditional faculties of theology often with a history of more than 500 years (my own faculty was founded in 1479), mostly representing an evangelical (fundamentalist) sort of Christianity. Theology's problems are well-deserved. It is not for nothing that the Church – the Catholic one – burned at the stake a Giordano Bruno (17 February 1600), or condemned a Galileo Galilei (1633). Theology earned a reputation which still creates problems in the scholarly world.

We have academic theology insisting on being a part of the academic world, while at the same time defending its main subject, which cannot be. University theology is accordingly attacked from two sides, on the one hand from evangelical Christianity in whose eyes it is liberal and God denying, and on the other from other parts of the academia, which considers its subject not part of the scholarly agenda. This is no problem for evangelicals who would definitely prefer to see a separation between theology and university – if the university cannot be converted to their own evangelical beliefs.

The problem with religion as we know it – apart from the problems already described – is that people really believe in what they believe. Religious people at large are of the conviction that they are right, that their belief in God is the correct one. The corollary of this is that people who happen to disagree with you must be wrong. Because it has to do with the right or wrong relationship to God, you/I live in God, and consequently other people cannot live; they are dead. The Old Testament has scores of expressions of this, most evident perhaps in the Prophets and Psalms. In the Book of Psalms, there are three actors present: God, the righteous and the godless. At the end of the collection, when all problems have been solved, only the righteous are present: "Let everything that breathes praise the Lord!" (Ps. 150:6; NSRV). The religious righteous has no need of the godless multitude that despises his righteousness. So we kill/burn/hang the godless because they are not living in God, they are already dead. Joshua's sin was not that he butchered the Canaanites but that he spared some.

The logic is perverse but has always been here, at least since the inception of sectarian religion as evidenced in ancient Judaism, Christianity, and later Islam. There are true believers and the godless. The religious mind knows of no more human categories.

## A Non-theological Sort of Biblical Studies?

In his Monash manifesto, Roland Boer attacks the interference of state and Church in biblical studies, a theme which develops as the manifesto proceeds. He opts for the independence of biblical studies from official censorship, and asks for a place for biblical studies among independent institutions, and here humanistic faculties would probably be preferable to theological ones.[1]

The title of this essay is a quote from the Russian engineer Kalashnikov, famous for having produced the most widespread family of handguns in the world today. What has Kalashnikov to do with this? Well, I would say, institutions do not interfere with biblical studies; people do. It is a human decision to enact control. Contrary to much political thinking, there are humans behind decisions, not institutions. Although I warn my students: At the end you will be supporting the great inquisitor against Christ, should Christ foolishly decide to return, as happens in Dostoyevsky's famous novel within the novel about the Karamazov brothers: Because Christ is going to destroy the Church! By the way, why has Roland Boer "forgotten" that novel? It says a lot about what we are talking about, because, as the late Robert Carroll framed it, the Bible is a wolf in a sheepfold.[2] Christ is a wolf to established Christianity (Kierkegaard's attack on the Church is another example) but the Bible is as well. Somehow it is not healthy for religious people to read that book.

Maybe there should be a ban: No religious person should be allowed within a hundred meters of that book. It is much too dangerous, and nothing good comes out of it when read by religious people! Maybe that should be my manifesto here.

To give just one example: Luther and his reforming colleagues expressed the principle of Sola Scriptura, the Bible alone, meaning that the Bible should always have the first and the last word when it comes to Christian doctrine. What happened in Protestantism? People understood Luther like they understand Deutero-Isaiah, where the God of Israel claims: I am the first and I am the last (Isa. 44:6).

So it came to be that the only book worth reading is the Bible. It is not far removed from the demand to the pious Jew: Study the Law day and night (Ps. 1:2). The consequence was that in the generation following Luther we already have the new orthodoxy: Here the Bible has not only the first but also the last word. It dominates everything and is directly and verbally inspired by God. It becomes the only authority, and soon it becomes God himself.

In contrast to Protestantism, you may say that the Trinity in popularized Catholicism has developed into a new Trinity: God, his son, and the Virgin Mary. In Protestantism following Luther, Calvin and the other reformers, a new Trinity came into being: God, his son, and the Bible, the Bible of course also representing the Holy Ghost (please, remember verbal inspiration).

It is clear from all of this that the Church and not the Bible is a problem to a Christianity which says that it is built on the Bible, as the Church has little if anything to do with the Bible. So how should we react when we are confronted with the Bible? Luther's main idea was to translate the Bible. He was not the first in his time to do it, but he did it very well, and his Bible was read. For a short time this seemed to spell the end of the Catholic Church, although it survived in its own way, not by presenting a competing translation – it took the Catholic Church another four hundred years to make translations acceptable to the Church – but simply through inertia. The Bible was never that important within Catholic circles. There was a vast Christian literature, hagiography of different kinds, only sporadically read by Protestant theologians.

You could say that the Church did not interfere with biblical studies. It simply had no room at all for anything like an independent – or even quasi-independent – branch of theology devoted to biblical studies. Guns don't kill, people do. The Church does not kill, its membership does – even today, although somebody will perhaps regret that it cannot happen anymore on Sunday afternoon bonfires after Church services.

Returning to the subject: More than a hundred years ago the leader of the fundamentalist branch of Danish Christianity, the Inner Mission in Denmark, Wilhelm Beck, in his famous (in Denmark) sermons thundered against his liberal colleagues: "Professors, on your knees in front of the Bible!" Did he have any official power as head of the Church, or within state administration? None at all; he was just the leader of this influential movement within Danish Christianity, and that leadership was formally unofficial, officially of no importance to the state. However, his action against the liberals was famous and still is both among liberals and conservative-evangelicals. He wanted to enact censorship; he was prevented from doing it officially, so his censorship had to be unofficial, and could not be traced back to either Church or state or both. However, his address shows how the Bible had been transformed into an icon, an image of God, not really to be opened nor read, at least not without guidance from the evangelical community itself. As James Barr has described the issue: "Don't read Wellhausen; read (conservative) books about Wellhausen"![13] This is the same as to say: Don't read the Bible, read conservative interpretations of the Bible!

## Free Access to the Bible?

Is there a free access to the Bible? The obstacles to a free access to the Bible may be of different kinds. First of all we have official organizations like the Church and the state. In its attitude to free access to the Bible, we have to distinguish between different strategies: Total banishment: No lay person is allowed read to the Bible. Partial banishment: They may read the Bible but only with official guidance. No banishment: They have access – however, often within certain limits (just try in an official environment of Church people – like a Bible Commission – to argue in favour of an "alternative" translation of Isa. 7:14). Whatever you propose, the Church will have the final word when it comes to the interpretation of scripture. Here we are close to Roland Boer's idea of Church control. A clear example of how it works can be found in a British context in the transformation of *The New English Bible* into *The Revised English Bible*. The New English Bible (1970) was – due to the secular interest of its driving force, G.R. Driver – in many ways revolutionary and inspiring. The Revised English Bible (1989) – published when Driver was no more (he died in 1975) – reverted to a much more traditional standpoint.[4]

The second way of presenting obstacles to the free access to the Bible is also more in the way of the presentation in the manifesto: Exegesis is allowed within certain limits. Thus *Divino Afflante Spiritu* from 1943, the encyclical of Pope Pius XII, announcing the Pope's decision to allow critical biblical scholarship, is often hailed as breaking the ground for a Catholic critical biblical discipline – in my years of studies at the University of Copenhagen, we had problems recognizing the consequences of this decision, as Catholic scholarship was in those days extremely cautious, very conservative and limited in scope. If you cannot oppose critical biblical scholarship, join it! Embrace it and make it tame! Kill it by being positive!

This could very well be a Church sponsored process. The Church allows its people to be involved in biblical studies, and it is the duty of the students as true soldiers of Christ to remain faithful to their commander or commanding institution, the Church. Be critical, but not too critical. If somebody gets too far, kiss him (or in our time her) on both cheeks, but don't reckon this scholar to be serious. The biblical scholar is here to entertain good Christians, but they are not serious theologians – indeed a very strange way of following Gabler's demand for non-dogmatic biblical studies.

We are familiar with a number of examples of how these tactics work. The first case might have been de Wette[5] two hundred years ago, although the Church did not have to interfere against this amazingly critical scholar, as the state reacted when de Wette supported a student who was planning to kill the King of Prussia. De Wette was exiled from Berlin to Basel, and his position given to Ernst Wilhelm Hengstenberg, an extremely conservative colleague, by all means a fundamentalist long before that concept was coined. Danger passed, and nothing happened for another 60 years before Julius Wellhausen's *Prolegomena*[6] was published. The next generation of biblical scholars – including Wellhausen's own students – and that is the beauty of it – spent most of their careers pacifying Wellhausen. Everybody accepted his greatness, and nobody followed him. You name these students: Hermann Guthe, Ernst Sellin, Rudolf Kittel among others, and the names of their students: Albrecht Alt, Martin and Gerhard von Rad (cf. Lemche, 1987–88).[7, 8]

The same happened in New Testament studies. When I was young, Rudolf Bultmann was the great old man in biblical studies, and his mythological and non-historical approach to the New Testament, including Jesus himself, was something that concerned everybody. What do they do in New Testament studies today: Elaborate on Bultmann? It is hardly the case. They cover him up and go for the historical Jesus and the Q-source. Nobody would say that Bultmann is not important, so read about him, don't read him.

When I and the people around me created what is known as the Copenhagen School, my old teacher, Eduard Nielsen, warned me that we would end up being totally forgotten like Maurice Vernes, who at the end of the nineteenth century claimed the Old Testament to be a Hellenistic Book. After Franz Buhl acted against him with the following remark: "He claims that the OT comes out of the Hellenistic Period like a shot from a pistol, nobody cared anymore about Vernes".[9] Reviewing the field today, we see a new historical trend coming up, proceeding as if nothing happened between Martin Noth and the new "historians". And soon the Copenhageners will be forgotten.

For the last few years I have been planning with a colleague to do a book about *minimalism* in biblical studies. The title was supposed to be "Back to Reason". With the present development within biblical studies, it might turn out to be "Goodbye to Reason" or "Back to Insanity". It will be the job of scholars one or two generations from now to study how this change occurred. Was it Church control or state control?

I do not think that it is primarily the state – not even in the USA or in Australia. In the Protestant parts of Europe, it is not likely that the state will interfere in biblical studies. Thus, the state does not interfere in what I am doing. My faculty is non-confessional (although there is definitely a very Lutheran overtone). I can write whatever I want within my subject without interference.

The interference comes not from institutions but from individuals who don't want to be disturbed; rather, they want to be confirmed in their beliefs. I agree that there will always be a strong tendency among human beings to "institutionalize" their ideas, to join other people sharing ideas and possibly create a network which will be able to lobby for some special cause. This is very obvious within religion, as already demonstrated in Paul's letters. However, as I began: No institution without people! Guns do not kill, people do. A Church without people is harmless; it's the people within the Church who create the problems.

The second institution mentioned by Roland Boer in his manifesto is the state. This is at the moment not a problem in Europe. On the contrary, the state has lost interest in the control of religion. Some would say that it has no part in the political agenda anymore.[10] Although I doubt that it is really true. The situation is most likely very different in the United States. Many Europeans shake their heads when it comes to recent religious developments within the United States which are unparalleled in Europe. This may change, and there are certainly persons who want it to change, but so far there is little danger. Why is it so? Simply because states are made up of people and without a large evangelical segment or even an evangelical majority, the state has only a peripheral interest in religious affairs.

However, I suppose that it is time to ask for independent *humanistic* biblical studies. We cannot ask theological institutions to part with their Bible, but we can create institutions – Bible departments – which are not bound to a Church but part of…well, that is another question, a part of what? Of literary studies as they have it in Israel today? Ancient Near Eastern departments? Departments of secular religious studies? Does it mean that all of this should be in one place? Hardly, the Bible as a secular book should belong to as many different departments as possible. Then it would be possible to establish networks. This would create no problems as long as such institutional units are traceable, that is, they have a recognized status.

In the end this would lead to a challenge to the usual institutions of biblical studies, within religiously oriented institutions. The Church – the "Christian" world – will definitely want to control such non-religious departments rather than negotiating with them (that is, exchanging ideas), and I am quite sure with some success. But we have to try.

## Endnotes

* The title of this essay is a quote from the Russian engineer Mikhail Timofeyevich Kalashnikov, famous for having produced the most widespread family of handguns in the world today.

** Niels Peter Lemche is Professor of Old Testament in the Department of Biblical Exegesis in the Faculty of Theology at the University of Copenhagen.

1. It is funny, and at the same time tragic, that there is nothing new here. Basically, Johann Philip Gabler said the same more than two hundred years ago, although his subject was slightly narrower: Bible studies should be liberated from dogmatic theology. Gabler's seminal lecture, delivered in 1787, is found in an English translation (the original is in Latin) in Ben C. Ollenburger (ed.), *Old Testament Theology: Flowering and Future.* Sources for Biblical and Theological Study, 1 (Winona Lake, IN: 2004), pp. 498–506.

2. Robert P. Carroll, *Wolf in the Sheepfold* (London: SPCK, 1991). The title of the American edition, *The Bible As a Problem for Christianity*, is most telling. The double role of the Bible, evident to Carroll's British readers, has to be cut out and framed in a North American religious environment.

3. James Barr, *Fundamentalism* (London: SCM Press, 1977), pp. 121–22.

4. We can illustrate the difference between the two versions of the English Bible by quoting the opening of the Bible (Gen 1.1–2): The NEB: "In the beginning of creation, when God made heaven and earth, the earth was without form and void, with darkness over the face of the abyss, and a mighty wind that swept over the surface of the waters". In the REB, we are back to normal: "In the beginning God created the heavens and the earth. The earth was a vast waste, darkness covered the deep, and the spirit of God hovered over the surface of the water".

5. Wilhelm Martin Leberecht de Wette (1780–1849). His *Beiträge zur Einleitung in das Alte Testament* (Halle: Bei Schimmelpfennig, 1806–1807), is still marvellous reading.

6. Julius Wellhausen, *Geschichte Israels* I. (Berlin, 1878), reprinted as *Prolegomena zur Geschichte Israels* (1882). ET: *Prolegomena to the History of Ancient Israel* with a preface by Prof. W. Robertson Smith, 1885 (Cleveland, OH: Meridian, 1957).

7. Niels Peter Lemche, "Rachel and Lea. Or: On the Survival of Outdated Paradigmas in the Study of the Origin of Israel, I." *Scandinavian Journal of the Old Testament* 2 (1987), pp. 127–53.

8. Niels Peter Lemche, "Rachel and Lea", pp. 39–65.

9. Lemche, "Rachel and Lea", pp. 39–65, 156–58.

10. Exemplified in the ongoing discussion about "dechristianizing" the charter of the European Union.

# Theological Secularity: A Response to Roland Boer

*Mark G. Brett**

> Secularization shall no longer be conceived of as abandonment of religion but as the paradoxical realization of Being's religious vocation (Gianni Vattimo 2002: 24).[1]

It is perhaps appropriate to note at the outset that I encountered the first version of Roland Boer's *"Manifesto for Biblical Studies"* a few years ago in Adelaide, at a meeting of the Bible and Critical Theory Seminar that took place in a "public house". That first version was tilted primarily against a common enemy of European biblical scholars for the last couple of centuries homogenized as *"the* church". In the course of time, the manifesto has become slightly more nuanced in relation to the church, and more inclusive in its list of enemies: now they include "the state". My first response was: Which church? Which state? I take it for granted that the manifesto will hold some value for biblical scholars locked in heroic struggle with right wing churches in America. But what about some non-Western contexts?

I tried to picture how our colleagues in Burma would read this manifesto, a country where Christianity is the main religion amongst the ethic minorities. To cut a long story necessarily short, the manifesto would be almost wholly irrelevant to them. The secular university environment there does not provide a fertile ground for emancipatory social imagination. Progressive political thought is constituted by an alliance of Buddhist and Christian groups outside the university.[2]

Perhaps the argument is thought to work for South Africa, since in the intriguing list of revolutionary movements listed at the end of the paper, the struggle against apartheid is mentioned. There is even a play on some of the recent discourse in South Africa, when this manifesto is represented as standing at a *kairos*: there may be an echo here of the *Kairos Document* in the anti-apartheid struggle which was indeed pitted against what was called "church theology". [3]

Yes, the universities did play a role in the anti-apartheid struggle – including a good number of biblical scholars. But one or two bishops played a role as well, paradigms of the institutional church. The *Kairos Document* was produced by politically-minded Christians, not by secularists. The African Independent Churches operate outside the clutches of Anglicanism, but they are nevertheless churches. And of course secular movements like black nationalism played a key role. But let me risk the suggestion that one movement played an insignificant role in fomenting popular resistance: the movement that promoted the secular use of the *Bible*. Political reading of the Bible tends to motivate people who are disposed to take the Bible seriously in the first place. In short, the suggestion that biblical study needs to be newly secularized in order to be more emancipatory is short-sighted.

This particular version of short-sightedness seems to be particularly at home in the West. If one looks at the advocacy of secularism in India, for example, it tends to be presented not as a militantly *irreligious* secularism, but rather, as a refusal to endorse any particular version of religion. In his recent discussion of "Indian secularism", Richard King[4] has suggested that irreligious secularism tends to reflect Western prejudices, and consequently a postcolonial approach to "religion" (even the category is largely a Western product) will therefore be better advised to adopt a "methodological agnosticism" (cf. Kwok Pui-lan, *Postcolonial Imagination and Feminist Theology*).[5]

Whatever one might think about King's overall argument, it needs to be pointed out that what he says about "Indian secularism" ironically has some notable affinities with classic understandings of secularity in Europe. The construction of a secular domain in Europe was, at least in part, an historical response to religious wars. The philosophical solution to religious conflict at the time was commonly seen to lie in principles of religious toleration and in a modern rationality that was distinguished from particular religious traditions or cultures. The Reformation provided one set of ideological resources for the political changes that were to see nation states emerge eventually as modernity's ideal of government. The tenor of these early modern arguments was not to exclude religion entirely, but rather, to exclude religious monopolies.[6]

This earlier tradition of secularity does not seem to be of great interest to another "new" secularist, Jacques Berlinerblau,[7] who in his book *The Secular Bible: Why Nonbelievers Must Take Religion Seriously*, advances his preference for a "mode of discursive aggression on Scripture and, by extension, those who hold it dear". The aim is to contest or refute dominant interpretations through developing the arts of "counterexegesis" – exegesis in "heckle mode", with no regard for the old philanthropic moorings of a now outdated secularism.

Those older philanthropic moorings often had a religious tint. Consider some of the heroes of political struggles named in Boer's Manifesto: Gerrard Winstanley, Thomas Müntzer and Martin Luther King are three who are mentioned. They were indeed people who fomented popular movements of resistance and who focussed on public matters. But they were all passionately religious, not secularists in this newly narrowed sense. And it is worth noting that Winstanley and his comrades, the "mechanic preachers", would have been puzzled by the very thought that revolutionaries could come from the ranks of university intellectuals. Contemporary critics in seventeenth century England attributed most of the social turbulence of the time to the "religious toleration that had allowed artisans to preach and the freedom of the press that had allowed them to publish".[8] The fight against slavery is mentioned in Boer's *Manifesto*, but the leaders of that fight are left unnamed. Perhaps there is some embarrassment in mentioning that the key parliamentary reformers in Britain in the early nineteenth century were evangelicals and Quakers, notably William Wilberforce. And after the *Slavery Abolition Act* of 1833, this group focused their humanitarian attention on Aboriginal people in the colonies.

Following in the footsteps of Wilberforce in the campaign against slavery, it was especially Thomas Buxton, James Stephen and Lord Glenelg who concerned themselves with the Indigenous peoples of Southern Africa, the Caribbean, Australia and New Zealand. Buxton's lobbying resulted, for example, in Glenelg's despatch to Governor D'Urban of the eastern Cape in December 1835 renouncing the annexation of Queen Adelaide Province on the grounds that "the original justice is on the side of the conquered, not the victorious party".[9] Apparently, at least some evangelicals have had a capacity for self-critical social imagination – although in many contexts today it would indeed be easy to overlook or to suppress that aspect of the tradition. One of the most interesting aspects of the discourses issuing from the Colonial Office in London in the 1830s was the blend of biblical language with human rights discourse – just in time to ensure that Maori in Aoteroa New Zealand were to have a treaty, but too late for the Australian context where British sovereignty was simply asserted without any treaty being negotiated with Indigenous people.

Would the social sciences, we may ask in passing, have provided a more revolutionary perspective on Indigenous peoples in colonial expansions in the nineteenth century? The short answer is no; the dominant social theories of the day had Aboriginal peoples securely tethered to the lowest rung of a hierarchy of races.[10]

Having drawn attention to the nineteenth century humanitarian Christian reformers, it must be acknowledged that many of them still harboured significant prejudices. An often uncritical conviction about the superiority of Western civilization lay behind the critiques of slavery, and it was commonly suggested that the eradication of such practices would do much to enhance the image of the "civilizing mission". Thus, these moments of prophetic Christianity were shadowed by their own dialectic of enlightenment.

At this point it may be appropriate to confess that one of my own intellectual heroes, Edward Said, regularly drew a sharp distinction between worldly and "theological" criticism because of the extent to which colonial violence had been underwritten by the Christian tradition of metaphysics.[11] But this sweeping (one might even say totalizing) dismissal of theology was unjustified. Following in the footsteps of Heidegger, and of his Jewish antagonist Levinas, there have been many theological attempts to overcome metaphysics that do not entail the banishing of theology to the domestic sphere.[12] And we do not have to wait for Heidegger's attack on metaphysics to encounter theological critique of colonialism.[13] It is precisely the history of public harm done by theology that provides sufficient reason not to eliminate that discipline from public discourse.

Philosophers such as Cornell West and Gianni Vattimo have, in different ways, illustrated how post-metaphysical theology may be undertaken and how emancipatory such projects can be.[14] These are Western theologians engaged with their own particular traditions, whereas when one turns to non-Western examples of liberation theology and postcolonial biblical studies the Western canon is regularly subjected to critique in markedly different ways. The outcome, however, is rarely the banishing of religion; more frequently, it amounts to the immanent *critique* of religion – which for some scholars is indeed theology in its most adequate mode.[15]

The manifesto also suggests that we should learn from the Peoples Republic of China and their exploration of biblical studies as a major source of Western culture. As a number of our Chinese colleagues have made clear, that is an ideal environment for the secular study of the Bible in universities. Equally, I would have thought that a Marxist cultural critic like Boer would have been interested, as many Chinese students are, in the

Taiping peasant rebellion in the mid-nineteenth century. But that appears to have slipped off the radar, perhaps because it was a popular movement combining a communist version of Christianity with traditional Chinese utopian thought, rather than an exercise of "secular" imagination in the newly narrowed sense.[16] Of course, the Bible has been used oppressively with relentless frequency, but it does not follow that reforms or revolutions cannot be fostered by religious readings of the text.

Perhaps Boer wants it both ways – both a more explicit secularism in biblical studies, as well as alliances with progressive movements within religious institutions. What is puzzling about the argument is the suggestion that these necessary alliances might be fostered by a more rigorous separation of institutional domains. It may well be the case that biblical studies generally has to be seen as a secular enterprise in order to secure state funding. But when it comes to the political business of fostering social change, and forging alliances with progressive religious elements, what would be the point of excluding theology from the university?

In one example close to home, the constitution of Melbourne University prohibits the teaching of theology, and the historian Geoffrey Blainey once described this institution as "probably the most secular university in the British Dominions".[17] But that has done very little to foster alliances around progressive causes. On the contrary, the arrangement seems to have fostered the idea that theology as a discipline need not be dignified with intellectual attention – although particular angles on theology may be provided by philosophers, literary critics, social scientists and historians. If, as it seems, religious convictions are influencing public policies in ways unforeseen in positivist dreams, demonizing the protagonists is not likely to bring strategic advantages.

Let me explore another example from my own experience. At present I work for an organization that provides anthropological and legal assistance to Aboriginal people in Victoria who are pursuing their "native title" rights. This political work is enabled by the *Native Title Act* of 1993, which provides that Indigenous people who have sustained their traditional law and custom since the assertion of British sovereignty can seek recognition of rights to land and waters in accordance with Aboriginal traditions. A key problem, however, is that the majority of the Aboriginal population is now Christian, and moreover, waves of mission and state bureaucracies have actively sought to extinguish the practices of traditional law and custom.

This might sound like a paradigm case illustrating that the Bible has been co-opted by church and state. And indeed, the tenor of much of the legal and anthropological work under the *Native Title Act* is understandably anti-Christian. The vast majority of anthropologists were trained in fiercely secular university departments. Yet historically, in the State of Victoria, some of the key Aboriginal leaders who have led the resistance against Government policies have been Christians, notably William Cooper and Douglas Nicholls.[18] Among the many examples of Indigenous resistance levered off Christian ideas, there is a letter written in 1900 by Maggie Mobourne to a local newspaper in southwest Victoria, complaining about the administrator of Lake Condah mission – that "he doesn't practice what he preaches…We who know his ways often wonder he is not punished by the Master he professes to serve".[19]

Aboriginal activists have often had non-Indigenous allies who were motivated by religious commitments. In this context, it would make little sense to undermine the alliance of progressive elements by advocating a version of secularism that prohibits such religious commitments. The anti-Christian tenor of Australian anthropology has often blinded it to emerging post-colonial forms of Aboriginal Christianity.[20] Part of the problem here is that "secularism" itself has not been sufficiently analysed. As already indicated, there are versions of secularism that prescribe the toleration of religious diversity rather than its extirpation from the public domain. One such version arises out of a non-conformist Protestantism that refused to succumb to state-sanctioned religious uniformity. That older tradition of non-conformism has a lot to commend it. To the extent that Boer's *Manifesto* promotes strategic alliances and adapts this tradition to build progressive political movements, I endorse it. There may also be advantages in locating religious specialists within departments of history, anthropology, sociology, cultural studies, medicine, law, economics and so on. Other versions of "newly" secular biblical study that are opposed to theological commitments, on principle, appear to be of dubious political value.

## Endnotes

* Mark Brett is Professor of Hebrew Bible, Whitley College, Melbourne, and Policy Officer at Native Title Services Victoria, Australia.

1. Gianni Vattimo, *After Christianity* (trans. L. D'Isanto; New York: Columbia University Press, 2002).

2. See, for example, the journal *Rays*, produced by the Myanmar Institute of Theology, a theological institution whose history enjoys the distinction of being led by three women Presidents in succession, until the recent retirement of Dr Anna May Say Pa.

3. Robert McAfee Brown (ed.), *Kairos: Three Prophetic Challenges to the Church* (Grand Rapids, MI: Eerdmans, 1990).

4. Richard King, *Orientalism and Religion: Postcolonial Theory, India and "the mystic East"* (London: Routledge, 1999), pp. 50–52.

5. Kwok Pui-lan, *Postcolonial Imagination and Feminist Theology* (Louisville, KY: Westminster John Knox Press, 2005), p. 204.

6. See especially Jeffrey Stout, *Flight from Authority: Religion, Morality and the Quest for Autonomy* (Notre Dame, IN: University of Notre Dame Press, 1981). William Cavanaugh has taken a different approach from Stout and argued that the exclusion of religious monopolies was often implied by – or conveniently compatible with – the project of establishing a monopoly of state powers. The British *Toleration Act* of 1689, for example, excluded Catholics in part because the international networks of Catholicism presented a challenge to state sovereignty. See William Cavanaugh, "The City: Beyond Secular Parodies", in John Milbank, Catherine Pickstock and Graham Ward (eds.), *Radical Orthodoxy* (London: Routledge, 1999), pp. 182–200.

7. Jacques Berlinerblau, *The Secular Bible: Why Nonbelievers Must Take Religion Seriously* (New York: Cambridge University Press, 2005), pp. 8–9, 102, 106.

8. Hill, *A Turbulent, Seditious, and Fractious People: John Bunyan and his Church 1628–1688* (Oxford: Clarendon Press, 1988), p. 14. See also, Christopher Hill, *The Religion of Gerrard Winstanley.* Past and Present Supplement 5 (Oxford: The Past and Present Society, 1978).

9. Quoted in Henry Reynolds, *The Law of the Land.* (Melbourne: Penguin, 2nd edn., 1992), p. 98, from the *British Parliamentary Papers* of 1836, pp. 39, 279.

10. See Marvin Harris, *The Rise of Anthropological Theory* (London: Routledge & Kegan Paul, 1968), pp. 97, 117; J.A. Barnes, "Anthropology in Britain Before and After Darwin" in *Mankind 5/9* (1960), pp. 37–74. Also see R. Evans, K. Saunders and K. Cronin, *Race Relations in Colonial Queensland: A History of Exclusion, Exploitation and Extermination* (St Lucia: University of Queensland Press, 2nd edn., 1988), pp. 12–13.

11. William D. Hart, *Edward Said and the Religious Effects of Culture* (Cambridge: Cambridge University Press, 2000).

12. Simon Critchley, "Introduction" to S. Critchley and R. Bernasconi (eds), *The Cambridge Companion to Levinas* (Cambridge: Cambridge University Press, 2002), pp. 1–32.

13. Among many other studies, see: R.S. Sugirtharajah, *The Bible and the Third World: Precolonial, Colonial and Postcolonial Encounters* (Cambridge: Cambridge University Press, 2001); Derek Peterson, "The Rhetoric of the Word: Bible Translation and Mau Mau in Colonial Central Kenya" in B. Stanley (ed.), *Missions, Nationalism and the End of Empire* (Grand Rapids, MI: Eerdmans, 2003), pp. 165–79; Gustavo Gutiérrez, *Las Casas: In Search of the Poor of Jesus Christ* (Maryknoll, NY: Orbis Books, 1993); and Henry Reynolds, *This Whispering In Our Heart* (St. Leonards: Allen & Unwin, 1998).

14. See especially Gianni Vattimo, *Belief* (Trans. L. D'Isanto and D. Webb; Oxford: Policy, 1999); Gianni Vattimo, *After Christianity* (trans. L. D'Isanto; New York: Columbia University Press, 2002); and Cornell West, *The American Evasion of Philosophy* (Madison, WI: University of Wisconsin Press, 1989).

15. The Maori rebellion led by Te Kooti would be another example, comparable with the Taiping. See Judith Binney, *Redemption Songs: A Life of the Nineteenth-century Maori Leader Te Kooti Arikirangi Te Turuki* (Melbourne: Melbourne

University Press, 1997, and Vittorio Lantenari, *The Religions of the Oppressed* (London: MacGibbon & Kee, 1963), pp. 248–59.

16. Hill, *A Turbulent, Seditious, and Factious People*, p. 375.
17. Geoffrey Blainey, *A Centenary History of the University of Melbourne* (Carlton: Melbourne University Press, 1957), p. 61.
18. Bain Attwood and Andrew Markus (eds), *The Struggle for Aboriginal Rights: A Documentary History* (St. Leonards: Allen & Unwin, 1999).
19. Penny Van Toorn, *Writing Never Arrives Naked: Early Aboriginal Cultures of Writing* (Canberra: Aboriginal Studies Press, 2006), p. 166.
20. Terence Ranger, "Christianity and the First Peoples: Some Second Thoughts", in P. Brock (ed.), *Indigenous Peoples and Religious Change* (Leiden: Brill, 2005), pp. 15–32.

# Is Boer Among the Prophets? Transforming the Legacy of Marxian Critique*

*Todd Penner***

> The word democracy was not forged by some expert concerned with identifying objective criteria by which to classify forms of government and types of society. On the contrary, it was invented as a term to 'indistinguish' things, to show that the power of an assembly of equal men could be nothing but the confusion of a formless and squawking horde, that this latter was to the social order what chaos was to the natural order  – J. Rancière[1]

> [S]uch a deconstruction…has remained faithful to a certain spirit of Marxism, to at least one of its spirits for, and this can never be repeated too often, there is *more than one* of them and they are heterogeneous  – J. Derrida[2]

For years now scholars like Philip Davies and others have been engaging in a sustained and at times raucous engagement over the way in which the Bible functions in scholarly discourse and educational institutions. Davies, in his well known collection of essays published over ten years ago, *Whose Bible Is It Anyway?*, raised fundamental issues regarding the need to bring the Bible into the realm of secular criticism, wrenching it from the grasp of those confessional and theological interpreters who refuse to read the Bible in a "truly critical" fashion. There has been widespread reaction to this counter-engagement of Davies and others, which has most recently been documented and engaged in a nuanced and illuminating manner by R. Barry Matlock,[3] who seeks to bridge "the great divide" that has emerged as a result of the critical interaction between the various groups in this debate. Roland Boer, who has offered up in this volume a *manifesto* of his own on the subject, promotes a similar radical agenda for the separation of the study of the Bible from the hands of those who would use such interpretation to "ignoble" ends, which largely focuses on the church, synagogue, and mosque as locations for socially dangerous and tyrannizing interpretations.

Reading through and thinking about Boer's manifesto has led me to that odd passage in the Hebrew Bible, where King Saul is encountered prophesying on the road to Gibeah (1 Sam. 10; cf. 1 Sam. 19). The spectators are astonished to see Saul in a prophetic frenzy, as he was clearly among those least expected to join in such inspired activities. Boer's own manifesto clearly has this prophetic edge to it. Indeed, he makes no attempt to hide his admiration for the "unruly" portions of the biblical text and those passages that inspire radical critique and interrogation of societal structures. Even more so, there is much in this short manifesto that aligns itself with those major prophets of a biblical ilk, particularly the prophetic denunciation of the Israelite religious establishment and priesthood. True, these same prophetic paradigms ought to be subjected to a hermeneutic of suspicion (and critique) – and Boer I am sure would not disagree. But in this essay I am interested less in the prophets of old and more in the visionaries among us today. Is Boer, to whom we are indebted for foregrounding Marxian readings of biblical literature and culture in his own work,[4] to be counted among the prophets? What does it mean for a Marxian interpreter to be so (easily?) invested in the Bible and its discourses? Is, finally, the Bible itself to be recovered in a Marxian interpretive framework? There is much in Boer's manifesto that bears a "Marxist spirit", which Derrida described as "a certain experience of the emancipatory promise...perhaps even the formality of a structural messianism, a messianism without religion, even a messianic without messianism, an idea of justice...an idea of democracy".[5] But before we become too enamored with the possibilities of this eschatology, one must also, I think, heed Derrida's thoughtful warning: Marx's "inheritance is never a *given*, it is always a task" and "this inheritance must be reaffirmed by transforming it as radically as will be necessary".[6]

My interaction with Boer in this essay is focused on what a radical transformation of the spirit of Marxian interpretation might mean in our contemporary context. There is much to write in response to Boer's blistering criticism of the ways in which the Bible has been shielded from ideological criticism and, even more so, has been wielded by those with/in power to establish hegemony in a world that has set the "liberal left" adrift (or made it irrelevant?). Many scholars of a confessional pedigree of one form or another, upon reading Boer's manifesto, will doubtless respond by saying "this is not *my* approach, this is not *my* institution". And there are clearly massive differences in the ways in which the Bible is engaged and used in academic and confessional contexts across say Asia, Africa, Europe, and North America. Much of what Boer writes makes more sense for a European setting, but less for even confessional contexts on the American scene (although, the Bible has played a particularly potent role in American politics in recent years). When Marx and Engels wrote their famous *Communist Manifesto* the world was much smaller and less diffuse (at least the world that they were addressing). But the situation has changed greatly in this period of late(r) capitalism, and Boer's manifesto has a larger audience in view, which also brings with it certain limitations that earlier manifestos did not have. My concern, however, is not to detail the various contextual nuances that have escaped Boer's assessment – this is, after all, a *manifesto*, and the genre itself mandates a particular kind of generalizing and overreaching in order to establish the essential claim. Those biblical critics and theologians who find themselves balking at Boer's scathing critique ought to remind themselves of the centrality of *genre* in their own work and, in fairness, give Boer a generous hearing – the manifesto is, after all, a form of prophetic discourse.

Boer's main point, it seems to me, immediately draws attention to the vital issues not just in biblical interpretation, but also in the broader confrontation of religious belief and practice in secular (particularly Western or Western-shaped) societies (one thinks of the issue of the Islamic headscarf in France and also the intermittent struggles in Turkey between a secular constitution and an overwhelmingly Muslim population). Boer's appeal makes most sense in a context in which there is already a commitment to secularism in politics and social formation, as well as secularization as a thoroughgoing process of citizen formation. Indeed, his rhetorical stance seems to rest on the premise that emancipation of Biblical Studies (and the Bible) is necessary precisely because such is mandated by larger social and cultural contexts. In his reading, the Bible is being held "hostage" by forces opposed to the secularizing influences of Western society.

My contention with Boer's manifesto is not so much with his hope to emancipate Biblical Studies – as formal principles, I am all in support of emancipation and transformation (even despite their not so covert theological origin[7]). Rather, my concern is with Boer's own embracing of this "other" – the implied culture of Western secularism. In his appeal to the work of Michel de Certeau,[8] Boer notes that the Bible unleashed particular discursive modes of analysis that are now being managed and controlled in terms of application to the biblical text itself. This may in fact be the case, but I am interested in something else that de Certeau observes in his impressive distillation of the process towards secularization:

> [A] dominant political ethics is born of the enormous effort that allowed the eighteenth century to create nations and pass from Christianity to modern Europe. It accredits the state with the role that until this time the Church had claimed, that of being the social mediation of common salvation – the sacrament of the absolute. This is a Catholic ecclesiology, but it is transferred to the state, which sets hierarchies among social orders, initiates liturgies for its power, distributes graces, and rationalizes individual interests...The imperative of state policy orders at once the criticism of Christian prohibitions and new prescriptions.[9]

Herein "Christian organizations are put to renewed use, in relation to an order which they no longer have the power of directing".[10] I am more circumspect of the degree to which this redirection ever totally stripped these structures of their Christian and theological character. De Certeau in fact still perceives traces of theology, as the emphasis on *progress* (in ethics and culture) is understood to be the principle that most embodies the remnant of Christianity.[11] Talal Asad's study of the genealogy of secularism illuminates certain aspects of this point. Drawing on the original usage of *saecularis* to designate the transition from the life of the monk to that of the "life of canons", Asad argues that there is a "remarkable ideological inversion" with respect to secularization: "In the discourse of modernity 'the secular' presents itself as the ground from which theological discourse was generated (as a form of false consciousness) and from which it gradually emancipated itself".[12] Moreover, as Vincent Pecora notes, for Asad the modern stress on "the universal character of human rights...is defined as no more than a projection of secularized Christian nation-states...That is, particular religious beliefs have supplied substantive norms that are then elaborated, self-interestedly, as 'universal'".[13]

In short, secularism is an ideology that is every bit as disciplining of its subjects as is religious belief proper.[14] Perhaps most critically, secularism posits by its very nature an opposite of "religion" or the "sacred" – the two have always existed in an uneasy yet necessary (and co-dependent) relationship. As Asad demonstrates in his recent essay on the French headscarf issue, secularism is caught in a bind between seeking to protect politics from the "perverting" force of religion and, vice versa, to protect religious liberty.[15] Further, Asad seems correct to read the contention over the headscarves of Muslim women in the French context as a sign pointing to broader conflicts and tensions within that particular form of secular society. One might helpfully turn here to Slavoj Žižek's formulation that such social mappings of the other by, in this case, the secular "conceal social antagonism" *within* by allowing us to "perceive social totality as an organic

Whole".[16] In other words, the "religious other" here projects into "concrete" reality the very disruption and discrepancy experienced from within the secular formation, but which cannot be admitted let alone confronted. In any case, it is evident that the conflict between secular and religiously (in)formed citizens represents a fundamental disagreement related to ideology, of the way in which that ideology is understood to be embedded in state politics and practices, and in the manner in which individuals choose to relate to the larger ideo-political context in which they are located. Following Alasdair MacIntyre, moreover, one might well argue that there is no basis upon which any resolution to this ideological conflict will be found through a process of rationalization, since there is no common set of traditions upon which these competing viewpoints are based and can thereby be adjudicated.[17]

So what does this all have to do with Boer's desire to liberate Biblical Studies from the grasp of theological interpretations and authoritative *loci* of religious power? I have several observations to make arising out of the above delineations, and I begin by tracing out three threads from the above discussion. First, it is commonplace to assert that the architects or "fathers" of modern biblical criticism sought to free the investigation of biblical texts (early Christian ones in particular) from the dogmatic structures of church authority. That said, religious experience *qua* experience was still valued if not understood to be quintessential in any historical reconstruction for many of these earlier practitioners. We should thus not be surprised that, as Stephen Moore notes, historical-criticism has always "genuflect[ed] before the icons it had come to destroy".[18] Biblical criticism never actually sought to destroy theology or religion, let alone the church structures – it ultimately only sought a space outside of those spheres of influence, but it was a space that was always in the shadow of the former, and that is where much of the discipline currently remains. A full emancipation of Biblical Studies, if there is to be one, must engage the genealogy of the discipline, particularly examining the discursive structures as they are fundamentally embedded in the socio-cultural and politico-historical contexts out of which biblical criticism arose. Russell McCutcheon has been engaged in a project like this for the study of religion more broadly, analyzing both the history of the discipline and its current structures from a secular(izing) perspective.[19] Boer himself has made similar forays into this territory.[20] Yet, so far we have just dabbled in this task, and a thoroughgoing manifesto needs to be rooted in precisely a genealogical exploration and explanation that details not only the theological – even if sublimated (or repressed?) – tendencies of biblical scholarship,[21] but also the way in which the "liberal left" or the "radical wing" of biblical criticism is in some sense still lying in the shadow of its former self, bolstering hegemonic discourse in the very act of trying to decentre it.

Second, following upon the observations of de Certeau regarding the way in which the modern nation-state became the heir apparent of Christianity's theological mantle, and including also the arguments by Asad on the ideology of secularism, I would suggest that we need to be alert with respect to from where, for whom, and to what end we are emancipating Biblical Studies – a Marxian project seems to demand this kind of questioning. In my estimation, the de-Christianization process that de Certeau touts is too optimistic. Christian theological structures have been reified on ever more universal levels through the political, social, and economic structures emerging out of Christianized nations. The "gospel" has perhaps become less explicitly theological (if by that we mean something to be identified with explicit historical theological tradents and traditions), but it has not necessarily thereby become less "Christian" or less imperialistic/colonizing. Indeed, the survival of Christian memes, if we use that conceptual category for the moment, is manifest precisely in the transition from church rule to state formation. But it has not stopped there. The political state has given way to larger global structures in terms of the domination of neo-liberal market economies. Has the process of universalization now moved to another level? David Harvey[22] has argued that political and market logics with respect to expansion and imperial control are still distinct even if tightly interwoven. Even if they are still separate, it is clear that "secularism" possesses not only its own ideological disciplining function, but that it also has become intercalated with broader forms of regulation and control arising through the globalizing power of the market. Thus, Asad's observations must be pushed – and urgently – to a new level of interaction, wherein we begin to assess more fully the ways in which so-called "liberal democratic secular" values are actually serving, even if covertly, larger imperial agendas. Recent work on neo-liberalism's exportation of capitalism abroad is illuminating the devastating (even if still inchoate) effects of globalization in terms of the recalibration of the value and marketability of the *human*,[23] and we, in the once "comfortable" West, are feeling the repercussions of this mass rescaling (cf. Appadurai 2006).[24] Further, if we take the recent insightful analysis of Tricia Sheffield into account, then we will also have a better sense of how the function of religion in previous societies has resurfaced in the era of American mass consumption, particularly through the totemic power of advertising.[25]

While space does not permit dwelling on these aspects at length, arising out of this admittedly thin sketch is the notion that there is something larger afoot on the global political and cultural scene, and that any emancipation of Biblical Studies must be attuned to these broader dynamics. In other words, what does the "liberal left" hope to gain by freeing Biblical Studies from alleged "theological tyranny"? Is this to be freed from Egypt only to die in the desert? In a recent essay in honour of the famed feminist critic Elisabeth Schüssler Fiorenza, herself a tireless advocate as of late for the role of the biblical critic in the political public forum, R.S. Sugirtharajah,[26] in his own manifesto with respect to the historical-critical study of the Bible, suggests that biblical critics need to seek a wider public than the "usual suspects". Fair enough. His suggestion of what this might look like, however, is unsettling: he figures that perhaps singer/songwriter Bono, of the Dublin rock group U2, might be better fitted to interpret the biblical text than biblical critics themselves. If that is our best option, I am all for keeping the Bible in the theology schools and under the thumb of conventional and less critical historical-critics (I believe there is more liberative potential in the latter, since "liberation" still has a substantive meaning for many in these traditions).

If Žižek has taught us anything, it ought to have been that at every step of the way, in our high-minded emancipatory rhetoric and action, we will always already reify the structures of the dominant discourse we are opposing. Even more so, the "liberal left" is in fact that element that allows the hegemonic to exist; the "liberal left" is the latter's projected antagonism. That would suggest that the first step in any emancipatory praxis ought to be liberating the Bible from *our own* grasp and *our own* hermeneutic. Added to this picture, at least on the North American scene, is the increasing participation of biblical scholars – especially that quadrant already "liberated" from theological repression – in the spectacles and simulations of the media ideological apparatus of dominant politics and society. Simply put, from the engagement over the *Passion of the Christ* and the *Da Vinci Code* to the recent hype swirling around the James ossuary and *The Gospel of Judas*, scholars are increasingly becoming sucked into the vortex of the culture of consumption and mass production.[27]

In a striking Platonic reversal, we have left the sunlight for the stark glare of the spotlight. Publishers are more interested in "scholarship light" because it sells better (both among the public and in the classroom), and scholars themselves often seem more fascinated with and mesmerized by simulacra than substance with respect to ideas and practices. This may sound like an argument for a return to elitism; in my mind, however, it is not. Rather, my concern is that the meaningful engagement and interrogation of ideas and paradigms, sustained by critical evaluation and judgment, has been, without us even noticing, wrenched away (or perhaps we gave it up much more willingly than that?) – where there once was predominantly *krisis* there is often now only *circus*.[28] Higher education, at least in North America, is fast following suit (how could it not?). Somewhere between the strategic intellectual organization of PowerPoint and the emergent fluidizing, amorphous neo-liberal moral value system, the new economy of learning and teaching has slowly reconfigured and rescaled education into a subsidiary of the market economy itself – and resistance seems futile! Finally, as Aijaz Ahmad[29] has astutely reminded those of us with penchants toward postcolonial and poststructural interpretative frameworks, "theory itself becomes a marketplace of ideas, with massive supplies of theory as usable commodity, guaranteeing consumers' free choice and a rapid rate of obsolescence", and the recent "turn to religion" in Continental philosophy seems not to be excluded from this critique. We might think that democracy itself were in jeopardy if that concept did not already mask the elite oligarchies that run much of Western society.[30] Even the once heralded prophet of "the end of history", Francis Fukuyama, seems more depressed these days. Thus, while I am very much in sympathy with Boer's broader emancipatory project and am willing to stand by his side in many respects, I cannot help but wonder who will liberate the liberators.

Third, returning to the political signification that Asad raised with respect to the headscarf affair in France, I think there is an element from that discussion that may also help one engage some of the issues that Boer raises in his manifesto. In particular, Asad's interest in reading the headscarf as a sign is intriguing, not in small part because I perceive a similar kind of signification operative in the debate between theological and secular biblical studies. It is a matter of argument who in fact is wearing the "headscarf" in this debate, and the answer to that depends on where and how one decides to unpack and delineate the structures of argumentation. The "liberal left" may well be in the minority (donning the headscarf, so to speak) before the court of final arbitration on such matters. Yet one can also assess the clarion call offered by Boer as the structural equivalent to the French insistence on the unscarfing or, even more fundamentally, unveiling of Muslim females in the public forum. I am less concerned here about matters related to religious motivation and intent or even the battle between secularism as a Western ideology and its apparent (resurgent) religious challenge. Rather, I am interested in the politics that underlie these attempts at unmasking and unveiling. At an essential level, then, this debate about who interprets the Bible and how it is interpreted is ultimately a political engagement *on both sides*, and it is useful to expose the debate as such. There is no doubt, in my mind at least, that at stake are alternative political visions, and the Bible is a central trope in that discursive play. Recognizing this possibility does not resolve anything, but it may bring some clarity to what precisely we are trying to be liberated from and towards. The *telos* is everything in this debate and, while we will still have diverse notions of the 'end' in various local and national contexts, we gain clarity, I believe, by at least placing these visions on the table in an open and honest way. Further, the urgency behind Boer's manifesto is not in small part dependent on the role that the Bible has come to play in American political discourse, in particular the "war on terror" that is terrorizing us all to some extent (although many beyond our borders are experiencing the repercussions in the most hellish of ways). As Bruce Lincoln has adroitly illustrated in his essay "Symmetric Dualisms: Bush and bin Laden on October 7", there is a disturbing similarity in the way that religious argumentation and tropes are couched *on both sides* to serve specific political ends.[31] That religious discourse should be so closely tied to politics should not surprise us – religious discourse *is*, after all, the sacred texture of human ideological aspirations. Jacques Berlinerblau is similarly concerned about this encroachment of religion into the public sphere, although he has gone about the task of engagement in a decidedly different fashion than Boer, discursively constructing the Bible as irrelevant for civic moral and political use.[32] In the end, however, the fundamental issue is weighing the balance of rights and freedoms in a republic – and one's theological or secular, embracing or critical, reading of the Bible may have little to do with that larger concern (although some will argue it is at the very least a barometer). In writing this, finally, I do not want to minimize what Russell McCutcheon[33] has recently pointed out, that "religion" as a category opposite of the "political" also functions to do much *political* work for our liberal democratic societies – and our radical dissent is palpably muted by our continual separation of an emotive, internal construction of "religion" juxtaposed to the "political". For precisely this reason, then, the demystification of the political dimensions of religious rhetoric is a critically important task.

Further along these lines, we are living in an era that Zygmunt Bauman has designated as "liquid modernity".[34] Alongside the abandonment of early modernity's commitment to progress as "an attainable *telos* of historical change", Bauman also highlights a second major shift in this new form of modernity: "the deregulation and privatization of the modernizing tasks and duties".[35] For Bauman, this shift from collective human rationalizing processes to the focus on the individual has resulted "in the relocation of ethical/political discourse from the frame of the 'just society' to that of 'human rights'...refocusing that discourse on the right of individuals to stay different and to pick and choose at will their own models of happiness and fitting life-style".[36] Bauman's main concern, then, is that in this new incarnation of modernity "the private colonizes the public space, squeezing out and chasing away everything which cannot be fully, without residue, expressed in the vernacular of private concerns, worries and pursuits".[37] Bauman concludes by arguing that "*any true liberation calls today for more, not less, of the 'public sphere' and 'public power'.*"[38] There are dangers in that desire, of course, but helpful in Bauman's observations is the notion that our intellectual and cultural roots have shifted dramatically in the past twenty years, keeping pace with the vast changes in political and especially economic structures – we are mimicking the broader patterns of globalizing (and totalizing) discourses and practices in our daily lives. The effort to separate the Bible from church dogmatics that was waged at the beginning of the era of modernity cannot be our battle today – it is time for a recalibration of aims and discourses in light of the rapidly morphing state of contemporary life. True, many American fundamentalists are bringing the Bible to bear on the public forum, toward ends that seem to restrict the individual liberties of some (if not many) people in both the US and abroad. Still, as noted above, I wonder if we do not do better to unmask the political nature of this (often facile) biblical discourse, rather than seeking to wrench the Bible out of the hands of the church and the seminaries (as if that were really possible anyway). To do the latter, it seems to me, confirms the belief that the Bible *is the thing* that matters most – but, in effect, it is not. Our attempt to grasp it fuels its power in the fundamentalist imaginary (and our own!), but it does not solve the problem on the level of politics and culture, which is where our attention needs to focus (where are the new Robert Bellahs and Jürgen Habermases?). Unveiling the oppressive structures of the Bible is easy – unmasking those in our culture is much less so – revealing our own is perhaps the most difficult. Herein there is also a noticeable tension between the Marxian project and that of biblical prophetic critique – the latter is committed to examining the human pretensions that have usurped biblical mandates, particularly social, while the former is dedicated to probing the always already cultural and social prison erected by biblical and religious discourse (even that language that focuses on social reform and liberating the poor). While the two are often interconnected (cf. liberation theology) and exist in a co-dependence somewhat like the terms "secular" and "religious", the inherent tension should not be passed over lightly.

Finally, and in somewhat of an ancillary vein, José Casanova's still pertinent observations on the critical role that religion can play in a secular society ought not to be ignored.[39] Casanova suggests that religion can sometimes be an ally in a secular society and "force modern societies to reflect publicly and collectively upon their normative structures". In line with Bauman's observations above, Casanova also perceives a shift in terms of the private increasingly encroaching on the public sphere.[40] Yet even when the more traditionalist religious beliefs enter into and encounter the public forum, they are also, according to Casanova, potentially changed in that interaction. The current shift in American evangelicalism with respect to traditionally "liberal" social issues may suggest that Casanova is right in some respects. Still, as Asad notes in his criticism of Casanova, the definition of appropriate religious "interference" is precisely one that supports rather than undermines the general value structure of the public forum,[41] and this observation then brings us back to one of the fundamental issues at stake in this whole discussion: whose public forum and whose social policy are we talking about? William Connolly has tried to force secularism to reengage some of these critical points, arguing that it has been too narrow in its understanding of public reason, therefore actually running interference with respect to the freedom and tolerance it so resolutely touts.[42] At the minimum, scholars like Paul Apostolidis argue that the disregard for conservative religion by secularists inhibits the latter's ability to engage effectively and radically the current political situation.[43] In the end, as the liquid slowly evaporates on this new mode of modernity, to be replaced by something possibly quite monstrous, I cannot help but wonder if we will not need the church and its theological interpretations as comrades in what comes next – and we will likely require new models of public engagement and collaboration to accommodate that shift.

In conclusion, I come back to something that Jacques Rancière has been stressing as of late: democracies are fundamentally unpredictable entities, and they are primarily about the decentring of hegemonic powers and discourses.[44] Moreover, democracies are always already co-opted by elite powers in society:

> the 'government of anybody and everybody' is bound to attract the hatred of all those who are entitled to govern men by their birth, wealth, or science. Today it is bound to attract this hatred more radically than ever, since the social power of wealth no longer tolerates any restrictions on its limitless growth, and each day its mechanisms become more closely articulated to

> those of State action ... [Democracy] is the action that constantly wrests the monopoly of public life from oligarchic governments, and the omnipotence over their lives from the power of wealth.[45]

Of course, it remains to be seen where academics/biblical critics will position themselves in this struggle – as part of the oligarchy or in resistance to such powers?[46] If the latter, it would appear that (future) manifestos will need to focus on how the Bible, secularly *and* theologically, confessionally across a wide spectrum of ideologies, can be used to liberate individuals from an increasing deracination of democratic impulses. In a moment of particular clarity, Žižek suggests that "instead of imposing our notions of universality, universality – the shared space of understanding between cultures – should be conceived of as an infinite task of translation, a constant reworking of one's own particular position."[47] As we think of manifestos, then, we should bear in mind these larger projects of translation and advocacy, always with an eye trained on the moments we continually (and by necessity) undermine our own valiant and vaunted ethics. Is Boer among the prophets? He is, most definitely, and it remains the task of those who seek to conjure up the Marxian spirits in the present to carry on grappling with this emancipatory legacy, both its meaning and application – come what may.

## Endnotes

\* In the course of writing this essay, I am indebted to several individuals. Steve Stell's forthright and insightful interaction over Boer's manifesto (from a decidedly Christian theological perspective) in the upper level Religious Studies methods seminar of spring 2007 helped both to foment and solidify my thoughts articulated herein. As this piece came to fruition, it was also readily apparent that the specters of my fall 2006 "Spectacle and the Death of History" course continued to haunt my thinking, and I am thankful for the many keen students who took that remarkable "liberal arts" journey with me. Special thanks goes to Tatiana Vakidis, for the continual reminder that "you probably suck more" (it is true, I do), and also to Ishan Sareen, for his astute challenge that my appeal to students to "touch the ark" (come what may) was actually an affirmation of biblical authority (in the very act of seeking to decentre it). Further, my newfound comrade, Milton Aylor, has been an immense (materialist and otherwise) source of inspiration in the short time I have known him. Finally, this essay is dedicated to the memory of Michael Reimer (Morden, Manitoba, Canada), who died 23 May 2007, after a five-month battle with pancreatic cancer. Michael was not a biblical critic, but he nonetheless struggled to understand the place of the Bible in his world (one in which the Bible was often held up as a standard judgment and exclusion). It may have come as some comfort for him to know that many of us who have made a career out of studying the Bible and asking questions about its meaning often find ourselves in a similar struggle to make sense of it all. *Amor animi arbitrio sumitur, non ponitur* (Syrus).

** Todd Penner is the Gould H. and Marie Cloud Associate Professor of Religious Studies, Austin College in Sherman, Texas, USA.

1. J. Rancière, *Hatred of Democracy* (trans. S. Corcoran; New York: Verso, 2006), p. 93.

2. J. Derrida, *Specters of Marx: The State of Debt, the Work of Mourning and the New International* (trans. P. Kamuf; Routledge Classics Edition; New York: Routledge, 2006), p. 95.

3. R. Barry Matlock, "Beyond the Great Divide? History, Theology, and the Secular Academy", in T. Penner and C. Vander Stichele (eds.), *Moving beyond New Testament Theology? Essays in Conversation with Heikki Räisänen* (Publications of the Finnish Exegetical Society 88; Helsinki: Finnish Exegetical Society and Göttingen: Vandenhoeck & Ruprecht, 2005), pp. 369–99.

4. Roland Boer, *Marxist Criticism of the Bible* (New York: Continuum, 2003).

5. Derrida, *Specters of Marx*, p. 76.

6. Derrida, *Specters of Marx*, p. 67.

7. G. Schulman, "Redemption, Secularization, and Politics", in D. Scott and C. Hirschkind (eds.), *Powers of the Secular Modern: Talal Asad and His Interlocutors* (Cultural Memory in the Present; Palo Alto, CA: Stanford University Press, 2006), pp. 154–79.

8. See Michel de Certeau, *The Writing of History* (trans. T. Conley; New York: Columbia University Press, 1988), p. 179.

9. de Certeau, *The Writing of History*, p. 176.

10. de Certeau, *The Writing of History*, p. 156.

11. de Certeau, *The Writing of History*, p. 178.

12. Talal Asad, *Formations of the Secular: Christianity, Islam, Modernity* (Cultural Memory in the Present; Palo Alto, CA: Stanford University Press, 2003), p. 192.

13. Vincent Pecora, *Secularization and Cultural Criticism* (Religion and Postmodernism; Chicago, IL: University of Chicago Press, 2006), p. 42.

14. Asad, *Formations of the Secular*, pp. 191–92.

15. Talal Asad, "Trying to Understand French Secularism", in H. de Vries and L.E. Sullivan (eds), *Political Theologies: Public Religions in a Post-Secular World* (New York: Fordham University Press, 2006), pp. 524; cf. 504.

16. Slavoj Žižek, *Welcome to the Desert of the Real* (New York: Verso, 2002), p. 32.

17. Alasdair MacIntyre, *After Virtue: A Study in Moral Theory* (Notre Dame, IN: University of Notre Dame Press, 1984, 2nd edn.), pp. 244–63.

18. Stephen D. Moore, *Poststructuralism and the New Testament: Derrida and Foucault at the Foot of the Cross* (Minneapolis, MN: Fortress Press, 1994), p. 117. Also see W. Blanton, "Biblical Scholarship in the Age of Bio-power: Albert Schweitzer and the Degenerate Physiology of the Historical Jesus", in *The Bible and Critical Theory* 2.1: 6.1–6.25 (2006).

19. See for e.g. R.T. McCutcheon, *The Discipline of Religion: Structure, Meaning, Rhetoric* (New York: Routledge, 2003).

20. See Roland Boer, *Novel Histories: The Fiction of Biblical Criticism* (Playing the Text 2; Sheffield: Sheffield Academic Press, 1997); S. Kelley, *Racializing Jesus: Race, Ideology and the Formation of Modern Biblical Scholarship* (Biblical Limits; New York: Routledge, 2002). Cf. W. Blanton, *Displacing Christian Origins:*

*Philosophy, Secularity, and the New Testament* (Religion and Postmodernism; Chicago, IL: University of Chicago Press, 2007).

21. Cf. W. Blanton, "Biblical Scholarship in the Age of Bio-power".

22. See David Harvey, *The New Imperialism* (New York: Oxford University Press, 2003), p. 183.

23. See especially A. Ong, *Neoliberalism as Exception: Mutations in Citizenship and Sovereignty* (Durham, NC: Duke University Press, 2006).

24. Cf. A. Appadurai, *Fear of Small Numbers: An Essay on the Geography of Anger* (Public Planet Books; Durham, NC: Duke University Press, 2006).

25. See Tricia Sheffield, *The Religious Dimensions of Advertising* (Religion/Culture/Critique; New York: Palgrave MacMillan, 2006); cf. W. Hamacher, trans. K. Wetters, "Guilt History: Benjamin's Sketch 'Capitalism as Religion'" in *Diacritics* 32 (2002), pp. 81–106.

26. R.S. Sugirtharajah (2003) "The End of Biblical Studies?", in F.F. Segovia (ed.), *Toward a New Heaven and a New Earth: Essays in Honor of Elisabeth Schüssler Fiorenza* (Maryknoll, NY: Orbis Books, 2003), pp. 133–40.

27. T. Penner and C. Vander Stichele, "Passion for (the) Real? *The Passion of the Christ* and Its Critics", in *Biblical Interpretation* 14 (2006), pp. 18–36.

28. Alongside these observations, I would also note that one other major concern at present is an accelerating repression of academic and broader cultural, social, and political freedom of expression in the United States. There is widespread involvement among both conservative and liberal forces to regulate speech acts so as to produce a neo-liberal illusion of justice and harmony. Academics, who were once a critical conscience of liberal democracy, have themselves become complicit in the control of knowledge production, thereby helping shape a generation of students and educational institutions that imbibe the same chimera.

29. A. Ahmad, *In Theory: Classes, Nations, Literatures* (New York: Verso, 1992), p. 70.

30. See Rancière, *Hatred of Democracy*, pp. 73–75.

31. Bruce Lincoln, *Holy Terrors: Thinking about Religion after September 11* (Chicago, IL: University of Chicago Press, 2003).

32. Jacques Berlinerblau, *The Secular Bible: Why Nonbelievers Must Take Religion Seriously* (Cambridge: Cambridge University Press, 2005).

33. Russell T. McCutcheon, *Religion and the Domestication of Dissent: Or, How to Live in a Less than Perfect Nation* (Religion in Culture; London: Equinox Publishing, 2005).

34. Zygmunt Bauman, *Liquid Modernity* (Cambridge: Polity Press, 2000).

35. Bauman, *Liquid Modernity*, p. 29.

36. Bauman, *Liquid Modernity*, p. 29.

37. Bauman, *Liquid Modernity*, p. 39.

38. Bauman, *Liquid Modernity*, p. 51.

39. J. Casanova, *Public Religions in the Modern World* (Chicago, IL: The University of Chicago Press, 1994); cf. Talal Asad, *Formations of the Secular*, pp. 181–87.

40. See Casanova, *Public Religions in the Modern World*, pp, 228–29.

41. Asad, *Formations of the Secular*, p. 183.

42. William Connolly, *Why I Am Not a Secularist* (Minneapolis, MN: University of Minneapolis Press, 1999).

43. Paul Apostolidis, *Stations of the Cross: Adorno and Christian Right Radio* (Durham, NC: Duke University Press, 2000); cf. Berlinerblau, *The Secular Bible*.

44. Rancière, *Hatred of Democracy*, pp. 41–42.

45. Rancière, *Hatred of Democracy*, pp. 94–96.

46. Cf. B. Robbins, "Secularism, Elitism, Progress, and Other Transgressions: On Edward Said's 'Voyage in'", in F. Afzal-Khan and K. Seshadri-Crooks (eds), *The Pre-Occupation of Postcolonial Studies* (Durham, NC: Duke University Press, 2000), pp. 157–68.

47. Žižek, *Welcome to the Desert of the Real*, p. 66.

Part C

THE END OF BIBLICAL STUDIES?

# The End of Biblical Studies as a Moral Obligation

*Hector Avalos**

The only mission of biblical studies should be to end biblical studies, as we know it. This essay explains why I have come to such a conclusion. In the process, it will summarize the history of academic biblical studies as primarily a religionist apologetic enterprise, despite its partial integration of secularist epistemologies. Our argument will be framed not only on historical and pragmatic grounds, but also on moral grounds.

For our purposes, we can summarize our plea to end biblical studies as we know it with the two following main premises:

1. Modern biblical scholarship has demonstrated that the Bible is the product of cultures whose values and beliefs about the origin, nature, and purpose of our world are no longer held to be relevant, even by most Christians and Jews.
2. Paradoxically, despite the recognition of such irrelevance, the profession of academic biblical studies still centres on maintaining the illusion of relevance by:
   i) A variety of scholarly disciplines whose methods and conclusions are often philosophically flawed (e.g., translation, textual criticism, archaeology, history, and biblical theology).
   ii) An infrastructure that supports biblical studies (e.g., universities, a media-publishing complex, churches, and professional organizations).

The first premise acknowledges that we have learned much new information about the Bible. The Dead Sea Scrolls (DSS) and the enormous archaeological treasures found in the ancient Near East in the last 150 years or so have set the Bible more firmly in its original cultural context. However, those very discoveries show that the Bible is irrelevant, insofar as it is part of a world radically dissimilar to ours in its conception of the cosmos, the supernatural, and ethics. In fact, in a 1975 report published by the American Academy of Religion, one scholar frankly admitted that "[i]ndeed, one of the enduring contributions of biblical studies in this century has been the discovery of the strangeness of the thought-forms of the biblical literature of the 'western' traditions to us".[1] In short, scholars of religion themselves, not just secular humanists, admit that the Bible is a product of a very different culture. If that is the case, then there is no reason to continue to expend scholarly effort on a book that is no more relevant to the modern world than numerous other works of antiquity, many of which still lie untranslated.

### *Irrelevance Defined*

"Irrelevant" here refers to a biblical concept or practice that is no longer viewed as valuable, applicable, and/or ethical. Thus, genocide might be regarded as objectionable among many Americans today, whereas that was not the case in many biblical texts. In fact, Michael Coogan[2] admits that some biblical practices are so objectionable that churches try to hide them:

> Conspicuously absent from lectionaries are most or all of such books as Joshua, with its violent extermination of the inhabitants of the land of Canaan at divine command, or Judges, with its horrifying narratives of patriarchy and sexual assault in chapters 11 and 19, to say nothing of the Song of Solomon, with its charged eroticism, or of Job, with its radical challenge to the dominant biblical view of a just and caring God.

Likewise, modern medicine does not use the supernatural explanations for illness found in the Bible, and so such explanations for illness are irrelevant today. Here are some more examples of scientific and scholarly "discoveries" that do or should render the Bible irrelevant.

1. Some biblical authors held the universe was created in six days, and modern science has demonstrated otherwise.
2. Slavery was often condoned or endorsed.
3. There is no independent evidence for the life or teachings of Jesus in the first century CE, and so most modern Christians are not even following Jesus' teachings.
4. Biblical authors generally believed that women were subordinate to men.

Even when many persons in the modern world still hold to biblical ideas (e.g., creationism), it is partly because academic biblical scholars are not sufficiently vocal about undermining outdated biblical beliefs. Instead, biblical scholars concentrate on maintaining the value of the biblical text in modern society. Maintaining the value of the Bible, in turn, helps biblical scholars make the argument that they are still relevant.

## Irrelevance by the Numbers

The idea that the Bible is irrelevant, even among those who regard themselves as Christian, can be demonstrated empirically very easily. For decades, the Gallup organization has conducted surveys on biblical literacy. These surveys show that, despite professed adherence to the Bible, most Christians are either ignorant of the Bible or their appeal to the Bible is very limited. For example, the 2005 Gallup poll shows that "[f]ewer than half of Americans can name the first book of the Bible".[3]

In September 2006, Baylor University's Institute for Studies of Religion published a comprehensive survey on American religion, which showed 21.9 percent of Mainline Protestants and 33.1 percent of Catholics "never" read Scripture (Bader, et al. 2005: 14).[4] Michael Coogan's observation is pertinent here, "[a]lthough the Bible is acknowledged in theory as an authority, much of it has simply been ignored".[5]

More importantly, it is conservative biblical scholars themselves who say that a lot of biblical materials are irrelevant. A good illustration is found in the work of Daniel J. Estes.[6] Estes is worried about irrelevancy, and even developed the following "scale" to measure the relevance (his term is "degree of transfer") of biblical teachings:[7]

| 0 | 1 | 2 | 3 | 4 | 5 | 6 | 7 | 8 | 9 | 10 |
|---|---|---|---|---|---|---|---|---|---|---|
| Obsolete precepts | | | Patterns | | | Principles | | Directives | | |

For Estes, the "degree of transfer" and "continuity" refers to how obliged a modern audience is to follow what is addressed to an "original audience" in the Bible. Something close to zero is obsolete, and something at 10 would be a directive that Christians must still follow.

He then provides the example of the law of first-fruits in Deut. 26:1–11, which commands Israelites to go to a location which Yahweh has chosen in order to provide the priest with the first yields of their agricultural season. Estes would rank this close to the zero side of the scale (obsolete precepts) because, among other things, most modern Christians no longer are farmers, nor do Christians recognize a central location that Yahweh has chosen.

Estes[8] recognizes that "[n]one of these specific items has a precise equivalent in the identity and experience of Christian believers today. Many of the Old Testament legal prescriptions are in this category, including, for example, the dietary regulations…" When pressed to find examples of "total continuity" between the original biblical audience and today's Christian audience, he admits "[i]ndisputable examples of total continuity between the two audiences are relatively rare".[9]

John Bright, one of the most prominent American biblical scholars of the last century, reflected a similar sentiment regarding the Sabbatical and Jubilee years in Leviticus 25. Bright[10] remarked that "the regulations described therein are obviously so little applicable to the modern situation that a preacher might be pardoned if he told himself that the passage contains no relevant message for his people whatever". In fact, if we went verse by verse, I suspect that 99 percent of the Bible would not even be missed, as it reflects many practices, injunction, and ideas not much more applicable than Leviticus 25.

### *Hiding the Irrelevance*

Our second major premise is that, despite this admission of irrelevance, the profession of academic biblical scholarship paradoxically and self-servingly promotes the illusion of relevance. This illusion strives to make believers think that they have "the Bible" when all they really have is a book constructed by modern elite scholars. So even if modern Christians said that the Bible was relevant to them, such relevance is based on an illusion because most readers falsely assume that modern versions do reflect the original "Bible". And, of course, throughout Jewish and Christian history there has been discussion about the relevance of certain passages, books, or even large sections of the Bible. One need only remember the notorious proposal of Marcion, the Gnostic writer of the second century, to eject the entire Old Testament from Christian life (see Blackman, Hoffman).[11] Friedrich Delitzsch made similar proposals in the twentieth-century, although they were tarnished by his anti-Judaism.[12]

Our argument is that there is really nothing in the entire book Christians call "the Bible" that is any more relevant than anything else written in the ancient world.[13] Therefore, biblical scholars should be shifting their attention to informing the modern world of how alien and inapplicable biblical concepts are to the modern world. By so doing, however, biblical scholars would eventually bring an end to their discipline. This is the altruistic solution.

## Translations as Marketing Instruments

Insofar as the general public is concerned, nothing maintains the relevance of the Bible more than translations. By the year 2000, the Bible had been translated into 2,029 languages[14] If it were not for translations, the Bible probably would have remained inaccessible and forgotten. Nearly as much is admitted in a report of a meeting of church leaders, which concluded that "the difficulty of modern man to see the relevance of the Bible in his life is one of the main impediments in the effective use of the Bible"[15] But even more surprising is that translations often are not meant to make the Bible relevant by faithfully translating the original. Rather, relevance is often maintained by using translation to hide and distort the original meaning in order to provide the illusion that the values and norms of biblical authors are compatible with those of the modern world.

It is not that translations mistranslate everything. But certainly, there are distortions or outright misrepresentations of the original meaning where it might make a difference to how a modern audience sees the Bible. Consider the translation of Lk 14:26 in *The Good News Bible* (GNB) which is famous for sugarcoating objectionable passages: "Whoever comes to me cannot be my disciple unless *he loves me more than he loves* his father and his mother, his wife and his children, his brothers, and his sisters and himself as well".

The GNB has expunged the word "hate" from Jesus' instructions, which are more accurately translated in the *New Revised Standard Version*: "Now large crowds were traveling with him; and he turned and said to them, 'Whoever comes to me and does not *hate* father and mother, wife and children, brothers and sisters, yes, and even life itself, cannot be my disciple.'"

According to this text, Jesus behaves like a cult leader who actively attempts to transfer allegiance from the believer's family to himself. Disciples must hate their parents. This, of course, contradicts the commandment to honour one's parents (Exod. 20:12) and makes for a bad image of Jesus in the modern world.

The *Contemporary English Version* (*CEV*) sanitizes Jesus' seeming endorsement of genital mutilation with this translation of Mt. 19:12:

> Some people are unable to marry because of birth defects or because of what someone has done to their bodies. Others *stay single* for the sake of the kingdom of heaven. Anyone who can accept this teaching should do so.

Compare this translation to that of the older *Revised Standard Version*:

> For there are eunuchs who have been so from birth, and there are eunuchs who have been made eunuchs by men, and there are eunuchs who *have made themselves eunuchs* for the sake of the kingdom of heaven. He who is able to receive this, let him receive it.

The *RSV* conveys much more accurately the idea that people can make themselves eunuchs, which literally might involve castration, for the sake of the kingdom of heaven. Jesus does not seem to object, and, in fact, can be interpreted to endorse the idea of self-mutilation. That this passage could be so understood is shown by the fact that Origen, the famous Church Father, is reported to have castrated himself in light of this verse.[16] The rendition of "stay single" seems most disingenuous in light of how the *CEV* is portrayed by its advocates: "The *CEV* is not a paraphrase. It is an accurate and faithful translation of the original manuscripts" (Bible Gateway online). Yet, commenting on the *CEV*'s translation, Stanley Porter, the New Testament scholar, remarked: "Is it possible, in light of the overtly evangelistic purpose of the *CEV*, that the New Testament has been toned down in some places so that it does not scare off those attracted to Christianity?"[17]

The Holocaust generated a lot of self-critical analysis on the part of many Christians. Some Christian scholars have acknowledged the anti-Judaism (Beck; Ruether),[18] while others have claimed that any anti-Judaism has been the result of misunderstanding crucial passages.[19] But, among those who think the anti-Judaism to be undeniable, we find this curious solution voiced by Irvin J. Borowsky:

> The solution to erasing this hatred is for bible societies and religious publishers to produce two editions, one for the public similar to the Contemporary English Version which reduces significantly this anti-Judaic potential, and the other edition for scholars taken from the Greek text.[20]

Orwellian double-speak could not be celebrated more fervently. The proposal is paternalistic because it assumes that readers need protection from their own Bible. Borowsky, adds, "[t]he stakes are high. People have been murdered because of these words".[21]

Such efforts only expose the fact that scholars themselves know that "the Bible" can be a violent and opprobrious document which must be sanitized to keep it alive. The same may be argued with respect to, among other things, including gender-neutral language to hide biblical patriarchalism and misogyny.[22]

## The End of the Original Text

Textual criticism, the scholarly discipline that seeks the reconstruction of the most original text possible, has also helped to end biblical studies. Unlike most works of antiquity, the textual criticism of the Bible carries crucial theological and moral consequences for those who believe they must have an accurate record of God's word to conduct their lives.[23] Yet, in the past few decades, there have been prominent textual critics who have predicted an imminent demise. Consider the depressing assessment of Eldon J. Epp:

> The reasons for this recent and rapid erosion of the field of NT textual criticism are elusive. Most of it has taken place in a little more than a decade. Whether the disappearance of opportunities for graduate study in the field is a cause or a symptom of the erosion is not clear, though certainly the discipline would seem to have no bright future in America and little hope of survival here without opportunities.[24]

Epp[25] later saw signs of progress. But one of the highlights of that progress – the shift away from the idea that we can recover an "original text"[26] – actually spells doom for textual criticism.

Indeed, the findings of textual critics devastate any claim that the Bible has been transmitted faithfully from any original text. For the Hebrew Bible, the earliest actual manuscripts are no earlier than the third century BCE.[27] For the New Testament, our earliest manuscript, P[52], is dated to the second century.[28] The gap between the earliest manuscripts and any supposed autograph means that we cannot know what has been added or removed within that gap.

Accordingly, Emanuel Tov, one of the most prominent textual critics of the Hebrew Bible, offers an ambiguous revised definition of "original text" in the second edition of his standard manual on textual criticism:

> In the *first edition of this monograph* (1992) such textual evidence, which is mainly from [the Septuagint] (such as the short text of Jeremiah), was not taken into consideration in the reconstruction of the original text, and was presented as (a) layer(s) of literary growth preceding the final composition, in other words, as mere drafts. Such thinking, however, attaches too much importance to the canonical status of [the Masoretic Text], disregarding the significance of other textual traditions which at the same time must have been as authoritative as [the Masoretic Text] was at a later stage.[29]

In the case of the New Testament, Helmut Koester deftly summarizes the current situation:

New Testament textual critics have been deluded by the hypothesis that the archetypes of the textual tradition which were fixed ca. 200 CE – and how many archetypes for each Gospel? – are (almost) identical with the autographs. This cannot be confirmed by any external evidence. On the contrary, whatever evidence there is indicates that not only minor, but also substantial revisions to the original texts have occurred during the first five hundred years of the transmission.[30]

Given the failure to find any original text, textual critics now must defend the value of texts that are really modern elite scholarly constructs. Epp comments, "the artificiality of our critical editions is a nonissue, for a critical edition of any ancient writing is by nature a reconstruction".[31] However, the problem is that the Bible is not regarded as just "any ancient writing". It is regarded as the word of God, and so any admission of reconstruction is an admission that we do not have the word of God as originally intended. As such, a reconstructed text becomes useless when measured against any perceived intended purpose of communicating God's original word to the masses.

Textual criticism of the Bible has always mattered to believers rather than to non-believers. But if what matters to believers is an original text on which to base their lives, then textual criticism is not going to matter to believers. And if it does not matter to believers, then we really do not see much use for textual criticism anywhere. It becomes more than ever an elite leisure pursuit akin to solving Sudoku puzzles, but with little benefit to anyone else.

### The End of Biblical Archaeology

Biblical archaeology lies in ruins, be it literally, socially, or metaphorically. In 1995, William G. Dever,[32] a doyen of the archaeology of ancient Israel, declared "American Syro-Palestinian and Biblical archeology are moribund disciplines; and archaeologists like me who have spent a lifetime in the profession, feel like the last members of an endangered species". In 2006, Ronald Hendel[33] remarked, "Biblical Archaeology doesn't really exist today in the way it once did" (see also Davis).[34] To be fair, Dever and Hendel are speaking of "biblical" archaeology in the sense of archaeology focused on supporting the historicity of the Bible. Dever himself once advocated the broader term, "Syro-Palestinian" archaeology, although now his terminology is more varied.[35] Yet, part of that problem lies in the fact that the study of biblical history, which has been intimately tied to biblical archaeology, is itself increasingly under attack. As Dever phrases it, "If the actual history of the Biblical world no longer matters, then archaeology is clearly irrelevant".[36] And, indeed, the debates about recovering Israelite history, and even establishing the existence of the reigns of David and Solomon, show only a downward direction.[37]

Despite the discovery of the Tel Dan Inscription, there is no indisputable extra-biblical evidence for the existence of the Davidic or Solomonic kingdoms.[38]

Within the Deuteronomistic History, it is reasonable to believe in the existence of the following kings based on independent corroboration in Assyrian and Babylonian documents:[39]

| Northern Kingdom | Southern Kingdom (Judah) |
|---|---|
| Omri (ca. 885–874 BCE) | |
| Ahab (ca. 874–853 BCE) | |
| Jehu (ca. 841–790 BCE) | |
| Joash (ca. 805–790 BCE | |
| Menahem (ca. 740 BCE) | Hezekiah (725–696 BCE) |
| Pekah (ca. 735 BCE) | Manasseh (696–642 BCE) |
| Hoshea (ca. 730–722 BCE) | Jehoiachin (605–562 BCE) |

Overall, this is a very impoverished yield for any sort of "biblical history" when one compares it to many of its Near Eastern neighbours. The result is that even a once self-described anti-minimalist such as Dever has signalled his retreat thusly: "I wrote to frustrate Biblical minimalists; then I became one of them".[40] Indeed, Dever's retreat also reaffirms Karl Popper's[41] contention that virtually all our claims about the past are based on trusting a nearly endless chain of authority rather than on our ability to verify if those authorities are correct (cf. White).[42] Similarly, historical Jesus studies have gone not far past what we found in Hermann Samuel Reimarus (1694–1768; cf. Avalos 2007).[43]

The problem remains that our actual earliest sources are no earlier than the Second century. Second, even the so-called Greco-Roman corroborating sources depend on manuscripts of Medieval date. As John P. Meier (1991: 100, n. 6),[44] the noted Jesus scholar, admits: "As with Josephus, so with Tacitus our observations must be tempered by the fact that the earliest manuscript of the Annals comes from the 11th century". This also means, of course, that any thought that modern Christians are following the teachings of Jesus is vacuous. We don't know what Jesus taught or did. And if the teachings of Jesus matter to modern Christians, then modern scholars should be telling believers that such evidence cannot really be found. If scholars did a good job, then less people, not more, would try to follow Jesus' teachings.

## Aesthetics as Apologetics

For our purposes, we use literary criticism to describe a suite of approaches unified by the idea that biblical texts have artistic merit. As David J.A. Clines and J. Cheryl Exum, two of its most influential current practitioners, observe in their own survey of literary criticism, "its primary concern is the text as an object, a product, not as a window upon historical actuality"[45] Such a description reflects what is called "New Criticism" in broader secular literary studies.[46] The New Criticism focuses on a work of art as an autonomous object whose beauty is independent of its historical context. A Rembrandt painting is beautiful no matter what historical forces brought it about.

One need not excavate deeply to find apologetic motives for literary analysis of the Bible among virtuosos such as Robert Alter (1991); Meir Sternberg (1987); and Frank Kermode).[47] Consider Robert Alter's comment on how ancient and modern readers have approached the Hebrew Bible:

> Subsequent religious tradition has by and large encouraged us to take the Bible seriously rather than enjoy it, but the paradoxical truth of the matter may well be that by learning to enjoy the biblical stories more fully as stories, we shall also come to see more clearly what they mean to tell us about God, man and the perilously momentous realm of history.

Indeed, any artistic merit in the Bible is often glorified as unique or superior to that of other works of literature. Yet, this is a subjective judgment. We can just as well make the case that the Bible consists of a lot of ugly and mangled narratives.

When asked what differentiated the Bible from Shakespeare, Phyllis Trible,[48] the renowned biblical scholar, could only reply "I ask myself that question, and if I had a clear answer, I would give it to you". Indeed, the bibliolatrous praise for the Bible's literary merit only diverts attention from many other equally or more deserving texts of antiquity that still lie untranslated in the backrooms of the British Museum, among many other places.

## *Why Recontextualization is Flawed*

Since scholars themselves acknowledge the alien nature of the biblical world, one of the most important techniques to maintain the value of the biblical texts in the modern world is recontextualization or reinterpretation. In a much-cited article, Krister Stendahl[49] argued that scholars should distinguish "what it meant and what it means".[50] Stendahl[51] realizes that the Bible is so alien to our culture that only reinterpretation could keep it alive: "This understanding leads to the puzzling insight that in the living religious traditions continuity is affirmed and achieved by discontinuity. Authority is affirmed and relevance asserted by reinterpretation". For Stendahl, disregarding the "original" sense of a text, is an "essential" function of scriptures:[52] "From a historical point of view, Paul did not mean what Augustine heard him say...For better or for worse, that is how Scriptures function, and, if so, we had better take note thereof also in our treatment of the history of ideas".

Yet, when considering the meaning of a biblical text, two positions can be identified for those who believe there is even such a thing as authorial intent:

1.  Authorial intent is the only one that matters.
2.  Authorial intent is not the only one that matters.

If one chooses 1, then biblical studies has been highly unsuccessful. We often do not possess enough information to determine what an author meant or even what the right socio-historical "context" should be. This is also why trying to determine whether an author meant something "literally" or "figuratively" is usually just as futile.

If one chooses 2, then the only result is chaos and relativism that renders all scholarly biblical studies moot and superfluous. Faith communities do not need academic biblical scholars to inform them about any original context in order to keep the Bible alive for themselves. So what is the purpose of academic biblical studies in such a case? The answer is that there is no purpose, except perhaps to preserve the status of biblical scholars.

The moral reprehensibility of recontextualization can be shown by the simple fact that any good exegete could "recontextualize" *Mein Kampf* and turn it into a text meaningful for today. All we have to do is divest it of the meaning it had in its original context, and – poof – the text becomes relevant for us. For example, we could pretend that "family" and "fellow community members", in Mein Kampf now means "everybody". We can pretend that "Jews" are a symbol that should not be taken seriously.

So why don't scholars do that? Because it would be absurd and immoral. There are excellent linguistic and contextual markers to determine what the original meaning of "German", as a racist term, meant for Hitler. It now would be ludicrous to reinterpret Hitler's "German" to mean "everybody". The "original meaning" of whatever Hitler said is sufficient to judge his book on moral grounds.

The same should apply to the Bible. Once we think we have established an original meaning for a biblical passage, then reappropriation is a morally sordid game just as reappropriation of *Mein Kampf* would be nothing more than a game of "let's pretend".

My analogies with *Mein Kampf* are deliberate here, for I see very little difference in the techniques used by biblical scholars to maintain the relevance of a text that we otherwise believe meant something in its original context that would now be morally reprehensible.

Moreover, any reappropriation of biblical texts leaves unexplained why we are investing so much effort in reinterpreting a book that we can do without. The very idea that the Bible *needs to be reinterpreted* signals our bibliolatry, as few other books of antiquity receive this sort of labor expenditure. Again, surveys show that most people are not reading the Bible or using very little of it, even when they do read it. Societies existed before the Bible, and there is no logical reason why they cannot exist without it. Equally important is that the violent potential of the few passages that are still being used poses threats unlike those we have faced before.[53]

### A Moral Obligation

Since scholars have long concluded that the biblical world is alien to the modern one, then our moral obligation is to inform modern human beings of that fact. To recontextualize or translate original passages to mean the opposite of what they mean is immoral if done for the sake of keeping a text alive.

Even now, bibliolatry binds conservative exegetes and Marxist biblical hermeneuticians. All biblical exegesis is premised on the idea that the Bible should matter to the modern world. But if we are advocates of any sort of liberatory or postcolonial hermeneutics, then de-privileging the text that lies at the centre of our profession is one way to help liberate the texts that are not privileged. My call is not so different from the call to the wealthy nations to give up some of their riches so that the rest of the world can have more.

Yes, biblical scholars have helped bring many Near Eastern texts to light. But there are still so many that lie untranslated, and so it is unconscionable that we still maintain so much focus on the Bible. It falls on biblical scholars to recover more of those ancient texts because biblical scholars form the largest pool of experts in Near Eastern languages that are now used mainly to supplement biblical exegesis. These skills can now be shifted to more non-biblical texts.

Ending the privileged status of the Bible will open up our "canon" to the thousands of ancient texts that still do not have a voice in the modern world. If the Bible has wisdom to teach, then maybe so do many other texts we have not read yet. If the Bible is to be prized for its beauty, then what about the thousands of other texts whose beauty has not even been countenanced at all?

## *Summary*

Biblical scholars have already been moving away from "biblical studies" and more toward the study of Christian and Jewish or Near Eastern "texts". But it is not moving fast enough. Nor is there enough consciousness of the fact that the Bible is more of modern scholarly construct that serves to keep our own profession alive. By making the Bible seem compatible with the modern world, when we otherwise admit it is not, we can justify this elite leisure pursuit called biblical studies.

If my plea is accepted, then one day, what we know as "the Bible" will be viewed as the particular elite scholarly construct of one of many groups that called themselves Christian or Jewish. If my plea is accepted, then liberation will be redefined to mean liberation from the idea that any text in the ancient world should be an authority in the modern world. And it is when biblical scholars realize that we are part of "the biblical empire", that we can come to appreciate the self-sacrifice required to de-privilege the very text that lies at the centre of our profession.

## *Endnotes*

* Hector Avalos is Professor of Religious Studies at Iowa State University, USA.
1. Paul G. Wiebe, "The Place of Theology in Religious Studies", in Anne Carr and Nicholas Piediscalzi (eds), *The Academic Study of Religion: 1975: Public Schools Religion Studies* (Missoula, MT: American Academy of Religion, 1975), p. 24.
2. Michael Coogan, "The Great Gulf Between Scholars and the Pew", in Susanne Scholz (ed.), Biblical Studies Alternatively: An Introductory Reader (Upper Saddle River, NJ: Prentice Hall, 2003), p. 7.

3.  Leonard J. Greenspoon, "What Americans Believe about the Bible", in *Bible Review* 21.5 (2005), p. 29.
4.  Christopher Bader, Kevin Dougherty, Paul Froese *et al.* (2006) *American Piety in the 21ˢᵗ Century: New Insights into the Depth and Complexity of Religion in the U.S* (Waco, TX: Baylor University Institute for Studies of Religion), p. 14.
5.  Michael D. Coogan, *The Old Testament: A Historical And Literary Introduction to the Hebrew Scriptures* (Oxford: Oxford University Press, 2005), p. 7.
6.  Daniel J. Estes, "Audience Analysis and Validity in Application", *BS* 150 (April–June 1993), pp. 219–29.
7.  Estes, "Audience Analysis and Validity in Application", p. 224.
8.  Estes, "Audience Analysis and Validity in Application", p. 224.
9.  Estes, "Audience Analysis and Validity in Application", p. 227.
10. John Bright, (1967) *The Authority of the Old Testament* (Nashville, TN: Abingdon, 1967), p. 152.
11. See E. C. Blackman, *Marcion and his Influence* (London: APGK, 1948); and R. Joseph Hoffmann, *Marcion, on the Restitution of Christianity: An Essay on the Development of Radical Paulist Theology in the Second Century* (Chico, CA: Scholars Press, 1984).
12. Bill T. Arnold and David B. Weisberg, "A Centennial Review of Friedrich Delitzsch's 'Babel und Bibel' Lectures". *JBL* 121 (2002), pp. 441–57.
13. Cf. Philip Davies, "Do We Need Biblical Scholars?", *The Bible and Interpretation* (June 2005); available on-line at: http://www.bibleinterp.com/articles/ Davies_Biblical_Scholars.htm (accessed 2 July 2006); Jacques Berlinerblau, *The Secular Bible: Why Nonbelievers Must Take Religion Seriously* (Cambridge: Cambridge University Press, 2005).
14. Philip C. Stine, *Let The Words be Written: The Lasting Influence of Eugene Nida* (Atlanta, GA: Society of Biblical Literature, 2004), p. 182.
15. Stine, *Let the Words be Written*, p. 66.
16. Eusebius, *Ecclesiastical History* 6.8. (1980), pp. 1–3; (trans. J.E.L. Oulton; Cambridge, MA: Harvard University Press; cf. Mathew Kuefler, *The Manly Eunuch: Masculinity, Gender Ambiguity, and Christian Ideology in Late Antiquity* (Chicago, IL: University of Chicago Press, 2001).
17. Stanley Porter, "The Contemporary English Version", in Stanley Porter and Richard Hess (eds), *Translating the Bible: Problems and Prospects* (London: T&T Clark, 1999), p. 39.
18. See Norman A. Beck, (1994) *Mature Christianity in the 21ˢᵗ Century: The Recognition and Repudiation of the Anti-Jewish Polemic in the New Testament* (New York: Crossroad, 1994); and also see, Rosemary Radford Ruether, *Faith and Fratricide: The Theological Roots of Anti-Semitism* (New York: Seabury, 1979).
19. Eugene Nida, "Meaning-full Translations" [Interview with Eugene Nida], in *Christianity Today* (7 October 2002), pp. 46–49 [48].
20. Kee and Borowsky, "Removing Anti-Judaism from the New Testament", p. 20; cf. Beck, *Mature Christianity in the 21ˢᵗ Century*.
21. Howard Clark Kee and Irvin J. Borowsky (eds), *Removing Anti-Judaism from the New Testament* (Philadelphia, PA: American Interfaith Institute/World Alliance, 1996).

22. Cf. D. A. Carson, *The Inclusive Language Debate: A Plea for Realism* (Grand Rapids, MI: Baker Academic, 1998); Hector Avalos, *The End of Biblical Studies* (Amherst, NY: Prometheus Books, 2007), pp. 53–56.

23. Norman Geisler and William E. Nix, *A General Introduction to the Bible* (Chicago, IL: Moody Press, 1986).

24. Eldon J. Epp, "New Testament Textual Criticism in America: Requiem for a Discipline", in *JBL* 98 (1979), p. 97.

25. Eldon J. Epp, "Issues in New Testament Textual Criticism", in David Alan Black (ed.), *Rethinking New Testament Textual Criticism* (Grand Rapids, MI: Baker Academic, 2002), p. 19.

26. Eldon J. Epp, "The Multivalence of the Term 'Original Text' in New Testament Textual Criticism", *HTR* 92. 3 (1999), pp. 245–81.

27. Emanuel Tov, *Textual Criticism of the Hebrew Bible* (Minneapolis, MN: Fortress Press/Assen: Royal Van Gorcum, 2001, 2nd rev. edn), p. 106.

28. Bruce Metzger and Bart D. Ehrman, *The Text of the New Testament: Its Transmission, Corruption and* Restoration (New York: Oxford, 2005, 4th edn.) p. 55.

29. Tov, *Textual Criticism of the Hebrew Bible*, p. xxxv.

30. Helmut Koester, Introduction to the New Testament (New York: De Gruyter, 2002).

31. Eldon J. Epp, "Issues in New Testament Textual Criticism", in David Alan Black (ed.), *Rethinking New Testament Textual Criticism* (Grand Rapids, MI: Baker Academic, 2002), p. 45.

32. William G. Dever, "Death of a Discipline" in *Biblical Archaeology Review* 21. 5 (September/October 1995), p. 51.

33. Ronald S. Hendel, "Is There a Biblical Archaeology?", *BAR* 32. 4 (July/August 2006), p. 20.

34. Thomas Davis, *Shifting Sands: The Rise and Fall of Biblical Archaeology* (New York: Oxford University Press, 2004).

35. William G. Dever, "Whatchamacallit" in *BAR* 29. 4 (July/August 2003), p. 60.

36. William G. Dever, "Death of a Discipline", p. 53.

37. Ronald S. Hendel, "Is There a Biblical Archaeology?" in *BAR* 32. 4 (July/August 2006), p. 20.

38. George Athas, *The Tel Dan Inscription: A Reappraisal and a New Interpretation* (London: T&T Clark, 2005).

39. Cf. Baruch Halpern, "Erasing History": The Minimalist Assault on Ancient Israel, in *BRev* 11. 6 (1995), pp. 26–35, 47.

40. Hershel Shanks, "Losing Faith", *BAR* 33. 2 (March/April 2007), p. 54.

41. Karl Popper (*Conjectures and Refutations: The Growth of Scientific Knowledge* (London: Routledge, 2002) [1963], pp. 29–30.

42. Hayden White, *Metahistory: The Historical Imagination in Nineteenth-Century Europe* (Baltimore: Johns Hopkins University Press, 1973).

43. Avalos, *The End of Biblical Studies*.

44. John P. Meier, *A Marginal Jew: Rethinking the Historical Jesus.* Volume 1: *The Roots of the Problem and the Person* (New York: Doubleday, 1991).

45. J. Cheryl Exum and David J. A. Clines (eds), *The New Literary Criticism and the Hebrew Bible* (Valley Forge, PA: Trinity Press International, 1993), p. 11.

46. Edgar V. McKnight and Elizabeth Struthers Malbon (eds), *The New Literary Criticism and the New Testament* (Valley Forge, PA: Trinity Press International, 1994; Frank Lentricchia, *After the New Criticism* (Chicago, IL: The University of Chicago Press, 1981).

47. See Robert Alter and Frank Kermode, *The Literary Guide to the Bible* (Cambridge, MA: Belknap Press, 1990); Robert Alter, *The Art of Biblical Narrative* (New York: Basic Books, 1991); Robert Alter, *The Art of Biblical Poetry* (New York: Basic Books, 1985); Meir Sternberg, *The Poetics of Biblical Narrative: Ideological Literature and the Drama of Reading.* (Bloomington, IN: Indiana University Press, 1987).

48. Phyllis Trible, "Wrestling with Scripture" [interview with Hershel Shanks]. *BAR* 32. 2 (March/April 2006), p. 49.

49. Krister Stendahl, "Biblical Theology, Contemporary", in George A. Buttrick *et al.*, (eds), *The Interpreter's Dictionary of the Bible* (4 vols; Nashville, TN: Abingdon, 1962), see vol. 1, p. 420.

50. Cf. E.D. Hirsch, *Validity in Interpretation* (New Haven, CT: Yale University Press, 1967), p. 8.

51. Krister Stendahl, "Biblical Studies" in Paul Ramsey and John F. Wilson (eds), *The Study of Religion in Colleges and Universities* (Princeton, NJ: Princeton University Press, 1970), p. 31.

52. Stendahl, "Biblical Studies", p. 31; cf. Hans-George Gadamer, *Truth and Method* (trans. Joel Weinsheimer and Donald G. Marshall; New York: Crossroad, 2nd rev. edn, 1989).

53. Hector Avalos, *Fighting Words: The Origins of Religious Violence* (Amherst, NY: Prometheus Books, 2005).

# RESPONSIBILITIES TO THE PUBLICS OF BIBLICAL STUDIES AND CRITICAL RHETORICAL ENGAGEMENTS FOR A SAFER WORLD

*Joseph A. Marchal*[*]

Lately some scholars have been asking the tantalizing and perhaps scandalizing question: "Have we reached the end of biblical studies?"[1] Asking after the end of biblical studies also echoes the beliefs of some American conservatives, who claim that we have reached the apex of society and, hence, the end of history, in line with Francis Fukuyama's famous assertion.[2] The question of the moment, though, is perhaps apocalyptically tinged in a direction not quite as grand as Fukuyama's arguments. The question implies the field of biblical studies has either: (1) reached its nadir, not its apotheosis, or (2) harmlessly drifted into a diffuse and obtuse obsolescence. Yet, for some scholars, biblical literature has not become irrelevant, but far too relevant, given the historically and horrifically unjust uses of biblical literature. I have to confess that, on reading quite a bit of biblical interpretation, I have more than once been inclined to think such unflattering things about the state of our field and the utility of much of our work. A great deal of work fails to measure up to a somewhat-basic test of "so what?" Yet, this is not always the case.

R.S. Sugirtharajah posed a very similar question (simply, "The End of Biblical Studies?") in an essay that also begins by contrasting itself with the echoes of Fukuyama.[3] Unfortunately, like Sugirtharajah, I also make my arguments aware that what I have to say is not particularly original, though it still seems incredibly central to our proceedings.[4] This essay aims to operate as a reminder or a "re-sourcing" of the possibilities for a transdisciplinary practice of biblical studies. By doing so, it departs from those calling for the increased presence of, or even a paradigm shift toward, a secular form of biblical hermeneutics.[5] Indeed, following this call would be an ambiguous and quite possibly unnecessary step, given the many potential connotations of the term "secular". Since the term secular derives from the Latin *saecularis* (of, or relating to, this time, this world, this generation, or this age; as opposed to the eternal or timeless), its explicitly temporal dimension offers one way to answer the question "is it time to end?" Yet, in its additional functions as an antonym to religious, the secular only raises further questions. How exactly is the secular not religious? The secular could mean a rejection of the religious or even the active elimination of religious influence; on the other hand, it might simply connote a lack of particular religiosity and, hence, a tolerance of religious variety.[6] Beyond these, the dimension of the term that most appeals to my sense of biblical studies' potential stresses worldly matters: those events, forces, and dynamics affecting all of us ("religious" or not). If we were to address this domain, then biblical studies would be concerned with what is happening to people now and live up to its distinctly public responsibilities.

Thus, my work in our field did not grow out of a love affair with the text, or some profound sense of loyalty to the Bible, a guild, or a religious body. It began with the realization borne out of my own (granted, limited) experience of how interpretations have an impact on our world. Historical and continuing uses of biblical or biblical-sounding arguments have had very real effects upon people, requiring a process of further ethical-political engagement and assessment. Like others in this volume will likely highlight, I raise the lingering effects of sexist, racist, imperialist and heterosexist claims (in and outside of the academy) to our collective consideration. The Bible is not and has not been an entirely harmless collection in this regard, and it is to these effects that I direct my comments.

The focus on the effects of biblical argumentation also begins to steer the analysis away from questions about the end of biblical studies. Even if biblical studies were to end, and even if everyone were to stop reading or "citing" the Bible tomorrow (an unlikely and perhaps unwarranted set of events), the effects of this literature and its field of study would likely continue. If the experiences "after" colonialism have taught us anything, it is that the effects of oppressive dynamics – material, cultural or rhetorical – linger well past their governing imposition. Thus, given the effective and authoritative manner in which they have been and are deployed, it seems unlikely that the use of biblical or biblical-sounding arguments will come to an end in the foreseeable future. As a result, there is a strategic need to develop skills for engaging such argumentation, shifting the analysis from answering a disciplinary question ("the end?") to refining a transdisciplinary practice for such engagement ("to what ends?"). This kind of scholarly activity, then, is less concerned with the preservation or elimination of certain traditional boundaries in the field, than the ability to address crucial issues for the use of biblical rhetorics. The question of secular vs. religious/theological, then, might be more profitably tabled for the moment.

As noted above, though, the move to this kind of practice is neither original nor without a history. When looking for resources for a critical engagement of gender, sexual, racial, and/or imperial dynamics, one need not invent new modes nor strain to find useful work by inspecting the most obscure corners, either within or without biblical studies. Rather, just within our own field, one can turn to the work set out by Musa Dube, Vincent Wimbush, Fernando Segovia, Kwok Pui-lan, or Theodore Jennings, among others. It is fitting that the reflections of Sugirtharajah cited above were published in a Festschrift for Elisabeth Schüssler Fiorenza, as she has been one of the most persistent advocates for the critical rhetorical practice of biblical studies as and within public-political discourse.[7] Understood as an activity that can (and should) have a practical and ethical impact, biblical studies becomes responsible to the wider public, but most particularly to those movements for transformative change and social justice.

A paradigm shift is already underway; it is now simply a matter of knowing our disciplinary history and making use of these resources. Remembering the resources that are available, one can shape an alternate history of biblical studies as a practice that can address the ends to which biblical arguments are used. As a part of this alternate history, the following reflections will especially concentrate upon the approaches of Krister Stendahl, Schüssler Fiorenza, and Ken Stone, as they interact with each other and a set of common interpretive interests. In doing so, we can: *address* this oppressive heritage, highlight the need for an *accountable* practice of interpretation, and utilize the *already available approaches*. The goal of these steps is to find a way to treat a touchstone topic for our contemporary context: what many have called salvation, but what might be better reformulated as safety or security.

## Addressing Its Use

If one were to survey the landscape of current public-political discourse, most especially in my "home" country, the U.S.A., it seems that there is no shortage of biblical or at least biblical-sounding arguments in use. Indeed, given the current context of omnipresent and possibly everlasting war, there has been a burst of scholarly analysis of the Bush Administration's employment of biblical rhetorics.[8] But why do people still use such arguments? On a practical level, doing so could bestow much needed *gravitas* and authority upon a speaker, presenting an implicit appeal to received wisdom and tradition. Still, as a biblical professor whom I used to assist was fond of saying to students: "we often can't tell the difference between Shakespeare and the Bible".[9] The "we" of the comment, whether it implied Christians, Episcopalians, seminarians, or just Americans, often cannot recognize the difference between biblical and biblical-sounding claims in "our" culture. The sound-alike arguments are imbued with authority by association. The reason could be because words and phrases from biblical and Shakespearean quotes hold a few things in common. The most obvious of these is that they both sound familiar, yet "old". Indeed, both "old-sounding" collections have long been treated as sources for teaching about the human condition and are "canonical" to an education in the Western world.

A far less obvious and less-commented-upon similarity between these two great sources for public speech is their contexts of production. Both were created, promoted, and maintained by elite males of certain prized ethnic, sexual, class, and imperial status. While Shakespeare wrote from within England during one of its first phases of colonialism, Kwok Pui-Lan has convincingly argued that the Bible "must also be seen as a political text written, collected, and redacted by male colonial elites".[10] While it is vital not to compress the differences between various imperial eras, it is striking how centrally interconnected gender, ethnic, sexual, and imperial dynamics are for both sources of public speech. It is precisely this history that is rarely, if ever, explicitly noted by those who use biblical or biblical sounding argumentation now. This should raise one's suspicion about the reasons for their use and heighten concern about the intended and unintended effects of such repeated use. It should also remind us that the use of such arguments is not new or unique, but old, with a considerable history.

In order for biblical studies to retain its critical place, then, it must elucidate and engage the historical heritage of how biblical arguments have been used toward oppressive ends. In order to explain of what use this field can be, we must understand to what use it has already been put. This reflects a process frequently extolled in Schüssler Fiorenza's work, that of a rhetoric of inquiry.[11, 12] A rhetoric of inquiry involves greater attention to and evaluation of past and present disciplinary practices, especially as they relate to dominant interests, assumptions, and frameworks. Once more, we are fortunate that we do not have to "reinvent the wheel" ourselves when it comes to a rhetoric of inquiry about biblical claims for sexist, racist, heterosexist, and imperialist ends. Our resources for a rhetoric of inquiry are not obscure; to the contrary, there have been a series of landmark works to address these issues. Schüssler Fiorenza's two-volume collection *Searching the Scriptures*, for example, addressed a range of issues interlocking with the sexism and androcentrism of biblical scholarship.[13] Cain Hope Felder's *Stony the Road We Trod*, and more recently Wimbush's *African-Americans and the Bible*, address the racist ends to which the Bible was used, particularly in America's past and present.[14, 15] One of the more compelling developments is the recent engagement with the historical use of biblical arguments in imperial and colonial relations, as could be found in Sugirtharajah's volumes *The Postcolonial Bible* and *The Postcolonial Biblical Reader* (among others).[16] In documenting and combating biblically-argued homophobia, one might turn to the groundbreaking work of Bernadette Brooten, Dale Martin, or Stone's volume on *Queer Commentary and the Hebrew Bible*.[17]

The above listing of "major works" was by no means meant to be comprehensive or prescriptive. It was meant to indicate what resources we already have in biblical studies for addressing the problematic heritage of how biblical argumentation has been used. These volumes are not the limit, but a demonstration of what one could find in dozens of other collections and monographs. The range of contributors and approaches within each of them testifies to the variety with which these issues are engaged, providing multiple points of entry for the scholar who consults their entries. Furthermore, each of them does not "just" treat sexism, racism, ethnocentrism, imperialism, or heterosexism as solitary and isolated phenomena, but they frequently address how these dynamics are intertwined and mutually influential. These are examples of biblical studies at its best: working across disciplinary questions and academic domains to address matters of public relevance.

Upon turning to texts from the biblical tradition and how they have been employed to argue in various public contexts, these social dynamics often coincide or collide. Historically, for example, Paul's letters have been wielded to justify women's subordination, slavery, homophobia, racial/ ethnic differentiation, anti-Semitism, colonizing missions, and all manner of political collaboration and quiescence. All of these came out of just one portion of the biblical canon for Christians. Given these kinds of dominating effects, Schüssler Fiorenza has argued that the contents of biblical texts should be marked with the label: "Caution, could be dangerous to your health and survival".[18] While Schüssler Fiorenza clearly has the concerns of sexual and domestic violence against women in mind in this quote, she is not alone in making such a determination. This is not just a "women's issue" that we need to address (not that, in and of itself, it would not be reason enough to reassess biblical argumentation). As Krister Stendahl wrote years ago:

> I would guess that the last racists in this country, if there ever be an end to such, will be the ones with Bible in hand. There never has been an evil cause in the world that has not become more evil if it has been possible to argue it on biblical grounds.[19]

Because of these historical and contemporary uses of biblical argumentation, biblical scholars must continuously question to what ends we interpret.

### Accountability

The dominating ends to which biblical argumentation is employed are not simply a matter of the past. It is necessary for these arguments to be continuously addressed because they are still being applied in a variety of contemporary contexts. Thus, on a strategic level, scholars concerned with sexism, racism, ethnocentrism, heterosexism, nationalism, and imperialism cannot afford to ignore the domain of religious or religious-styled argumentation in so many of our current contexts. Whether we see it as legitimate or not, people continue to use biblical arguments to found or reinforce a variety of destructive social-political movements. Again, just in my immediate context, one must consider: the recent panicked efforts of various states to "protect marriage" from lesbian and gay Americans, the infantilizing curtailment of reproductive rights across the country (but now most noticeably in South Dakota), the increasing feminization of poverty and the ritualized scapegoating of especially ethnic women for this lack of class mobility, and the muscular masculinism of militarized invasions and imperial-international interventions. Biblical claims have played a central role in some of the most frightening aspects of our contemporary landscape.

To not engage such argumentation is to cede a still vibrant and effective rhetorical domain to those moving against the safety, survival and social justice of the disempowered. To adopt a supposedly neutral and value-free stance with regard to such efforts is not a bulwark and boon for academics, but a destructive lapse into complicity that works not toward justice, but toward an exploitative status quo. This might be a convenient and comfortable position of self-interest for most scholars, as we are mostly members of the upper and upper-middle classes. However, for those against whom biblical argumentation is still used, and those who attempt to stand in solidarity with them, this is not a viable option. We cannot afford to *not* prepare and enact a transdisciplinary practice of biblical studies. To address this situation, biblical studies should adopt processes that engage and assess how biblical or biblical-sounding arguments are implemented toward oppressive ends. In order to recognize these kinds of argumentative effects, biblical studies need to cross disciplinary boundaries and learn from the contributions of feminist, anti-racist, postcolonial, and queer analytic practices. Furthermore, if these groups should have any hope of countering such problematic, but effective, argumentation, movements of social justice need the committed contributions of biblical scholars. Indeed, here is a primary way that the field of biblical studies can show its continuing utility and relevance for the contemporary context.

By undertaking or renewing a responsibility for our actions and their potential effects upon others, then, biblical scholars would find a way to enliven our inquiries. This is of immediate import for those still victimized by certain forms of biblical argumentation. This critical rhetorical form of biblical studies is also suited to reflections about the past and for the future. One learns about the past so as not to repeat or perpetuate their oppressive mistakes in the future. Sharpening an analytic ability to identify how biblical arguments have worked in the past aids in future critical thinking. Learning to identify the dynamics of gender, sexuality, race/ethnicity, and empire in the first instance of past biblical arguments is a pragmatic and forward-looking technique for assessing all rhetorical forms, no matter where such argumentation appears (or reappears). Thus, biblical studies as a critical rhetorical practice becomes worthwhile for an analysis of public-political speech, in general, not just when it directly or explicitly relates back to the Bible.

As a result, adopting what Schüssler Fiorenza has alternately called a rhetorical-political, rhetorical-ethical, or rhetorical-emancipatory paradigm of biblical studies involves a specific relationship to the politics and processes of identification.[20] Unlike most malestream biblical scholars (particularly in Pauline studies), one cannot unproblematically *identify with* a particular biblical author or text.[21] Certainly, it becomes crucial to *identify what* rhetorically the text or author attempts to accomplish. Still, the turn to a critical rhetorical approach responsible to a wider public cannot pause at this task. One must be able to assess and critique the interwoven gender, sexual, ethnic, and imperial trajectories represented within the text, especially as they are still evident in our world today. Such an approach stresses the difference between identifying these biblical rhetorics and identifying *with* them. As discussed above, the scholar is ethically and politically compelled to be accountable to those who suffer under the imposition of such rhetorical and material conditions. In this manner the biblical scholar strives to identify not with the text, but with the efforts of those laboring against oppressive argumentation.

To remain relevant, then, biblical studies should be increasingly accountable to sociopolitical movements for change. This approach might never be entirely completed. Instead, interpretation will be a continuously vigilant process, requiring the practitioner to be critically reflexive, especially as movements for change (even against their best intentions) have often managed to reinscribe dominating modes and mindsets. Once more, this might be the specific utility of crossing disciplines: in order to heighten an awareness of multiple intersecting systems of subjection so as to identify their resurfaced coincidence and conjoined reinforcement.

Commendably, those scholars arguing either for the end or the increased secularization of biblical studies have often recognized just such problematic dynamics in the history of biblical interpretation. However, their collective solutions, suggestions, and theses frequently fail to specifically address *how* to resist and undo these dynamics. To eliminate the field would surrender the power of these forms of argumentation to those who have and likely will continue to move against the safety, survival and social justice of the dominated and exploited. Yet, it is precisely the historical and continuing fates of these people that are enlisted in these scholarly arguments for a moral close or a secular reform of biblical studies. To borrow a term from the (secularly?) political realm of the U.S., scholars like Berlinerblau, Boer, and Avalos have implemented the topics of gender, sexuality, ethnicity, and empire as "wedge issues" in order to convince us of their own prescriptions for change. However, just as quickly as they introduce these issues, their focus lapses away from the analysis and critique of institutionalized forms of sexism, racism, heterosexism, and colonialism on to their own primary interests and investments. In this manner, their strategies are not that far astray from those social, political, economic, and moral forces with whom they see themselves in conflict. It is this lack of persistent focus on such reoccurring dynamics, characteristic of most biblical scholarship, that a rhetoric of inquiry responsible to a wider set of publics seeks to remedy. The pragmatic outcome of implementing explicitly feminist, postcolonial, queer, and anti-racist approaches is the unabated sharpening of skills for identifying, assessing, resisting and undoing the effects of multiple intersecting forms of oppression and subordination.

Following such a pragmatic strategy could facilitate a renewed relevance and an increasing accountability for biblical studies as a discipline. As scholars, we need to ask ourselves not just what we can identify in a text, but with what forces do we identify now. With whose safety or survival are we concerned?

### Approaches Already Available: Stendahl, Schüssler Fiorenza, and Stone

As highlighted several times above, the efforts to enact just such a disciplinary practice have been repeatedly examined and advocated by Elisabeth Schüssler Fiorenza. Schüssler Fiorenza's work shows that the history of biblical interpretation is not wholly one of "bad news" when it comes to recognizing and resisting dominating rhetorics. To further demonstrate this point here, I could select a number of scholars, past and present, who attempt to initiate and act in ways described above. In this section, though, I will briefly treat some of the observations made by Stendahl, Schüssler Fiorenza, and Stone. This should demonstrate that we can construct an alternate history of and for biblical interpretation. Biblical studies can still be a resource against the oppressive ends to which biblical arguments have been used.

In recalling Krister Stendahl, we find that questions about the good of the public who uses biblical literature are not entirely new to the field of biblical studies. As one of the more prominent figures in Pauline studies, Stendahl famously argued for a new perspective on Paul.[22] What most troubled Stendahl were the anti-Semitic implications of the scholarly conception of Paul as over against a monolithic and univocal first-century Judaism. In the same era, he became increasingly concerned about the conservative views of what most of his colleagues in the Church of Sweden held the Bible (and particularly Paul's letters) "says" about women's roles. In light of both of these issues, Stendahl proposed that biblical studies adopt the mentality of a department of public health, since "the whole scriptural tradition has had a clearly detrimental and dangerous effect".[23] In Stendahl's early insights, the dangers of biblical interpretation must not be downplayed or hidden, but should be identified and countered, particularly in the case of sexism and anti-Judaism. Yet, biblical argumentation is not simply cast aside, instead "the problem calls for frontal attention to what I have called the public health aspect of interpretation. How does the church live with the Bible without undesirable effects?"[24] Thus, decades ago we find biblical scholars worrying over the effects of interpretation and conceiving of ways to manage such dangers and difficulties as central to the task of interpretation.

Because of these efforts, perhaps it should not be so surprising to find many allusions to Stendahl in Schüssler Fiorenza's own efforts to initiate a paradigm shift that attends to the dangerous, destructive, and dominating dynamics of biblical interpretation.[25] Suggesting that Stendahl's was "an ingenious proposal", Schüssler Fiorenza seeks to elaborate upon it to explicate an ethics of interpretation and a rhetoric of inquiry that will be concerned with a wider public health.[26] As early as her own public presidential address in 1987 ("The Ethics of Biblical Interpretation: Decentring Biblical Scholarship"),[27] she has argued for "an ethics of accountability that stands responsible not only for the choice of theoretical interpretive models but also for the ethical consequences of the biblical text and its subsequent interpretations".[28] Since the approach matters, Schüssler Fiorenza denies the false interpretive divide between description and application within which Stendahl first proposed his public health department. An ethical rhetorical process is not just a matter of "application", but critically reflects upon what is claimed to be inscribed within the text and how these claims are created in scholarship.

This also becomes a matter not just of how "the church" lives with the text, but also of a responsibility to a wider public. As Schüssler Fiorenza cogently argues, because political arguments often make public claims using the Bible, biblical scholarship must have a wider audience than religious and academic institutions. This is necessary because biblical or biblical-sounding arguments have an impact larger than "the church", as they continue to shape social and political life. As to the relevance of this for biblical scholarship, I can find no better words than those that sum up Schüssler Fiorenza's remarks in 1987:

> In short, if the Society were to engage in a disciplined reflection on the public dimensions and ethical implications of our scholarly work, it would constitute a responsible scholarly citizenship that could be a significant participant in the global discourse seeking justice and well-being for all. The implications of such a re-positioning of the task and aim of biblical scholarship would be far-reaching and invigorating.[29]

While the effects of this approach could be far-reaching and though Schüssler Fiorenza has been deliberately, vigorously, and repeatedly explaining and refining this paradigm in the years since 1987, it is still a paradigm rarely considered by biblical studies. One of the few exceptions in this regard is Ken Stone's recent reflections in his *Practicing Safer Texts: Food, Sex and Bible in Queer Perspective*. As a route to explicate his own reading strategies, Stone endorses Schüssler Fiorenza's refusal to choose between failing to recognize the negative effects of interpretation and rejecting the Bible because of these dangers.[30] It is this combination of ethical evaluation with persistent critique (not abandonment) that Stone connects to the title's wonderfully apt pun of learning to "practice safer texts". Schüssler Fiorenza's approach can be extended by way of this analogy to the "safer sex" approach of contemporary AIDS activists, since safer sex also offers a route besides denying the risks of certain practices for HIV transmission or rejecting sexual activity absolutely.[31] Both Stone and Schüssler Fiorenza reflect a pragmatic approach to a situation that is potentially hazardous, but also possibly life-affirming.

Stone's concept of "safer textual practice" helps to refashion where the perils and problems lie in the process of interpretation. Safer sex emphasizes that HIV transmission is not attributable to the gender, number, or location of one's partners, but to very specific practices in particular situations. To make both sexual and textual practices safer, one should attempt to avoid or modify only these particular practices and cultivate safer practices of textual intercourse. Just as one might question the absolutism of the practices of denial or relinquishment, Stone[32] argues that one cannot invest this practice with the hope of providing total safety. Hence, the emphasis is upon making interpretation "safer". In fact, any argument that claims to offer complete safety or security is an argument almost always worthy of suspicion. As a result, a safer textual practice will need to be critically reflexive, evaluative, and pragmatic. It will be aware that certain "safer" messages work better for different people in different situations. Such practices should be adaptive and attentive to difference, as they cannot be simplistically universalized based on the effectiveness for only one population.

Stone closes his book with further reflections on Schüssler Fiorenza and feminist scholarship, pausing also to recall Stendahl's proposal for biblical studies' public health. As if to answer those who wonder if biblical studies is at its end, Stone argues:

> to rule out the possibility that one can learn a great deal from the careful study of texts with which one, in the end, fundamentally disagrees, or which one can show to have had damaging effects in the past or to have potentially damaging effects in the present or the future, would be as foolish as a decision to restrict research into those pathogens, that, by way of food or sex, cause potential harm to our bodies. It may be the case that those texts which are most troubling, or for which the most damaging effects can be imagined, are precisely the texts that most need to be taught, with all the care and critical attention that good teaching entails.[33]

## Conclusions

Each of these scholars maintain that we cannot and should not evade our responsibilities for critically appraising and vigorously resisting such oppressive dynamics. To be accountable to the health and safety of a range of publics requires addressing these issues directly. Rather than adopting a specifically secularist approach, then, emphasis is placed on the uses of biblical literature and their connections to intersecting systems of sexism, racism, ethnocentrism, imperialism, and heterosexism. This is not simply a matter of identity politics, but of which resources to use, which approaches to take, and which questions to prioritize. Yet, the priorities described above often differ from some of the suggestions for a more secular approach to biblical studies.

This need not be the case. One could prioritize these critical practices of reconstruction and resistance for similar ethical and political purposes in either secular or religious contexts. Interestingly enough, in conceptualizing a response to these questions about the ends and purposes of biblical studies, I did not pause to reflect upon the relative religiosity of scholars.[34] Indeed, Stendahl, Schüssler Fiorenza, and Stone have trained both academic and religious professionals in their careers. Given their appointments at seminaries and divinity schools (and Stendahl's years as Bishop of Stockholm), one might be hard pressed to describe them as secularists. Yet, this differentiation seems less pressing than whether our methods are pragmatic in focus, remaining ethically and politically responsible to a public wider than those who claim to be "religious". These scholars' contexts did not prevent them from attempting to develop just such methods. The questions that remain are not where we do this,[35] but if and how we as scholars have the convictions and the collective will to engage and resist this problematic historical heritage and its ongoing present-day effects. If we are to seek safer practices for a wider public health, it remains to biblical scholars to develop ethically accountable and critically rhetorical engagements for a safer world. The dangers cannot be denied, but the task cannot be given up.

## Endnotes

* Joseph A. Marchal is Assistant Professor of Religious Studies at Ball State University, Muncie, Indiana.

1. The original context for a large portion of this essay was the author's answer to this query for a section of the International Meeting of the Society of Biblical Literature, as well as a limited response to an early version of Hector Avalos,

"The End of Biblical Studies As a Moral Obligation", in this volume. An abbreviated version of this essay appeared in *The SBL Forum*. See Joseph A. Marchal, "To What End(s)? Biblical Studies and Critical Rhetorical Engagement(s) for a 'Safer' World," *SBL Forum* 4:6-7 (August–September 2006).

2.  Francis Fukuyama, *The End of History and the Last Man* (New York: Free Press, 1992).

3.  R.S. Sugirtharajah, "The End of Biblical Studies?" In F.F. Segovia (ed.) *Toward a New Heaven and a New Earth: Essays in Honor of Elisabeth Schüssler Fiorenza* (Maryknoll, NY: Orbis Books, 2003), pp. 133–40.

4.  Sugirtharajah, "The End of Biblical Studies?", p. 13, is similarly concerned with the relevance of the field: "What strikes one immediately about contemporary biblical studies as practised in Western academies is that it is dull, mechanical, repetitive, cliquish, and totally out of touch with the issues people face".

5.  J. Berlinerblau, *The Secular Bible: Why Nonbelievers Must Take Religion Seriously* (Cambridge: Cambridge University Press, 2005); see in this volume, Roland Boer, "A Manifesto for Biblical Studies".

6.  For a brief, but engaging reflection on the different senses of the secular as it effects interpretations of the Establishment Clause (regarding the separation of church and state) in the U.S. Constitution, see Berlinerblau, *The Secular Bible*, pp. 131–35.

7.  One can point to the large body of Schüssler Fiorenza's work that has sought to define and refine a feminist emancipatory practice of biblical studies, including her more recent efforts. See for e.g. Elisabeth Schüssler Fiorenza, *Rhetoric and Ethic: The Politics of Biblical Studies* (Minneapolis, MN: Fortress Press, 1999); Schüssler Fiorenza, *Wisdom Ways: Introducing Feminist Biblical Interpretation* (Maryknoll, NY: Orbis Books, 2001).

8.  See for e.g. E.A. Castelli and J.J. Jakobsen (eds), *Interventions: Activists and Academics Respond to Violence* (New York: Palgrave Macmillan, 2004); E.A. Castelli, "Globalization, Transnational Feminisms, and the Future of Biblical Critique." In K. O'Brien Wicker, A. Spencer Miller, and M.W. Dube (eds), *Feminist New Testament Studies: Global and Future Perspectives* (New York: Palgrave Macmilan, 2005), pp. 63–78. Also see, S. Scholz, "The Christian Right's Discourse on Gender and the Bible", *Journal of Feminist Studies in Religion* 21.1 (Spring 2005), pp. 81–100.

9.  The quote is likely an inexact remembrance of a humorous and useful comment made by L. William Countryman, in and to an introduction to New Testament class. My apologies to Dr. Countryman if I have preserved neither the candid wit nor the precise utility of this comment.

10.  See L.E. Donaldson, *Decolonizing Feminisms: Race, Gender, and Empire-Building* (Chapel Hill, NC: University of North Carolina Press, 1992), pp. 13–31; H. Baker Jr, "Caliban's Triple Play", in *Critical Inquiry* 13 (1986), pp. 182–96; Kwok Pui-lan, *Postcolonial Imagination and Feminist Theology* (Louisville, KY: Westminster John Knox Press, 2005), pp. 8–9.

11.  Elisabeth Schüssler Fiorenza, "Challenging the Rhetorical Half-turn: Feminist and Rhetorical Biblical Criticism", in S.E. Porter and T.H. Olbricht (eds), *Rhetoric, Scripture, and Theology: Essays from the 1994 Pretoria Conference*

28–53 (Sheffield: Sheffield Academic Press, 1996); Schüssler Fiorenza, *Rhetoric and Ethic*, pp. 83–102.

12. On the rhetoric of inquiry, see J.S. Nelson, A. Megill and D.N. McCloskey (eds), *The Rhetoric of the Human Sciences: Language and Argument in Scholarship and Public Affairs* (Madison, WI: University of Wisconsin Press, 1987); H.W. Simons (ed.), *Rhetoric in the Human Sciences* (Newbury Park, CA: Sage Publications, 1989); C. Blair, J.R. Brown and L.A. Baxter, "Disciplining the Feminine", in J.L. Lucaites, C.M. Condit and S. Caudill (eds), *Contemporary Rhetorical Theory: A Reader* (New York: The Guilford Press, 1999), pp. 563–90.

13. Elisabeth Schüssler Fiorenza, *Searching the Scriptures: A Feminist Introduction* (New York: Crossroad, 1997, 2 vols).

14. Cain Hope Felder (ed.), *Stony the Road We Trod: African American Biblical Interpretation* (Minneapolis, MN: Augsburg, 1991).

15. Vincent Wimbush (ed.), *African-Americans and the Bible: Sacred Text and Social Texture* (London: Continuum, 2001).

16. R. S. Sugirtharajah (ed.), *The Postcolonial Bible* (Sheffield: Sheffield Academic Press, 1998); *The Postcolonial Biblical Reader* (Oxford: Blackwell, 2006).

17. Bernadette Brooten, *Love Between Women: Early Christian Responses to Female Homoeroticism* (Chicago, IL: University of Chicago Press, 1998); Dale Martin, *Sex and the Single Savior: Gender and Sexuality in Biblical Interpretation* (Louisville, KY: Westminster John Knox, 2006); K. Stone, *Practicing Safer Texts: Food, Sex and Bible in Queer Perspective* (London: T and T Clark International, 2005).

18. Schüssler Fiorenza, *Rhetoric and Ethic*, p. 14.

19. Krister Stendahl, "Ancient Scripture in the Modern World", in F. E. Greenspahn (ed.), *Scripture in the Jewish and Christian Traditions: Authority, Interpretation, Relevance* (Nashville: Abingdon Press, 1982), 201–214. Quote is from page 205.

20. Schüssler Fiorenza, *Rhetoric and Ethic*, p. 44.

21. Elisabeth Schüssler Fiorenza, "Paul and the Politics of Interpretation", in R.A. Horsley (ed.), *Paul and Politics: Ekklesia, Israel, Imperium, Interpretation: Essays in Honor of Krister Stendahl* (Harrisburg, PA: Trinity Press International, 2000), pp. 40–57.

22. K. Stendahl, "The Apostle Paul and the Introspective Conscience of the West", in *Paul Among Jews and Gentiles, and Other Essays* (Philadelphia, PA: Fortress Press, 1974), p. 85, reprinted from *Harvard Theological Review* 56 (1963), pp. 199–215.

23. Krister Stendahl, "Ancient Scripture in the Modern World".

24. Stendahl, "Ancient Scripture in the Modern World".

25. Schüssler Fiorenza, *Rhetoric and Ethic*, pp. 31–32; Schüssler Fiorenza, "Paul and the Politics of Interpretation", pp. 40–45.

26. Schüssler Fiorenza, "Paul and the Politics of Interpretation", p. 40.

27. Schüssler Fiorenza, *Rhetoric and Ethic*, pp. 17–30.

28. Schüssler Fiorenza, *Rhetoric and Ethic*, p. 28.

29. Schüssler Fiorenza, *Rhetoric and Ethic*, p. 30.

30. Stone, *Practicing Safer Texts*, pp. 12–13.

31. Stone, *Practicing Safer Texts*, pp. 8–9, 13.

32. Stone, *Practicing Safer Texts*, p. 13.

33. Stone, *Practicing Safer Texts*, p. 148.

34. As noted above, the initial contexts of these arguments I'm making were not in considerations of secular vs. religious/theological approaches, but in questioning the ends or purposes of biblical studies. Thus, the selection of these three scholars and their interpretive emphases was made somewhat independently of the structuring purpose of this volume.

35. Indeed, the liberal, progressive, or radical (and in some cases, secular) confidence in the university as a locale for these forms of critique might be mislaid, given how notoriously slow to change academic institutions have been and are, especially in comparison to the agile flexibility of market-based motivations in other institutional loci. The more historically entrenched, elite, or "competitive" a university might be, the less likely they are to change and, thus, disrupt their reputations as repositories of tradition (not unlike some religious institutions).

# A German Landscape: Currents and Credits of New Testament Studies in Germany During the Past Decades

*Heike Omerzu\**

## *The Problem – Which Problem?*

Germany was not only an important cradle of critical biblical scholarship itself. German exegesis also held a leading position within the international field of the discipline and concurrently participated in general theological or philosophical debates throughout major parts of the twentieth century (for example, in liberal and dialectical theology). While the situation has changed since then in many respects, German biblical scholarship has only begun to reflect its fading impact as concerns the international stage as well as broader discourses in theology or the humanities and social-sciences, not to speak of general public debates.

Because of the limitation of space I will confine my subsequent observations to New Testament studies. I will first briefly take stock of current research interests and sketch the way the discipline sees itself, its state and its present and future tasks. Second, I will examine at least some of the reasons for the increasing loss of influence of German (speaking) exegesis since about the 1970s. On this basis, I will finally outline recent emerging reactions to this development and discuss the ensuing impulses to meet future challenges of the discipline which will not only appear as a national agenda.

## *The State of Affairs*

Most of the research achieved in Germany during the last three to four decades was and still is indebted to historical criticism with its inherent emphasis on philological and historical analyses. Meanwhile, the – if even often controversial and short-lived but nevertheless fruitful – debates on new approaches to biblical studies (arising, for example, from structuralism, deconstruction or new literary criticism) have almost taken place without German contribution on the level of *theory* (in contrast, for example, to France, Great Britain, and the United States). Regarding the *practice*, innovative methods are often adopted – if at all – in a half-hearted way and scholars who apply them are viewed rather sceptically. This phenomenon also pertains to elsewhere "established" methods such as feminist or socioscientific exegesis.[1] Literary-critical approaches such as rhetorical, narrative or reader response criticisms are more acceptable.[2] That alternative methods in Germany are still met with reserve can be illustrated by Martin Hengel's[3] account of the tasks of New Testament studies on the occasion of his presidential address towards the "Societas Novi Testamenti Studiorum" in 1993. He rejects such new approaches as a "postmodern playground" resulting in an "anything goes" alienation of biblical texts. Their arbitrariness made these methods inadequate tools for the interpretation of the Bible. Instead, Hengel[4] claims that the only appropriate way to understand the lasting truth of the Christian kerygma, is to reveal what the New Testament author has meant and what he wanted to express with respect to his audience, his hearers and readers. Though most German biblical scholars will not share this extreme author-centred position any longer, in his conservative disposition and the implicit devaluation of new trends as superficial and transient,[5] Hengel is nevertheless representative of a predominant inclination.

This tendency does not only affect methodological aspects but also important research issues, for example, the Third Quest for the historical Jesus and the New Perspective on Paul. Both are international discourses, yet mainly conducted in English and – in contrary, for example, to Scandinavia – with rather few contributions of any initiative by German speaking scholars. Such exceptions are Gerd Theißen,[6] Wolfgang Stegemann,[7] or Michael Bachmann.[8] In Germany, the pertinent debates are often reflected with a considerable delay[9] and from a rather sceptical[10] point of view. Finally, though New Testament studies claim their position within the canon of theological disciplines, they have only little impact on general theological debates.[11] Exegetical research does not affect discussions within the church or in academic and public discourse.[12]

### When and Why?

I will try to suggest at least some reasons for this development. Thomas H. Olbricht[13] has designated the beginning of the 20th century up to the

First World War as the "Germanic Period" of biblical interpretation in North America. Only in considering the great impact of the *Formgeschichte* method of Martin Dibelius and Rudolf Bultmann and of the *Redaktionsgeschichte* method of Hans Conzelmann and Ernst Haenchen, as well as the contributions of Rudolf Bultmann and Ernst Käsemann to wider theological discussions,[14] it is evident, that German exegesis at least exerted an important influence until the end of, and some time after, World War II.[15] Even if Germany no longer held the leading position, it still maintained a significant role in international exegesis as well as in systematic-theological and philosophical discourses.

The years 1933 through 1945 severely shocked everyone, including biblical scholars. This resulted – among other things – in an increased sensibility for a centuries-old tradition of anti-Jewish readings of the New Testament which were also supported by biblical scholars, not only German ones[16] Yet, corresponding to the larger political developments and the altered power relations after World War II, the higher critical agenda originating among, and having been dominated by, German exegetes became more and more disputed.[17] The emancipation especially of North American exegesis, from a German biblical-exegetical hegemonic hold was surely facilitated by English becoming the *lingua franca* of the scientific world. Thus, it is symptomatic of the current situation that a growing number of particularly American scholars only possess a basic knowledge of German while simultaneously the amount of German exegetical research translated into English is decreasing.[18]

Is Wolfgang Stegemann[19] really right in blaming German exegesis for its provinciality and therefore entitling his account on the condition of New Testament studies: "'Amerika, du hast es besser!' (America, you are better off!)?" Is Anglo-American exegesis really at an advantage compared to Germany?

I suggest not. At least it seems as if those on the other side of the sea are not on the safe side either. This impression is corroborated by various recent observations by international scholars.[20] Independent of their different backgrounds, implications and aims, there seems to be a general consensus that the main reasons for the current – poor – state of our discipline is related to the globalization and pluralization of society (or societies).[21] In 1997, for example, Ulrich Luz[22] devoted his presidential address to the Society for New Testament Studies' group to the topic "The tasks of exegesis in a religiously pluralistic society". Only a few months later, Larry Hurtado[23] argued in his inaugural lecture on "New Testament Studies at the Turn of the Millennium: Questions for the Discipline" that "the pluralising of our society ... makes it even more important and relevant for the scriptural texts of the Christian faith to be a university subject". One of the latest assessments has been presented by the Society for New Testament Studies' President of 2004, Wayne A. Meeks,[24] who states that in contrast to our "more or less post-Christian age", about "half a century ago the difficult questions had to do with *how*, not *why*, and certainly not *whether*"[25] to study the New Testament. Inquiring on possible motivations to study the New Testament he points out the various audiences modern exegetes have to address. These are besides the *Christian* communities the *intellectual* community represented by the academy with which we should enter into an effective and *mutual* discourse. The most important challenge to face, however, and at the same time the largest audience is the non-Christian majority of the world. To speak to them should not aim at mission but at a new dialogue and understanding.[26] Given the complaints uttered by Meeks and others about the isolation of the discipline from ecclesiastic, academic and societal discourses, one could conclude that Germany simply participates in a "global crisis" of exegesis – perhaps with the only difference that it lacks an equivalent to especially North American forms of "civil religion".[27] At first glance this impression of a general calamity might be further approved by my subsequently presented considerations on how to stop the misery and demise of German biblical studies. These claims include a reformulation of the historical and theological task of the discipline after the linguistic turn and the emphasis that exegesis must not be separated from hermeneutics.[28] Probably, this does not appear to be thrilling, new and ingenious but at least it reveals a rising consciousness for the need of deeper theoretical and methodological reflection. At this point we are back at Wolfgang Stegemann's longing look at America and his plea for methodical innovations. One must assert that new methods are not per se fruitful (here Hengel is absolutely right), even though they do at least foster debates on methodology. While some scholars, such as Stanley E. Porter[29] have recently characterized the problems of North American exegesis as being caused by "fragmentation" and "multiformity" on account of too much theory, Germany's crisis is – in my perception – mostly due to a lack of theory (i.e. of methodological and hermeneutical reflection). So aside from the general "global situation", there is also a more specific cultural aspect to this matter.

## On Our Way Out

As already noted, for the past decade a debate on the present state and on future perspectives of New Testament studies has been going on in Germany. Contributions to this discussion come, apart from those exegetes already mentioned, from scholars such as Stefan Alkier,[30] Christof Landmesser,[31] Eckhart Reinmuth,[32] Jens Schröter,[33] and Oda Wischmeyer.[34]

An important stimulus of the debate is the growing discontent with the fact that the various exegetical methods, old and new, historical-critical and literary, diachronic and synchronic, are usually employed additively and without integration into a theoretical concept of text interpretation.[35] Such an overlooked but strongly demanded text theory does not only have to consider the epistemological, linguistic, and philosophical presuppositions of each single method, but it also has to reflect the conditions of understanding and interpretation of texts in general. Fundamental to this striving for a theory of text-comprehension are the insights associated with the term "linguistic turn",[36] which originated in various intellectual movements (e.g. analytical philosophy, structuralism) and was adopted in the humanities in the 1970s. Decisive for the linguistic turn is the recognition of language as structuring thought and constructing reality. There is no direct relation between the world created by, and in, a text and the non-linguistic reality to which it refers. Language rules the boundaries of our knowledge and thought.

The question for the conditions of the comprehension of linguistic utterances relates (at least) back to the hermeneutics of Friedrich Schleiermacher for whom interpretation required the re-construction of meaning.[37] This has been refined by modern textual linguistics and discourse studies, which characterize interpretation as a process involving producer/author, recipient, and text alike, yet still laying a strong emphasis on the reader. Very influential in this respect were the concepts of Wolfgang Iser,[38] featuring the idea of an implicit reader, and of Umberto Eco[39] featuring the idea of a model reader. Both pay special attention to the active part of the reader in the act of interpretation. This cooperation (cf. Eco: "*la cooperazione interpretativa*") does not necessarily imply a conscious interaction, yet it does suggest permanent decisions as regards the actualization of specific aspects of the "cultural encyclopaedia" of the reader. This encyclopaedic competence is, for instance, performed when deciding between different possible grammatical or semantic choices a text offers and when filling gaps in the text. However, while this presupposition facilitates a pluralisation of interpretation, it does not result in arbitrary perspectives, because every realization is restricted by certain predispositions of the text itself.

Turning to the German scholars mentioned above, while Wischmeyer[40] explicitly defines her exegetical approach as text hermeneutics, Landmesser primarily seeks, by means of philology, to develop the "linguistic potential" of the New Testament texts,[41] Alkier is predominantly engaged in semiotics and the ethics of interpretation[42] and Schröter (and, in a similar way but interwoven with postmodern issues in a more general mode, also Reinmuth)[43] seems to envisage an even broader project by linking current insights of linguistics and historical theory. Schröter wants to strengthen ties between text, reality, *and* history, by the idea of a (moderate) constructivism with its fundamental assumption that humans have no access to any ontic reality, but that all reality is dependent on knowledge and thus subject to construction. Reality appears to be the product of ascribing and relating meaning to events in order to make sense of them.[44]

Adopting the above mentioned linguistic perspectives,[45] Schröter holds that the New Testament writings are comparable with any other text as they all constitute reality via the medium of language.[46] But language does not only structure our access to, and the perception of, reality, it also mediates between past and present.[47] Drawing among others on the works Paul Ricœur (Finke Verlag, 1991), pp. 294–311 and Hayden White Schröter[48] emphasizes the constructive character of history in general, including Early Christian history and our own perception of it. Thus, the quest for the origins has to be regarded as a cultural construction as well.[49] Faction and fiction, history and historiography cannot be split up. The establishment of relations in meaning is an important prerequisite for the reception of the past, and meaning is not inherent to facts and reality but has to be created by interpretation.[50] Thus, like all other *historical* texts, the Early Christian writings describe the reality they relate to in a selective and interpretative way.[51] But if we can acquire the past only in the mode of fictionality, Schröter demands as a necessary consequence that the question for the truth of history must not be identified and mixed up with that of its verification.[52] So far my remarks on Schröter's stimulating considerations are on the relation of text, reality and history that open the field for discussions with many other disciplines.

In short, it is in these newer hermeneutical developments in Germany that I see some significant hope for a renewed German-speaking contribution to the field of biblical studies and for a possible way out of the current state of isolation we are facing.

## Concluding Remarks

It is not only generally to be welcomed that a discussion on theory has been inaugurated in German exegesis, but also that these efforts seek for an integral connection between exegesis and hermeneutics. An integrative theory that considers both the creative act of text interpretation, necessarily including, alongside an appropriation of the first century "encyclopaedia", the critical historical and philological skills that Hengel rightly, even if too one-sidedly, demands and the idea of the constructive character of history, appears to be a promising way out of the isolation of German exegesis. Of course, I am not promoting a return to German hegemony, but rather a move to "interdisciplinary" and "international" discourse and exchange. The constructive notion of reality and history draws on international discourses in literary studies, linguistics, historical, and philosophical sciences, and thus may inaugurate debates within the theological context as well as with non-theological partners. If all reality is construed and linguistically mediated, this is also true for the biblical texts. As a consequence, we can only strive for an *adequate* interpretation, but not for the one and the only true one,[53] a point that is critically relevant in the debate within theology, nationally and internationally. If there is no direct connection between the signs of a text and the designated non-linguistic reality, the biblical texts just provide *one* possible interpretation of reality.[54] This recognition opens the space for dialogues with other, non-theological disciplines on the basis of a rational, negotiable methodological basis.[55] Theology can then be an autonomous partner in the discourse on competing drafts of interpretation of the world, of history and reality.[56]

Regarding the public eye, the idea of the constructive nature of reality and history may be in fact appealing because it perfectly corresponds so well to our every day experiences. Our co-operation is asked everywhere – in the supermarket, at the cash machine, when having a coffee break at a Starbucks or lunch at a Burger King. We book our flights via the internet and print the tickets at the airport. So, why not cooperate in producing meaning?

Time will prove whether these ideas are fruitful. For the moment they offer a discourse and a promising path to be followed. Maybe this path will not lead us to blossoming landscapes; at least it might provide exegesis a place in the global village.

## *Endnotes*

\* Heike Omerzu is Professor of New Testament in the Department of Biblical Exegesis in the Faculty of Theology at the University of Copenhagen.

1. See G. Theißen, "Von der Literatursoziologie zur Theorie der urchristlichen Religion". In E.-M. Becker (ed.), *Neutestamentliche Wissenschaft. Autobiographische Essays aus der Evangelischen Theologie* [UTB, 2475] (Tübingen, Basel: A. Francke Verlag, 2003), pp. 176–85, p. 183. Theißen identifies academic hierarchies as a means of inhibition of the creativity and autonomy of aspiring scholars: "Habilitationsschriften widmen sich immer seltener innovativen Ansätzen".

2. Cf. O. Wischmeyer, "Das Selbstverständnis der neutestamentlichen Wissenschaft in Deutschland: Bestandsaufnahme. Kritik. Perspektiven. Ein Bericht auf der Grundlage eines neutestamentlichen Oberseminars". *Zeitschrift für Neues Testament* 5 (2002), pp. 13–36, p. 28. Wischmeyer notes, "Die letzte Generation hat neue Fragestellungen erschlossen, neue Methoden übernommen, neue Ergebnisse formuliert, ohne allerdings dabei an Bedeutung zu gewinnen. Das Fach stellt sich etabliert, nicht aber innovativ oder gar führend dar".

3. M. Hengel, "Aufgaben der Neutestamentlichen Wissenschaft". *New Testament Studies* 40 (1994), pp. 321–57, p. 337.

4. M. Hengel, "Aufgaben der Neutestamentlichen Wissenschaft", pp. 349, 351.

5. Cf. M. Hengel, "Aufgaben der Neutestamentlichen Wissenschaft", p. 352, notes "Die Frage der Methode klärt sich immer wieder von selbst. Haben wir noch 10–20 Jahre Geduld!"

6. Cf. G. Theißen and D. Winter, *Die Kriterienfrage in der Jesusforschung*. Vom Differenzkriterium zum Plausibilitätskriterium [NTOA 34] (Göttingen et al.: Vandenhoeck & Ruprecht, 1997); G. Theißen and A. Merz, *Der historische Jesus. Ein Lehrbuch* (Göttingen: Vandenhoeck & Ruprecht, 2001, 3rd edn).

7. Cf. W. Stegemann, B. J. Malina and G. Theißen (eds), *Jesus in neuen Kontexten* (Stuttgart et al.: Kohlhammer Verlag, 2002); E.W. Stegemann and W. Stegemann, *Urchristliche Sozialgeschichte*. Die Anfänge im Judentum und die Christusgemeinden in der mediterranen Welt (Stuttgart et al.: Kohlhammer Verlag, 1997, 2nd edn.).

8. Cf. M. Bachmann, "Rechtfertigung und Gesetzeswerke bei Paulus". *Theologische Zeitschrift* 49 (1993), pp. 1–33. M. Bachmann, "4QMMT und Galaterbrief, ma'ase ha-torah und ERGA NOMOU". *Zeitschrift für Neutestamentliche Wissenschaft* 89 (1998), pp. 91–113; M. Bachmann, "Vorwort". In M. Bachmann (ed.), *Lutherische und Neue Paulusperspektive* [WUNT, 182] (Tübingen: J. C. B. Mohr, 2005), pp. VII–XIII; M. Bachmann, "Keil oder Mikroskop? Zur jüngeren Diskussion um den Ausdruck 'Werke des Gesetzes'". In M. Bachmann (ed.), *Lutherische und Neue Paulusperspektive*, pp. 69–134. Cf. also C. Strecker, "Paulus aus einer 'neuen Perspektive'. Der Paradigmenwechsel in der jüngeren Paulusforschung". *Kirche und Israel* 11 (1996), pp. 3–18.

9. Theißen, "Von der Literatursoziologie zur Theorie der urchristlichen Religion", p. 183, speaks of indications of a retarded development in Germany; cf. J. Schröter *Erinnerung an Jesu Worte*. Studien zur Rezeption der Logienüberlieferung in Markus, Q und Thomas [WMANT, 76] (Neukirchen-Vluyn: Neukirchener Verlagshaus, 1997); J. Schröter and R. Brucker (eds), *Der historische Jesus*.

Tendenzen und Perspektiven der gegenwärtigen Forschung [BZNW 114] (Berlin, New York: Walter de Gruyter, 2002).

10. Cf. similarly W. Stegemann, "'Amerika, du hast es besser!' Exegetische Innovationen der neutestamentlichen Wissenschaft in den USA". In R. Anselm, St. Schleissing and K. Thanner (eds), *Die Kunst des Auslegens*. Zur Hermeneutik des Christentums in der Kultur der Gegenwart (Frankfurt/M. et al.: Peter Lang, 1999, pp. 99–114, pp. 111–13; Bachmann, "Vorwort", VIII, examines with regard to the "New Perspective" a tendency of a too rash rejection.

11. Cf. K.-W. Niebuhr, "Neues Testament – ein akademisches Fach im Übergang". In Becker (ed.), *Neutestamentliche Wissenschaft*, pp.186–95, p. 192: "Im Zusammenspiel der theologischen Disziplinen hat das Neue Testament gegenwärtig offenbar nicht viel zu sagen". Taeger (J.-W. Taeger, "Die neutestamentliche Wissenschaft als theologische Disziplin". In Becker (ed.), *Neutestamentliche Wissenschaft*, pp. 374–82, p. 376) relates the loss of acceptance and influence to a lack of theology in exegesis itself: "[D]as Zu-kurz-Kommen des Theologischen ist ein Grundproblem heutiger neutestamentlicher Wissenschaft. Im letzten Viertel des vergangenen Jahrhunderts ist dieser Aspekt unseres Faches, der etwa von R. Bultmann und E. Käsemann noch so imponierend vertreten wurde, ungeachtet einschlägiger Veröffentlichungen immer stärker verblasst. (…) Über längere Zeit hat sie [sc. New Testament studies] nämlich zu gering von sich gedacht, sich statt dessen viel zu eilfertig dorthin zurückgezogen, wo sie einige ihrer Vertreter und erst recht andere Disziplinen der Theologie ohnehin am liebsten sehen, auf das Feld des (nur) Historischen und des (nur) Literarischen". Cf. also E. Reinmuth, "Diskurse und Texte. Überlegungen zur Theologie des Neuen Testaments nach der Moderne". *Berliner Theologische Zeitschrift* 16 (1999), pp. 81–96, p. 79: "Die Frage nach den Aufgaben der neutestamentlichen Wissenschaft kommt an der Frage nicht vorbei, was diese Disziplin zu einer theologischen macht".

12. Cf. Wischmeyer, "Das Selbstverständnis der neutestamentlichen Wissenschaft in Deutschland", p. 29: "Gesamttheologisch gesehen verhält sich die Disziplin unauffällig, anspruchslos und eher konservativ. Kirchliche oder gar gesellschaftliche Resonanz wird nicht beansprucht". See also p. 22: "[D]as Neue Testament [ist] eine fest etablierte philologische und religionsgeschichtliche Wissenschaft …, die ihre Ergebnisse allerdings kaum nach außen hin mitteilt". But cf. the similar evaluation for the anglo-phone context by J. Berlinerblau, "'Poor bird, not knowing which way to fly': Biblical Scholarship's Marginality, Secular Humanism, and the Laudable Occident". *Biblical Interpretation* 10 (2002), pp. 267–304, p. 268. He points to the "complete lack of interest that our sister disciplines in the humanities and our cousins in the social-sciences evince for our research".

13. T.H. Olbricht, "Biblical Interpretation in North America in the 20th Century". In D.K. McKim (ed.), *Historical Handbook of Major Biblical Interpreters* (Downers Grove, IL: InterVarsity Press, 1998), pp. 542–45.

14. Cf. Theißen, "Von der Literatursoziologie zur Theorie der urchristlichen Religion", p. 183. See also, Taeger, "Die neutestamentliche Wissenschaft als theologische Disziplin", p. 374.

15. The period from 1916–1945 is labelled as the "British" one by Olbricht, "Biblical Interpretation", pp. 545–48.

16. W. A. Meeks, "Why study the New Testament?". *New Testament Studies* 51 (2005), pp. 155–70, p. 160.

17. Niebuhr, "Neues Testament – ein akademisches Fach im Übergang", p. 193; Theißen, "Von der Literatursoziologie zur Theorie der urchristlichen Religion", pp. 183–84.

18. W. Stegemann, "'Amerika, du hast es besser!'", p. 101 with note 7; Niebuhr, "Neues Testament – ein akademisches Fach im Übergang", p. 193.

19. W. Stegemann, "'Amerika, du hast es besser!'", pp. 99–114.

20. In 2002, Oda Wischmeyer (Wischmeyer, "Das Selbstverständnis der neutestamentlichen Wissenschaft in Deutschland", pp. 27–8) attested the international, predominantly English speaking forum of SNTS-meetings constancy, persistence, and continuity in exploring major New Testament topics: "Hier dokumentiert sich ein ungebrochenes Vertrauen in das Fach und seine eigenen Fragen und wissenschaftlichen Debatten. Als die primäre, ja fast einzige Welt 'hinter' und 'neben' den ntl. Texten wird die Welt des antiken Judentums verstanden. Wirklich relevante andere wissenschaftliche Kontexte sind nicht in Sicht. Schon die hellenistisch-römische Welt ist deutlich marginal. Das christliche zweite Jahrhundert fehlt. Hermeneutische Fragen stehen ganz am Rand. Einige neue Methoden aus dem literaturwissenschaftlichen Bereich werden in der Diskussion erprobt. Insgesamt ist die thematische Innovation gering. Wesentliche Anschlußbereiche wie Religionswissenschaft und Sozialwissenschaft bzw. Kulturanthropologie fehlen. Das wundert umso mehr, als eine deutliche Dominanz der Wissenschaftler aus den USA festzustellen ist. Eine Anbindung an die allgemeine Theologie schließlich unterbleibt in auffallender Weise". This evaluation is, of course, qualified by the presidential addresses of Ulrich Luz (1997; cf. U. Luz, "Kann die Bibel heute noch Grundlage für die Kirche sein? Über die Aufgabe der Exegese in einer religiös-pluralistischen Gesellschaft". *New Testament Studies* 44 [1998], pp. 317–39) and Wayne A. Meeks (2004; cf. W. A. Meeks, "Why Study the New Testament?", pp. 155–70), who both pick up the challenges of the discipline as central theme. Besides, Meeks' paper proves Wischmeyer ("Das Selbstverständnis der neutestamentlichen Wissenschaft in Deutschland", p. 27) wrong who (earlier) considered that, as during the past decade only the two German speaking presidents Hengel and Luz presented papers on the tasks of New Testament studies, this could mean that "deutschsprachige Exegese sich ihrer Schwierigkeiten eher bewußt ist oder ... sie tatsächlich größere Schwierigkeiten hat".

21. H. Räisänen, "Biblical Critics in the Global Village". In H. Räisänen et al. (eds), *Reading the Bible in the Global Village: Helsinki* (Atlanta, Ga: Society of Biblical Literature, 2000), pp. 9–28, 153–66.

22. See Luz, "Kann die Bibel heute noch Grundlage für die Kirche sein?"

23. L. W. Hurtado, "New Testament Studies at the Turn of the Millennium: Questions for the Discipline". *Scottish Journal of Theology* 52 (1999), pp. 158–78, p. 159.

24. Meeks, "Why Study the New Testament?", see p. 167 especially.

25. Meeks, "Why Study the New Testament?", p. 155.

26. See Meeks, "Why Study the New Testament?", pp. 167–70.

27. But cf. the critical remarks on the religious landscape in America by Meeks ("Why study the New Testament?", p. 163): those Christian denominations

becoming more and more popular are predominantly fundamentalists or evangelicals and often "either ignore or deplore the kind of scholarship we do".

28. Luz, "Kann die Bibel heute noch Grundlage für die Kirche sein?", pp. 317–39.

29. St. E. Porter, "New Testament Studies in the Twenty-First Century: Between Exegesis and Hermeneutics. Observations from an Anglo-American Perspective". In Becker (ed.), *Neutestamentliche Wissenschaft*, pp. 361–73, see especially pp. 362, 365.

30. Cf. S. Alkier, "Es geht ums Ganze! Wider die geschichtswissenschaftliche Verkürzung der Bibelwissenschaften oder Aufruf zur intensiveren Zusammenarbeit der theologischen Disziplinen". In M. Rothgangel and E. Thaidigsmann (eds), *Religionspädagogik als Mitte der Theologie?* Theologische Disziplinen im Diskurs (Stuttgart et al.: Kohlhammer Verlag, 2005), pp. 165–70; S. Alkier, "Neutestamentliche Wissenschaft – Ein semiotisches Konzept". In C. Strecker (ed.) *Kontexte der Schrift II*. Kultur, Politik, Religion, Sprache (Stuttgart et al.: Kohlhammer Verlag, 2005), pp. 343–60; S. Alkier and R. Brucker (eds), *Exegese und Methodendiskussion* [TANZ, 23] (Tübingen: A. Francke Verlag, 1998).

31. Cf. C. Landmesser, *Wahrheit als Grundbegriff neutestamentlicher Wissenschaft* [WUNT, 113] (Tübingen: J. C. B. Mohr, 2001); C. Landmesser, "Neutestamentliche Wissenschaft und Weltbezug". In O. Wischmeyer (ed.), *Herkunft und Zukunft der neutestamentlichen Wissenschaft* [NET, 6] (Tübingen, Basel: A. Francke Verlag, 2003), pp. 185–206.

32. Cf. Reinmuth, "Diskurse und Texte", pp. 81–96; E. Reinmuth, "In der Vielfalt der Bedeutungen. Notizen zur Interpretationsaufgabe neutestamentlicher Wissenschaft". In U. Busse (ed.), *Die Bedeutung der Exegese für Theologie und Kirche* [QD, 215] (Freiburg i.Br.: Herder Verlag, 2005), pp. 76–96.

33. J. Schröter, "Zum gegenwärtigen Stand der neutestamentlichen Wissenschaft: Methodologische Aspekte und theologische Perspektiven". *New Testament Studies* 46 (2000), pp. 262–83; J. Schröter, "Neutestamentliche Wissenschaft jenseits des Historismus. Neuere Entwicklungen in der Geschichtstheorie und ihre Bedeutung für die Exegese urchristlicher Schriften". *Theologische Literaturzeitung* 128 (2003), pp. 855–66.

34. Wischmeyer, "Das Selbstverständnis der neutestamentlichen Wissenschaft in Deutschland", pp. 13–36; Wischmeyer (ed.), *Herkunft und Zukunft der neutestamentlichen Wissenschaft*.

35. See also, Alkier and Brucker (eds), *Exegese und Methodendiskussion*, p. ix; Schröter, "Zum gegenwärtigen Stand der neutestamentlichen Wissenschaft", p. 267; A. Reichert, "Offene Fragen zur Auslegung neutestamentlicher Texte im Spiegel neuerer Methodenbücher". *Theologische Literaturzeitung* 126 (2001), pp. 993–1006.

On the contrary Stegemann's ("'Amerika, du hast es besser!'", p. 114) interest is not aimed at theory but at the participation in current discourses for example, universalism, ethnicity, social and gender discrimination: "Die Fragestellungen und Aufgabenstellungen der Exegese wurzeln in der Gegenwart!". Perhaps, this initiative would result in more resonance towards exegetical questions and research – but were these issues still theologically relevant or just other contributions within cultural studies?

36. Cf. R. Rorty, *The Linguistic Turn* (Chicago, IL: University Press, 1967).

37. Schröter, "Zum gegenwärtigen Stand der neutestamentlichen Wissenschaft", pp. 262–83.

38. Cf. W. Iser, *Der implizite Leser*. Kommunikationsformen des Romans von Bunyan bis Beckett (München: Wilhelm Fink Verlag, 1979, 2nd edn); W. Iser, Der Akt des Lesens. Theorie ästhetischer Wirkung (München: Wilhelm Fink Verlag, 1994, 4th edn [= The Act of Reading: A Theory of Aesthetic Response, Baltimore: Johns Hopkins University, 1978]).

39. Cf. U. Eco, *Opera Aperta* (Milano: Bompiani, 1962); U. Eco, *Lector in fibula* (Milano: Bompiani, 1979).

40. O. Wischmeyer, *Hermeneutik des Neuen Testaments*. Ein Lehrbuch [NET, 8] (Tübingen, Basel: A. Francke Verlag, 2004).

41. Cf. C. Landmesser, "Neutestamentliche Wissenschaft und Weltbezug", pp. 185, 203: "Die neutestamentliche Wissenschaft hat die fundamentale Aufgabe, innerhalb der christlichen Theologie das Sprachpotential der neutestamentlichen Texte in angemessener Weise zur Geltung zu bringen. ... Innerhalb der christlichen Theologie werden die neutestamentlichen Texte als solche Texte gelesen, die etwas von der Welt zu verstehen zu geben beanspruchen".

42. Cf. S. Alkier, "Hinrichtungen und Befreiungen: Wahn – Vision – Wirklichkeit in Apg 12. Skizzen eines semiotischen Lektüreverfahrens und seiner theoretischen Grundlagen". In Alkier and Brucker (eds), *Exegese und Methodendiskussion*, pp. 111–33; S. Alkier, "Ethik der Interpretation". In M. Witte (ed.), *Der eine Gott und die Welt der Religionen*. Beiträge zu einer Theologie der Religionen und zum interreligiösen Dialog (Würzburg: Religion & Kultur-Verlag, 2003), pp. 21–41. S. Alkier, "Fremdes verstehen – Überlegungen auf dem Weg zu einer Ethik der Interpretation biblischer Schriften. Eine Antwort an L. Lawrence Welborn". *Zeitschrift für Neues Testament* 6 (2003), pp. 48–59; S. Alkier, "Neutestamentliche Wissenschaft – Ein semiotisches Konzept", pp. 343–60.

43. Cf. E. Reinmuth, "Historik und Exegese – zum Streit um die Auferstehung Jesu nach der Moderne". In Alkier and Brucker (eds), Exegese und Methodendiskussion, pp. 1–20; E. Reinmuth, *Neutestamentliche Historik – Probleme und Perspektiven* [ThLZ.F, 8] (Leipzig: Evangelische Verlagsanstalt, 2003); cf. also E. Reinmuth, "Diskurse und Texte", p. 83: "Es könnte ja sein, daß der gegenwärtige Glaubwürdigkeitsverlust der Theologie und ihrer Gegenstände auch als Teil des Glaubwürdigkeitsverlustes der Moderne zu verstehen ist".

44. Cf. Schröter, "Zum gegenwärtigen Stand der neutestamentlichen Wissenschaft", pp. 262–83; J. Schröter, "Neutestamentliche Wissenschaft jenseits des Historismus. Neuere Entwicklungen in der Geschichtstheorie und ihre Bedeutung für die Exegese urchristlicher Schriften". *Theologische Literaturzeitung* 128 (2003), pp. 855–66; J. Schröter and A. Eddelbüttel (eds), *Konstruktion von Wirklichkeit*. Beiträge aus geschichtstheoretischer, philosophischer und theologischer Perspektive [ThBT, 127] (Berlin, New York: Walter de Gruyter, 2004).

45. P. Lampe, "Neutestamentliche Theologie für Atheisten? Konstruktivistische Perspektiven". *Evangelische Theologie* 64 (2004), pp. 201–11, argues in a very similar way but neglecting linguistic factors as he restricts his perspective to constructivism.

46. Cf. Reinmuth, "Diskurse und Texte", pp. 81–96.

47. Cf. Schröter, "Neutestamentliche Wissenschaft jenseits des Historismus", pp. 855–66.

48. Cf. P. Ricoeur, "Erzählung, Metapher und Interpretationstheorie", *Zeitschrift für Theologie und Kirche* 84 (1987), pp. 232–53; P. Ricoeur, *Zeit und Erzählung III: Die erzählte Zeit* (München: Wilhelm Fink Verlag, 1991). H. White, *Metahistory: The Historical Imagination in Nineteenth Century Europe* (Baltimore, London: Johns Hopkins University Press, 1973); H. White, *Tropics of Discourse: Essays in Cultural Criticism* (Baltimore, London: Johns Hopkins University Press, 1978).

49. Cf. Reinmuth, "In der Vielfalt der Bedeutungen", p. 87: "Die Aufgabe lautet folglich nicht mehr, das Überlieferte und Übliche in fragloser Geltung zu halten, sondern die Konstruktion unserer Herkünfte zu reflektieren und zu verstehen".

50. Cf. Schröter, "Zum gegenwärtigen Stand der neutestamentlichen Wissenschaft", p. 281.

51. Schröter, "Zum gegenwärtigen Stand der neutestamentlichen Wissenschaft", p. 274.

52. Cf. Schröter, "Zum gegenwärtigen Stand der neutestamentlichen Wissenschaft", especially p. 281; also W. A. Meeks, "Assisting the Word by Making (Up) History. Luke's Project and Ours". *Interpretation* 57 (2003), pp. 151–62, especially p. 160: "The way we assist the Logos is, like Luke, to construct a narrative ... There is no avoiding the task of *construction*. The narrative is not given; it is made up. It is always incomplete and imperfect, shaped by the structures of plausibility that are part of our mentality, dependent upon our time, place, and culture. Nevertheless, although history is always fictive, it does not make up its story whole. It interprets *something* that, however dimly we may perceive it, really happened".

53. Schröter, "Zum gegenwärtigen Stand der neutestamentlichen Wissenschaft", p. 267.

54. See Luz, "Kann die Bibel heute noch Grundlage für die Kirche sein?", pp. 328–29. Luz claims that exegesis because of the discovery of interpreted history and reader response criticism is a "Vorbereiterin des religiösen Pluralismus".

55. H. Omerzu, "Die Pilatusgestalt im Petrusevangelium. Eine erzählanalytische Annäherung". In T. Nicklas and T. J. Kraus (eds), *Das Evangelium nach Petrus. Text – Kontexte – Intertexte* [TU, 158] (Berlin, New York: Walter de Gruyter, 2007), pp. 323–42; H. Omerzu, "Neuere Methoden und Einsichten der neutestamentlichen Wissenschaft". In C. Bizer, R. Degen, R. Englert, H. Kohler-Spiegel, N. Mette, F. Rickers and F. Schweitzer (eds), *Bibel und Bibeldidaktik* [JRP, 23] [Neukirchen-Vluyn: Neukirchener Verlagshaus, 2007), pp. 38–50; H. Omerzu, "Apostelgeschichte als Theologiegeschichte. Apg 19 als Beispiel konstruktiver Paulusrezeption". In D. Marguerat (ed.), Reception of Paulinism in Acts – Réception du paulinisme dans les Actes des apôtres [BEThL, 229] (Leuven: Peeters, 2009), pp. 157–74.

56. Schröter, "Zum gegenwärtigen Stand der neutestamentlichen Wissenschaft", p. 283.

# Private or Public? The Challenge of Public Theology to Biblical Studies

## Philip Chia*

Given my social and geopolitical context, I will approach the topic of secularism and the Bible from my specific location known as the Greater China Region (China mainland, Hong Kong, Taiwan, Macau) and Southeast Asia in general. Hopefully, my contribution will also be a response to the ongoing discussion/debate on the Future of the Society of Biblical Literature, especially the essay by Hector Avalos in this volume.

So, let me begin from a slightly different perspective, i.e., coming from a global market economy's point of view and asking the fundamental economic demand-supply question, that is, *whose interest has the discipline of biblical studies been serving? And which market segment or public benefited most from the discipline? How well is that market or public projecting, is it diminishing or growing?* Such are only some of the realistic questions coming from a globalized market economy environment. Without the existence of a market, a product will have difficulty surviving; so will the discipline come to a natural death without any market demand for it. But judging from some of the responses to Hector's article, naturally the market is far from diminishing (e.g. Michael Fox's observation), so what makes Hector so unhappy about the profession or the Society? Hector impresses me with his utter dissatisfaction with the discipline's inability and incapacity to interact, integrate and contribute directly toward the current global human conditions, such as inequality, poverty, injustice, human rights, etc., which make the profession, its learned society, the discipline of biblical studies utterly irrelevant to our current global human reality. In frustration, there comes the call to abandon the profession, opting perhaps for legal or medical studies, those disciplines that seemingly would benefit people most. As a matter of truth, I believe it is the *relevancy of biblical studies to public life* that is at the core of the dissatisfaction and discussion, at least from my own contextual understanding. But even if the discipline is not immediately relevant to public life, that does not imply that there is a shortage in demand for the discipline or the profession. In fact, it may well be the direct opposite as some respondents to Hector's article have suggested. In other words, there has been, among certain segments of the public, a distinct market demand for the discipline and profession. To be sure, the Church/Ecclesia and the Academia are two such mature markets constantly demanding the supply from the discipline and profession. We shall discuss this at a later stage. The only problem is whether the Society/Profession/Discipline is supplying what they are demanding. As an example, the Ecclesia/Church has often complained (at least in the Chinese context) about the inadequacy of seminary training for their purpose.

But first, we shall need to get a brief sketch of our current global human condition relating to the nature and scope of the issue. For this, I shall borrow from the British political-economic sociologist, Anthony Giddens, in attempting a sketch of our current global condition, then present a contextual situation, looking at the discipline of biblical studies within my given context, and finally suggest an approach for consideration as a possible direction for the discipline of biblical studies which I would like to call a *Public Turn* for Biblical Studies, to move *beyond* being a religious text, such as a proof text for church dogma or doctrines (cf. Boer's "Manifesto"), and *beyond* being a literary text, such as the literary studies of the text from Form Criticism to Rhetorical Criticism in the last century, taking the role of being a *public* text, a legacy of human wisdom and civilization.

### Our Current Global Conditions

We do not live today in a world of the modern, and not so much in the world of the post-modern or second modern either; they were not so *certain, predictable, regulable* and *calculable*,[1] after all. We live, instead, in a world of reality, which painstakingly and penetratingly was characterized as a "*runaway world*" by none other than the renowned sociologist and critic, Anthony Giddens,[2] the previous Director of the London School of Economics:

> The world in which we find ourselves today, however, doesn't look or feel much like they predicted it would. Rather than being more and more under our control, it seems out of our control – *a runaway world*. Moreover, some

of the influences that were supposed to make life more certain and predictable for us, including the progress of science and technology, often have quite the opposite effect.

As also warned by the German sociologist Ulrich Beck,[3] "we are living in the hazardous age of creeping catastrophe".

What, then, has the Bible to do with such a condition of human socio-reality? How, then, should the Bible be read and understood in response to such a world of reality and address such human society, if characterized as a "runaway world"? *In what way(s) could the Bible function as a resource, being a wisdom legacy of human civilization and religious inspiration, for human direction in search of alternative(s)? The challenge remains that the profession and/or the Society needs to address issues and problems of the current human condition, especially from the discipline of biblical studies, which is both part of the human sciences and sacred text of a major world religion, Christianity.* In a way, such a challenge is also encouraged and anticipated by Anthony Giddens'[4] hopeful and imaginative statement: "we shall never be able to become the masters of our own history, but we can and must find ways of bringing our runaway world to heel".

The challenge to relate the profession with our global human condition, inevitably raises the issue of the *relevancy of biblical studies* in particular, and Christian beliefs in general *to public life.* Concerning such relation between Christian beliefs and public life, the British public theologian and politician, Lord Raymond Plant has stated: "if we assume that liberal societies need to have some kind of moral foundation and be based upon a substantial set of moral beliefs, then how far can or should Christian beliefs contribute to that set of beliefs which would be foundational for liberalism?" And in facing the current situation of the Church's attitude towards society and politics, Lord Plant[5] continues to challenge the Church, theologians and biblical scholars alike:

> Is it possible to draw out of Christian beliefs/Bible anything very determinate in terms of social, economic or political insights, or is it better to see Christianity as more concerned with issues of private and personal morality and personal salvation? Only if it is possible to claim that Christian beliefs could produce a reasonably determinate set of social and political insights would it make sense to link, questions relating to Christian beliefs about politics with issues to do with the moral foundations for liberal democratic societies. If social and political theology is impossible, then it is rather redundant to go on to ask what could or should be the role of Christian beliefs about politics in justifying the moral framework of a liberal democratic and pluralistic society.

The challenge to political theologians like Raymond Plant also forms a challenge to the profession of biblical studies, as Plant[6] puts it forcefully, "not just in terms of the assumption that liberal society needs a moral basis, but whether it is, in fact, possible to develop a Christian political theology". In other words, the challenge for biblical studies, as a discipline and as a profession, whether it is possible *to develop the discipline of biblical studies into a publicly relevant profession.*

As the Scottish public theologian Duncan Forrester[7] puts it,

> Public theology is thus confessional and evangelical. It has a gospel to share, good news to proclaim. Public theology attends to the *Bible* [italics mine] and the tradition of faith at the same time as it attempts to discern the signs of the times and understand what is going on in the light of the gospel.

Similarly, German public theologian, Jürgen Moltmann,[8] also points out that, "Its subject alone makes Christian theology a *theologia publica*, a public theology. It gets involved in the public affairs of society. It thinks about what is of general concern in the light of hope in Christ for the kingdom of God". In Jürgen Moltmann's view, as summarized by William Storrar and Andrew Morton, "*Public theology has to do with the public relevance of a theology which has at the core of its Christian identity a concern for the coming of God's kingdom in the public world of human history*".[9] If such a public theology of the Christian faith for the global public is to be based on the Bible, then the discipline of biblical studies has a lot to contribute towards the development of such a theology.

In order to relate biblical studies to public theology, biblical interpretation is a key element. Thus, an immediate concern must be given to hermeneutics, when considering the relations between biblical studies and the runaway world. *No reading is neutral and no understanding is without a context.* To make sense out of the ancient text for a contemporary world, there is a crossover between texts and the interaction between time and space. Reading strategy is often closely connected to contextual interests, and in turn, reality of time and space that nurture such interests. *Given the brief sketch of the current global context, one might consider legitimately, how to read the text in terms of: whose interests are served in which contexts?*

### *The Context: In Whose Interest? For Which Public?*

In whose interest does the discipline of biblical studies serve both at the local location and at the global level? For this essay, the location of the GCR and Southeast Asia is the concern. The Church as a community public (Pc) and the academy profession as yet another seclusive public (Pa), as two distinct "publics", are what the discipline of biblical studies has been serving, at least historically and traditionally in the West as well as in the GCR.[10] Thus, the ecclesial and the academic formed two distinct publics, and *the politics and power relations within these two publics play an important role in the formation of biblical understandings and thus their application.* Despite the difference between the two "publics" and their interests, they still fall primarily within the inner circle of religious public interest. This reality of inward religious public interest which constituted the lack of concern for the general social public (P) as well as the inability to engage in general public discourse on issues of public interest, has ultimately and seriously challenged the very core substance of their biblical confessional doctrine of Creation and Salvation, whereby humanity and creation are the ultimate concern and interest of the God of the Bible.

The common religious languages of the inner circle of the Church public (Pc) and learned terminologies or highly technical language of the academy public (Pa) also contributed directly toward their *inability to actively engage themselves in public (P) discourses.* Thus, *biblical studies*, in advocating the message embedded within the ancient texts or normative documents of the biblical religions, *needs a paradigm that can adequately address the relevancy of its text to the general global social public interest within the current global risk society*, a paradigm which engages in public discourses of these risk societies, at both local and global levels, and contributes responsibly towards the advancement of human civilization, which has been seriously threatened as humankind entered into the 21st century. *Biblical studies in particular and Christian/religious studies in general have been seriously challenged with a call for public relevance and market value, thus situating the discipline at the crossroad of human inquiry.*

Elisabeth Schüssler Fiorenza[11] has rightly pointed out that even as the hermeneutical-postmodern paradigm of biblical studies has "successfully destabilized the certitude of the scientific objectivist paradigm in biblical studies, it still asserts its own scientific value-neutral and a-theological character... and *cannot address the increasing insecurities of globalized inequality*".[12] To this I would add that biblical studies should seriously consider taking on a "*public turn*" to make public relevance a primary task of the profession and its intellectual discourse, expand its capability of engagement in public interest, as a response to Schüssler Fiorenza's proposal of an "ethical-political turn". In fact, earlier in her argument, she points out that "[t]his call for a public-ethical-political self-understanding of biblical studies has become even more pressing today".[13] Perhaps this call for a self-understanding of biblical studies also *voices a sense of identity crisis within the discipline, asking: whose interest and which public do we serve?* How should we position the discipline? Is it as a private discipline serving a small community of the profession for its own self-interests? Or should it be a global discipline, given the nature of the Bible and its text, addressing general and specific human conditions? It is imperative that the new paradigm must be able to address a variety of general and specific public-ethical issues concerning humanity's well being, engaging public discourses in areas such as global economy, global warming, environmental ecology, life-sciences such as Stem Cell research, DNA manipulation projects, life cloning, etc. This question also poses the greatest challenge to biblical studies in the GCR because of a distinct cultural tradition, embedded within its history, of understanding human value, which is quite different from the creation concept of the biblical text in the West. Biblical studies should see itself as a "public discipline" in that its professionals are "public intellectuals" (e.g. like Susan Sontag perhaps, and many others as pointed out by Jacques Berlinerblau).[14]

*A Public Turn? The Challenge of Public Relevance for*
*Biblical Studies*

As the GCR increasingly opens up its doors for knowledge and social transformation, as impacts of information technology and changes in social intellectual demography are taking effects on the region (and at a world scale), biblical studies in particular and theological or Christian studies in general, can *no longer remain as a privatized educational program,* limiting itself to the *Church public* where members share a common faith. In the academy public, students of theological and biblical studies can no longer be limited to Church members or religious people who share a similar faith. Un-Churched intellectuals trained in social science and humanities, regardless of their religious faith, are increasingly interested in taking on the task of studying Christianity for whatever reasons there may be, though often linked *to the search for religious value in nation building and ancient wisdom for human problems.* Thus teaching biblical studies to students in a non-faith based environment is becoming a common challenge, at least in the GCR. Constantly, in courses of biblical studies, *the discipline has been challenged with regard to its contemporary and public relevance.* As pointed out by Jürgen Moltmann, "Christian theology ought to get itself involved in the public affairs of the society.[15] *Thus, it is only natural and relevant that students of biblical studies want to know how biblical studies or religions can contribute as a resource for discourses in public issues, social development and nation building* (italics mine)".[16] They challenge the usage of exclusive language of the Church public in biblical or Christian studies, which themselves created communicative barriers for participation public discourse. Thus the biblical text not only served as a normative document for biblical religions (Pc), *but it is also and increasingly being required and expected to serve as a collection of ancient texts,*[17] *like other Chinese classics or ancient texts, that would provide wisdom for human inquiry and advancement.* The challenge from the academy for the "public character"[18] or "public-ness" of biblical studies is also increasingly matched with the demand from within the Christian public for the relevance of biblical teachings, urging the need to engage in public discourses on pressing public issues with the hope of contributing the values of biblical teachings towards the development of healthy public policies and nation building.

### From Public Relevance to Public Theology

As a reader of the Bible, it is natural for me to read the biblical text with an interest that is identifiable with the people and societies of the GCR. To identify a reading strategy with the GCR is to relate such readings of the biblical text to the public interest of the GCR and to engage the social, political, economic and cultural aspects of the GCR with the text. This engagement itself inevitably drives the result of those readings of the biblical text into formulating some sort of a "localized" biblical theology, and, in a way, contributing towards the development of a kind of critical public theology that is based on critical biblical scholarship and contemporary hermeneutics, as compared to philosophically based or politically based political theology in Western Europe. In this way, there is a meeting of biblical studies and public theology.[19]

As with any given contextual situation, the discipline of biblical studies and the general cultural context of the GCR are, and should be, closely attached to each if social location means anything to biblical studies or reading strategy. When detached from its context or social location biblical studies is merely a scientific positivist academic exercise. In addition to this, the split between exegesis and application is unhealthy and irresponsible, if not unethical.[20] It is rightly pointed out that "the once reigning hermeneutical division of labor between the exegete who describes what the text meant and the pastor/theologian who articulates what the text means has been seriously challenged in the past two decades and been proven to be epistemologically inadequate".[21]

To engage biblical studies with the public relevance of the GCR, one needs to delineate the culture of the GCR public (P). Although the cultural situation of the GCR is a complex phenomenon given the effect of globalization, political economy and market economy in any social location in the twenty-first century, not to mention the political history of the GCR. But suffice to say, all fall within the current global risk society.

To highlight simply and summarize forcefully, the central issue of the culture of the GCR and its primary public relevance and/or interest, as demonstrated by various academic and intellectual traditions, has been for the last century and still is the relation between the constitutional order and the rule of law within a political system. This issue is evidenced in the recent economic and political development within the GCR, and such interest has since sharply escalated both at the local and global level.

How then, should biblical studies be made relevant and be able to engage in public discourses of various scales of magnitude? How should the "public character" or "public-ness" of biblical studies be delineated? Hermeneutically, the biblical text is the primary resource, historical scholarship must be acknowledged, multiple interpretive models should be engaged, methodology should be shifted from the scientific-positivist paradigm to the *public-ethical paradigm*, evaluating its ability and effectiveness in critical engagement with its scholarship on discourses of public issues. The functional aspect of the discipline in engaging with public issues should not be undermined either.[22]

Biblical studies will be an end in itself as a discipline in a globalized world of reality if it continues to be a privatized discipline within the profession without having any relevance for public life, especially within an increasingly interconnected global risk society. The contemporary public relevance of biblical studies challenges its ability as a discipline to engage with the challenge from the emerging discipline of public theology. Issues of public interest such as global economics, environmental ecology, global inequality, religious conflicts, local and global governance, etc., are some of the public concerns that demand responses from biblical studies if creation and humanity continue to be key contemporary concerns of biblical studies. The need to construct a publicly relevant biblical theology is eminent. The task calls for a close interaction and cross engagement between biblical studies and interdisciplinary studies.

## *Endnotes*

\* Philip Chia is a Lecturer at Chinese University of Hong Kong and Conjoint Fellow at the University of Newcastle, Australia.

1. As noted by Ulrich Beck in "Risk Society and the Provident State", in Scott Lash, Bronislaw Szerszynski, and Brian Wynne *(*eds*)*, *Risk, Environment & Modernity: Towards a New Ecology* (Sage Publications, London, 1996), p. 40, "[T]he pre-industrial epochs and cultures were societies of catastrophe. In the course of industrialization these became and are becoming societies of calculable risk, while in the middle of Europe late industrial society has even perfected its technological and social providential and security systems as fully comprehensively insured societies".

2. Anthony Giddens, *Runaway World: How Globalisation is Reshaping Our Lives* (London: Profile, 2003), pp. 2–3.

3. Beck, "Risk Society and the Provident State", p. 40.

4. Anthony Giddens, *Runaway World*, p. 5.

5. Raymond Plant, *Politics, Theology and History* (Cambridge: Cambridge University Press, 2001), p. 2.

6. Plant, *Politics, Theology and History*, p. 2.

7. Duncan B. Forrester, *Truthful Action* (Edinburgh: T&T Clark, 2000), pp. 127–28.

8. Jürgen Moltmann, *God For a Secular Society* (London: SCM Press, 1999), p. 1.

9. See William Storrar and Andrew Morton (eds), *Public Theology for the 21st Century: Essays in Honour of Duncan Forrester* (London/New York: T&T Clark, 2004), p. 1.

10. The term "public" here serves better than the term "community" as demonstrated by Duncan Forrester, the Scottish public theologian. In Andrew R. Morton's characterization, "Whereas 'community' places strong emphasis on what is common to its members, shared by them, 'public' puts more emphasis on what is not common, not shared". See Andrew R. Morton, "Duncan Forrester: A Public Theologian" in William Storrar and Andrew Morton (eds), *Public Theology for the 21st Century: Essays in Honour of Duncan Forrester* (London/New York: T&T Clark, 2004), p. 29. Morton explains that "In a public, as distinct from a community, there is space or distance in the sense of difference and either disagreement or absence of agreement...a space which allows and indeed encourages encounter with that which is different...a public would not be a public unless its members had something in common. At the very least a public has a common language and form of discourse...What is shared in a public is space more than substance; there is some togetherness but with large spaces in it; its weave is open."

11. Elisabeth Schüssler Fiorenza, "Rethinking the Educational Practices of Biblical Doctoral Studies", *Teaching Theology and Religion* 6 (2003), p. 73.

12. See also Beck, "Risk Society and the Provident State", p. 40 [italics mine].

13. Schüssler Fiorenza, "Rethinking the Educational Practices of Biblical Doctoral Studies", p. 69.

14. Cf. Richard A. Posner, *Public Intellectuals: A Study of Decline* (Cambridge, MA: Harvard University Press, 2001).

15. Further, Moltmann (see *God for a Secular Society*, London: SCM Press, 1999, p. 1), states in his preface, "Its subject alone makes Christian theology a *theologia publica*, a public theology. It gets involved in the public affairs of society. It thinks about what is of general concern in the light of hope in Christ for the kingdom of God". Compare with Philip Knight, "Pragmatism, Postmodernism and The Bible as a Meaningful Public Resource in a Pluralistic Age" in John M. Court (ed.), *Biblical Interpretation: The Meanings of Scripture – Past and Present* (New York: T & T Clark, 2003), pp. 310–25.

16. See Moltmann, *God for a Secular Society*, p. 1.

17. "The same rhetorical tension remains... Should it be viewed as a collection of ancient texts or as a normative document of biblical religions?" See Schüssler Fiorenza, "Rethinking the Educational Practices of Biblical Doctoral Studies", p. 72.

18. "Since the socio-historical location of rhetoric as the public of the polis (*sic*), the rhetorical-emancipatory paradigm shift seeks to situate biblical scholarship in such a way that its public character and political responsibility become an integral part of its contemporary readings and historical reconstructions. It insists on an ethical radical imperative that compels biblical scholarship to contribute to the advent of a society and religion that are free from all forms of kyriarchal inequality and oppression". Schüssler Fiorenza, "Rethinking the Educational Practices of Biblical Doctoral Studies", p. 73.

19. Until recently, the commonly adopted pedagogy has been the "scientific-theological positivist" paradigm, adopting standards of excellence from the West. It is also a continuous interest of this study to develop some kind of a critical public-biblical theology to form as the platform for contextual public engagement with biblical studies.

20. Schüssler Fiorenza, "Rethinking the Educational Practices of Biblical Doctoral Studies", p. 69.

21. She also speaks of "how the seven critical feminist hermeneutical strategies could overcome the split between exegesis and application, between what the text meant and means, between history and hermeneutic/theology, which can also become fruitful for shaping doctoral education". See Schüssler Fiorenza, "Rethinking the Educational Practices of Biblical Doctoral Studies", p. 69.

22. One suggested option is to take the Creation in Genesis as a point of departure and work its way through the biblical text, from Old to New Testaments, constructing some sort of a "Critical Sino-Public Biblical Theology" model which could form a basis for further engagement in public issues. Such a theological construction is informed by both historical critical scholarship the hermeneutical-postmodern paradigm, though not limiting itself to those paradigms. It seriously takes on issues of public relevance as a focus of its interpretive reading strategy.

# Part D

## The Paradoxes of Secularism

# NEITHER RELIGIOUS NOR SECULAR: ON SAVING THE CRITIC IN BIBLICAL CRITICISM

*Ward Blanton**

To begin with a tip of the hat to Hegel, it is clear that biblical scholarship's insight about its own operations, about its own identity if you will, has not yet caught up to the true mode in which it functions today. Moreover, it is precisely this gap between the two, operation and insight, that guarantees biblical studies a smooth ride into that oblivion of acritical or apolitical repetition within which it seems to live, move, and have its being at the moment. As Marx loved to say about revolutions, namely, that they always misrecognize themselves in the portraiture of their non-contemporary predecessors, most contemporary accounts of biblical scholarship seem to me oblivious to the peculiar cultural logics of our own time, logics that go hand in hand with recent advances in religious studies and cultural theory. Missing these, biblical scholarship misunderstands its own potential to rework both itself and these new contextual logics in creative – even unprecedented – ways.

In this essay, I am particularly keen to consider a peculiar logic whereby those stalwart modern categories, "religion" and the "secular", have undergone an inversion, a scrambling of codes, and ultimately a collapse into indistinction in terms of their respective critical or political potentials.[1] Needless to say, this particular oppositional scrambling and collapse affects a rather sensitive spot for biblical scholarship as we know it today, which is to say as we continue to portray it to ourselves, even if according to conventions of a world that no longer makes sense of what we are doing. What are we, after all, if not those who can translate ancient religion *into something else*, whether modern historical reason, sociological knowledge, or some such "critical" form?[2]

Indeed, what are we? As will become clear, my fundamental assertion is that, in order to remain critical, intellectually and politically vigilant, it is no longer helpful to organize a self-definition by way of the old certainty that there is any substantial difference between religion and the secular. Not in any way an easy-going "post-" to the risky critical aspirations of self-consciously "modern" biblical scholarship, what we desperately need today is to push modern critique of religion yet further, indeed, to its limit where it begins to include in its self-surveilling purview that fundamental distinction which makes its operations possible in the first place. The unfinished modern project of biblical studies is, therefore, to allow the very difference between religion and its other, "modern" or critical thought in its many guises – history, sociology, literature, autonomy, etc. – to fall under the *epoché* of modern critique itself. It is only as we do so, I want to argue further, that we will be able to give an account of ourselves that is in keeping with the peculiarly aporetic or global cultural logics of our time. In short, it is only as we risk the loss of old certainties, above all that "religion" and historical "reason" are ontologically distinct states of affairs, that these names designate something "out there" in the world, so to speak, that we can attempt to save the power of modern critique itself from what is its current collapse within biblical studies into a (late) modern "historical-critical" mythology.

What is this mythological function of contemporary historical-criticism? It is its general refusal to question that fundamental modern *doxa* whereby it presents itself as the operation that translates *religion into something else.* It is with this goal in mind – the salvaging of that unruly, risky energy of critique, the scandal of which once meant lost jobs, ecclesiastical outrage, and official governmental censure – that I praise the only true stance left to the contemporary biblical critic: neither religious nor secular.[3] The twists of the dialectical screw have revolved multiple times since the political and social dramas of Enlightenment biblical scholarship, the subsequent efforts to translate theology into anthropology, and the general nineteenth-century complexification and profaning of the otherworldly book.[4] The contemporary political and conceptual task, therefore, is to articulate biblical studies in ways that do not refuse to question the basic operations, or paradigmatic questions, by which these two poles – the religious and the secular – have emerged into the light of modern cultural perception as the all-encompassing oppositional pair they have become. Without this risky next step in the progress of biblical scholarship, all the urging of the religious or the secular to take up their respective banners of identitarian faithfulness to the cause seems to me irredeemably retro, a diversionary misrecognition of our current critical potential in the bygone battles of earlier biblical scholars. In order to unearth or renew this critical potential, to save the critic in biblical criticism, we need to be aware of the way the old names of the religious and the secular have long since become dusty placards under museum glass.

## A Single Discourse of Religion-and-Secularity

What might it mean to articulate biblical studies in a world without these old compass points? First and foremost, it means that our analysis is compelled to invent new modes of orientation, new modes of critical thought, or new modes of intervening in a discourse about religion, secularity, and history that has been of central importance in the political and academic self-constitution of the West. We should take our cue here from what I find to be the most significant academic insight in the past three decades of research about the role of "religion" in the modern world, namely, that the modern West may be read as a self-organizing, expanding (or "universalizing") system that, we should never forget, operates free of the implied constraints we continue to imagine as inhering in a substantial distinction between religion and the secular (see below). Unfortunately we continue to have faith in this distinction, as if it were a kind of locational, conceptual, or political *terra firma*, an ultimate limit to which one could, in theory at least, move disputes to a point of ultimate stability (which is to say a point of ultimate incommunicability).[5]

To be sure, the ever-expanding discourse of religion-and-the-secular continues to develop hand in hand with Western notions of governance, concepts of human rights, and market interests. As Edward Said argued admirably for so long, one may even read this academic and social distinction between religion and the secular as a primary motor of the self-expansion of the modern, rational West.[6] As Foucault argued so persuasively, however, this operational motor can only work to the degree that this fundamental distinction is made intelligible by the proliferation of a massive apparatus intended to measure, count, and otherwise *reveal* the difference between, alternately, local, traditional, irrational "religion", and the autonomous, self-constituting, "modern".[7] Biblical studies has, in the past, functioned as just such a technology for the revealing of this distinction, making clear the difference between modern, rational subjects of study and pre-modern, religious objects of research. Nor do we have any reason to think that biblical studies will become less significant in the production and fixing of such distinctions, particularly as the quest to distinguish the specifically limited from the generalizable "human" has not diminished but only grown more aggressive as we enter the age of military intervention in the name of "human rights"[8] Jacques Derrida[9] repeats the same general observation about modern intellectual and political history more succinctly, formally, or theoretically than Said in his important "Two Sources of Religion" essay. Like Said, he describes the modern West as a system that organizes and expands itself precisely *by way of this distinction* between the (excessive or particular) religious and the (general, universal, or global) secular.[10] In other words, the very naming of people, places, ideas, or events as religious or secular has been one of the fundamental tactics of a singular modern form of systemic self-expansion that Derrida calls "globalatinization". The critical point to recognize is that to claim that the system works by way of the production and tactical exportation of this distinction between religion and the secular is not at all – this would be the worst mistake in the world – to claim that there is anything about the self-organizing modern system of the West which is controlled or limited, *as if from the outside*, by these terms. Rather, these are distinctions internal to this system, produced and exported precisely in order to expand and reorganize itself along new lines.[11]

We should not be afraid to evaluate such systems' analytic diagnoses against the backdrop of an everyday experience, the simplicity of which conceals the demand for a radical reconceptualization of the distinction between religion and the secular, and particularly the way biblical studies participates in the inflation and proliferation of these terms. Simply put, in the history of the modern West, people have been excluded, forcibly governed, and murdered both for having an excess of religion and for having a disconcerting lack of it. Either designation operates well to justify those exclusions, forced submissions, and production of corpses that have constituted a not insignificant part of this great modern adventure of the West. In this respect, one of the most important developments in postcolonial theory in recent years has been its increasing sophistication in utilizing colonial histories to dislodge modern, Western categories about religion and secularity.[12] Against the identitarian hysterics of the religious or the secular, the reason for this critical development is not that modernity has lost its nerve in its quest for worldly or profane understanding, much less that the world would have escaped the political disasters of the twentieth century had it never strayed from the substance of religion (these two tales being the typical interpretive jeremiads of such developments by the avatars of the secular and the religious). Rather, the postcolonial dislodging of the aura the modern West finds in secular readings of religion increasingly began to seem necessary if critical theory were to be able to recognize genuine political acts within postcolonial contexts. They needed to disenchant disenchantment, to exorcise the aura from Western reason's ability to dispel the sacred aura of the other.[13]

Dipesh Chakrabarty for example, reminisces about the founding of *Subaltern Studies* and its collective postcolonial sense at that time that it was necessary to contest modern notions of the secular, inasmuch as this name was held out by the Western Left against Indian religion, kinship structures, caste structures – in short, all its "gods, spirits, and supernatural agents" – as that purgative space through which all must pass in order to attain to the genuinely political. When the recognizably political is the self-constituting secular, the designation of the traditionally religious implies that the right to make real, recognizable political decisions must be reserved elsewhere, usually on some Western isle of the *terra firma* or by those living safely behind the liberal Western veil of the secular. As Chakrabarty makes clear, the distinction between religion and the secular, not to mention the politics flowing from it, is a basic – perhaps inextricable – element of the definitions of a self-constituting modern, critical West.[14] Again, the point we need to formalize in our rethinking of biblical scholarship is the way the modern West has used the designation religion as the name of that for the sake of which others must be ignored, or that which is the obstructive supplement to an autonomy these others would otherwise be recognized to possess.[15] So goes the story from the land of the *terra firma*, at any rate, where this oppositional pole is itself imagined to be a mere, rather than an agonistic or political, difference.

On the other hand, as anyone tinkering inventively with imagined biblical family values in recent years in the United States knows very well, censure (and much, much worse, actually) are reserved by the modern West as well for those who can be designated to have an inappropriate *lack* of religion. Or, to stick with the colonial archive just mentioned, if John Stuart Mill and Eric Hobsbawm could be criticized by *Subaltern Studies* for treating the excess of religion as precluding a group from the sphere of the political, we should not forget that the modern West has a long, copiously documented history of excluding, imposing governance, and murdering others whose religion seems, somehow, not enough.[16] Simple as are these recurring everyday realities, therefore, the demand for critical thought to address this more abstract system within which the old identitarian options play themselves out can be quite shocking to us who have become such docile subjects of this expansionistic system. And what is the symptom of our docility as biblical scholars within it but precisely the way we take seriously, as "identities" in need of appropriate representation, the distinction between religion and the secular? Critical thought, if it is not to jump at every invocation of the relative goodness or badness of religion or secularity (or every accusation that one has too much or not enough of the one or the other), must invert this focus on identity in order to consider the larger system within which this *distinction between religion and secularity* emerges and is set into oppositional poles. It is only as the critic allows these "identities" to collapse into a zone of indistinction and radical indifference that we stand a chance to contest the way an expanding, self-organizing system, the "modern West", is perfectly able to make operational – like so many missiles stored away in a bunker for safekeeping – either religion or the secular.[17] If a docile ethos convinces most biblical scholars that, as historians (rather than fundamentalists, for example) our translations of religious texts into something else are, because of this operation, more tolerant, pacifying, and redemptive, the larger systemic truth of our field operates behind our backs and with complete unconcern for our naïve faith that there is any ultimately stabilizing, limiting role of religion or the secular.[18]

### *Escaping the Doppelganger Effect*

In short, as I have shown at length elsewhere, the modern, secularizing study of the Bible is stamped indelibly by a basic operational structure: religion and secularity are identities or methodological stances that remain incoherent without an implicitly comparative moment between the modern, rational historian and the mirrored other *as* non-modern or *as* the embodiment of a form of the religious that the modern *is not*. Modern secularity is thus only ever able to grasp itself by way of this mirror game and the politically disastrous doppelganger effect it sets in motion. As D. F. Strauss put it after he lost his academic post due to the scandal caused by *Das Leben Jesu*: "If antiquity found it valuable to treat nothing as alien to humanity, the watchword of modern times [*die neueren Zeit*] is to regard everything as alien [*Alles as fremd*] which is not human and natural".[19] One discovers the "purely human" (as Strauss liked to put it) by recognizing, designating, and excluding from one's analysis the "alien" other, a kind of alterity Strauss frequently called the "mythical" and the "dogmatic". My interest in recalling such a paradigmatic modernizing (or secularizing) biblical scholar is to highlight the obvious, operational secret sharing at work between religious and secular identities in such an academic pronouncement, a sharing that is necessitated by the systemic "modern" demand that one grasp the "purely human" by way of making clear the "alien" other as that which must be recognized and excluded or subordinated. It was an historical critical method that was likewise repeating itself at the level of modern politics.

The current mantra of biblical studies about its (often racist, colonial, and anti-Semitic past) is that we should be kinder, gentler, and more open than our "essentializing" or "universalizing" predecessors. Against this generally accepted notion, what we need to do is rather to take up the modern logic, to push it yet further, to its limit. Mantras of commitment to individual kindness are insufficient weapons against a *systemic* violence that is buried deep within the heart of our enterprise as biblical scholars, much less against a "West" that expands itself now more than ever by way of the same old tricks.[20] Again, we should speak rather of the unfinished project of modern critique, meaning in our case that we need to rethink our discipline in terms of a form of analysis that does not reify or depoliticize this essential identitarian hierarchy between non-modern religion and modern (historical) reason, but that instead uncovers the *shared or contested* historical and systemic space within which these conjoined twins emerged and operated so effectively as a culturally central either/or.

### Looping Religion and Secularity: Critical Thought in a Global Environment

Or, as Marshall McLuhan used to say regularly (in a mediological prelude to our sociologies of a "risk society"), modernity begins to experience its own limit when it enters a situation in which all identities become "looped", as if driven crazy, by virtue of the fact that they can no longer take themselves seriously except *reflexively*, as *potential* causes of global effects.[21] In such a scenario (a madness he located within his notoriously reflexive "global village"), identity loses its self-contained substance and becomes virtual, a possible cause of some (media) registered effect in the world. Such is the hyper-modern or properly global reflexivity which modern biblical studies, that wonderful potential for religiosecular cultural critique and the translation of religion (and now the secular!) into the immanent space of "the world", must now recognize within itself in order to find new critical modes for its work. Such is the only way to discover anew, rather than to repeat in a hamstrung mythological mode, the critical force of earlier biblical studies. Far from merely representing the imagined, self-contained island of *terra firma* – whether religion or secularity – in a "looped" or global environment we must take up shelter within these old identitarian territories knowing that in doing so we are *negotiating* identity, imaginatively *projecting* and *mirroring* it, and all this with the most concrete effects on others.

In a global space that has thus become "looped" in every sense of that term, no fetishizing of the religious or the secular can save us from an interconnectedness, a modern problematic, and the weight of a colonial history, that has long since turned all of our identities inside out. Strauss already "knew" this, though without himself yet realizing what he was saying, when he claimed that the identity of the "modern" (or "purely human") can *only* be present to itself *through* the "alien" other. Far from liberal fantasies about being kinder and gentler individuals than were our modernist predecessors, what we need to do today is to repeat these logics anew, making clear what is being said therein. And while most only lament the loss of immediacy and self-identity such a repetition certainly implies in our "looped" environment, we should rather take consolation that these inverted identities are now turned out, irrevocably, *toward the other*. The generically human, and indeed the "critical" self, emerges only through the alien other.

Indeed, biblical scholarship is in desperate need to flesh out such insights today, as most seem to be missing them, in the renewal of the religious-or-secular Bible wars most of all. Today the space of viable critique, viable political thought, *is* such a looped space, and all the current paroxysms about recovering religion from a secularist detour (on the one hand) or remaining faithful to the secularist heritage against religion (on the other) are equally fetishistic disavowals of this fact. If only we remain secular or religious, we continue to tell ourselves (as if we had lost *our* jobs almost two centuries ago when Strauss lost his), all will be well. Again, the fundamental mistake that governs these two retro stances is that they base themselves on the belief that the globalizing or expansionistic West (whether parsed as colonial aggressivity, capitalist machinations, or even humanitarian military intervention) submits to – as if to a limiting outside – these names, the secular and the religious. This is the lie that seems to be pressing itself upon us with renewed vigour in the returned wars between the secular and the religious, a lie that convinces players on both sides that these names are stable, safe, self-enclosed, and unscathed identities within the otherwise looping madness of the global.

So long as biblical critics thus remain cocooned inside of one of these identities or another, (or to put it more provocatively) so long as they remain sane and healthily unscathed by the looped space of the global, it is to just such a degree that they remain docilely submissive to the larger, globalizing system within which they live, move, and have their being. *Therefore the only step "outside" the single discursive and expansionistic machine of religion-and-secularity – the war to define the immanent here and now of what will be countable or real over against the sphere of unfounded desire or mere fantasy – is a radical indifference to the stated stakes of this discursive game altogether.* We either begin to question the rules and the pre-determined countable "goals" of the game into which we have been thrown, or we continue to feed the fire of that expanding form of the global that is happening all around us.

In this specific sense, Giorgio Agamben is on the right track when he attempts to redeploy the radical *epoché* of Pauline messianism in 1 Corinthians 7 – living "as if one were not" what one's identity says one is – as a figure of resistance in an age of the global or universal.[22] Biblical studies could learn from this figure, and this redeployment, which may also be found within Agamben's work under the name of Melville's Bartleby the Scrivener.[23] It is only in a radical passivity and refusal before the face of a demand to settle the account being shoved upon us that we will be able to salvage a critical potential in relation to those disorienting global or worldly logics within which our "religion" or our "secularity" have been thrown, looped beyond recognition.[24]

## *No Stable Religion or Secularity: Singular Modernities*

But my rationale for unplugging critique – and the radical *critic* in biblical criticism – from this larger discursive network about which we (unlike Strauss) can no longer claim naiveté, is not merely systemic or structural. It rather emerges from my explorations of the role of secularizing modern biblical critics and my increasing awareness of just what singular affairs these moments of secularizing scholarship in fact were. One way to describe this generally unrecognized lesson of our disciplinary history is to say that there never has been an agreed upon definition of what would constitute, say, a secularizing or profaning reading of biblical texts. Nor has there ever been a stable rendering of what it would mean to guarantee the "religion" in these texts.

This is all to say, for example – and in a way that demands a more substantial cultural theory than we tend to employ in the guild – that in the history of biblical scholarship, what creates profaning scandal has often been surprising or unexpected, and frequently considered completely irrelevant by the "same" religious groups decades before or after these unexpected traumas. Consider, once more, the case of Strauss, whose biblical scholarship was self-consciously an attempt to locate the "purely human" by way of a disclosure of that which is "alien" to this merely human realm in the biblical texts. Who would have thought that Strauss' profaning "critique" of the heteronomous, alien powers of the sacred book would hinge entirely on a kind of literary and aesthetic argument?

His famous deployment of the category "myth", after all, was essentially an argument about the mode of literary production by which the Gospel texts came into existence. In this case, the alienating, traumatic revelation about the Gospels was that they were not written so much by authors as they were rehashed by "relaters" of a collective *mentalité*, less than conscious or even automatic expressions of a background cultural mood.[25] How surprising that the idea caused such a scandal! One could just as well imagine Strauss's nineteenth-century readers being, theologically and religiously, thrilled at this news, banding together to offer him a cushy promotion, perhaps. Strauss was, after all, repeating a way of understanding the production of literary texts that was extremely popular among the pious only a few decades before! When Vico, Herder, or Lowth described biblical texts as unconscious productions of a collective *mentalité*, they were rather praising these wonders from the blissful "childhood of the human race" than profaning religion. By the mid-point of the nineteenth century, however, the diffuse assemblage of disparate material and ideal elements that were quilted together under the name "religion" was much different from what had taken cover there previously. Far from considering Strauss a hero, full of outrage, made "Strauss-sick" (as George Eliot famously described herself on reading his book), they joined together to oust this profaner from the academy altogether.

Our rich disciplinary history indicates the way such shifts in what counted as religious or secular occurred again and again. This is a revelation (to those of us who still read our own disciplinary history, anyway) about how what is still our dominant form of self-narration, historical reason's progressive overcoming of prior religious prejudice, is necessarily thrown off the rails. There simply *is no stable understanding* of what would count as a "secularizing" reading of "religion" over time, if one is taking one's cues from the actual history of the field. Again, we need forms of self-understanding that do not imply religion or the secular to be self-identical islands, things, places, realities existing independently over time, even if all we claim to do with these names is to describe our historical "method". Rather, the religious and the secular were, and will continue to be, singular, fugitive, contingent events of cultural transformation that have nothing to do with a metaphysical givenness about what, always and already, is the case about ourselves, about our object of study, or our audiences. It is in this sense that biblical studies must learn to run the gauntlet of *our singular modernities.*[26]

To say the same thing more formally, we must not forget that there has never been what Lacan referred to as the big Other, a metalanguage of religion or secularity which observes us complacently from the outside, as if hanging around to make a final judgement about the difference between the really real of history over against the invasive presence of religious fantasy or the inappropriate intrusions theological desire. Rather, the designations of the religious and the secular are themselves involved, productive acts of players within a larger cultural game that they do not themselves control (which is to say, in modernity, that they do not understand). Consider, for example, that the designation "secular" has frequently been the *theological* accusation levelled by one religious group against another, the one disavowing the other as having profaned or transgressed something that must remain recognized tradition or sacred. Never mind that such accusations were often levied by one Christian group against what was imagined (by the competing group) to be pious theological labor.

One thinks of competing religious struggles to develop theories of Gospel interdependence, attempts to uncover the authentic eschatological hopes of Jesus, or even attempts to establish the "proof" of Jesus' miracles by way of modern knowledge about magnetism or psychology. The pious securing of one theological community becomes the transgressive, profaning abomination of another, with no outsider standing by in order to guarantee the genuine limits of theology, faith, or religion, just as there is no external landmark by which to validate the authenticity of atheistic critique or devastating profanation.[27] To recall my discussion of (a Levinasian) McLuhan, without any stable foundation in either religion or secularity, *our* religion or secularity will be decided by another whom we do not know and could never control. And this reality of being turned inside-out, looped, will remain in effect despite any hysterical effort to collect ourselves, to protect ourselves, and even to name ourselves according to a "method" that is one or the other.

And is not this reality made especially clear to us who teach biblical studies year by year? You will all know well the experience that it is sometimes the damnedest of random details to which your students will append either the ecstasy of faith or the horror of profaned precious hopes, and this always beyond what you could have expected or planned for them. Such weekly occurrences should *mean something* to the way we narrate the religious or the secular, as we know better than most that to name these names is to designate hodge podge assemblages of contingent desires and sensibilities that have come to be quilted together (as Lacan says) under these names that have been elevated above all names, the religious or the secular. Who would have guessed that it would be secular or religious to translate the Bible, to publish it as a contemporary teenie-bopper magazine, to present it without chapter headings, to have it sent to yourself as a text message, to interpret Gospel texts in ways that did not always refer back to a (modern) individual Jesus, to read Paul as Jewish, to find literary sophistication in the Pastoral Epistles?

Indeed, who would have guessed? And if we would not have guessed it, then perhaps we need to stop assuming that we are re-presenting pre-fabricated "identities" so that we can start exploring new and unprecedented ways that we might reconfigure the subterranean forces inhering in these names. Who knows what will yet become of the "secular" or the "religious"?

### *Neither Religious Nor Secular: How to Ignore the Disembodied Voice from Offstage*

Believe me...I am acutely aware of the fact that a becoming-indifferent to one of the major "stakes" of our modern discipline – indeed, of our modern academy – is a risky venture. To speak colloquially, in my probing of a potential critical praxis that is "neither secular nor religious", and therefore radically indifferent to a particular understanding of criticism (and critical theory) as we have received it, I too have sensed the surprisingly overwhelming suspicion of such a project. In lecture halls, interviews, colloquia, and chapels, my mapping of this intellectual and critical space has often been received as if I were pretending, as if I were being annoyingly coy, as if I were not "playing cricket", or as if I were somehow desecrating an unspoken rule of the game I am supposed to be playing. It is not simply that I find academic colleagues, students, and online interlocutors thinking that surely, surely, underneath it all I am *really* secular or religious. Rather, I am even more struck by the *implicit demand* from all involved that I not obstruct their access to a beloved point of orientation – the all-hallowed distinction between the religious and the secular.

This in itself I find a clear symptom of the state of affairs into which we are thrown today, a symptom I read, once more, against the backdrop of the Lacanian notion of the quilting point, the necessity for a radically relative or complexly interrelated system of signs to fix itself, to guarantee its intelligibility, by way of a controlling or hegemonic designation. As Lacan[28] states very simply in his discussion of Racine, "It's the point of convergence that enables everything that happens in this discourse to be situated retroactively and prospectively".[29] In this case, we should subtract Lacan's concept from his interest in the systemic rules of language in order to make clear the significance that the distinction between religion and the secular has had within modern colonial history in global contexts. Disoriented, finding itself only relatively and ambiguously located within the spaces and times of the global, the West organized – and hierarchized – a world of information by way of the religion-secular distinction. This, as I have mentioned already, I take to be the radical illumination of recent postcolonial theory or a book like Tomoko Masuzawa's, *The Invention of World Religions: Or, How European Universalism Was Preserved in the Language of Pluralism.*

Always inaccessible of itself, the hegemonic distinction of the quilting point nonetheless organizes or hierarchizes otherwise indifferently diffuse spheres of information. Indeed, precisely *because* it is inaccessible of itself, the driving hegemonic question here is able to colonize the most disparate territories in order to assert *there* its organizational authority, to demand of this otherwise disparate or unmapped sphere that it submit to the hegemonic name, that it declare itself in relation to this authority. Again, it is worth saying that my interest in saying no to, and rearticulating, this powerful machinery for organizing words and things arises directly from my work on the modern, avowedly "secularizing" history of New Testament scholarship. If the history of debate between religion and secular interpretation makes *anything* clear, it is that there has never been in this field a "religion" – or a "secular" critique of it – that does not shift, continually and unpredictably, over time. It is in this precise sense that our conversations about the past and future of biblical studies should reject fuzzy and merely ideal repetitions of these terms, as if they represented a world in which this pluralism were not the case. Rather, informed by this history in all its diversity, we must explore the fact that, to borrow the lingo of Bruno Latour, *we have never been secular-or-religious,* or that this distinction does not refer to self-same identities over time or geographical space. To do so, of course, means that our discipline, and ourselves as individuals, must risk the obvious question in light of what we know from our own history. Since these names do not designate ideal or self-same entities over time or across ethnic and national borders, *from where does this unseen pressure arise,* this compulsion, to confess ourselves – and to rat out others – in relation to an (inaccessible and obfuscating) either/or?

Like a voice coming from offstage, actors within different spheres – eating, caressing, dressing, exploring, intervening, or studying the Bible – all find themselves incited to act out in these diverse spheres their versions of a hegemonic, pre-scripted, and inaccessible stage direction: *indicate whether you are doing this or that religiously or secularly.* And, I freely admit it, the pressure of this offstage demand on the sphere of biblical scholarship is perhaps at its most acute. Rather than to lament this fact, we should rather rejoice (as in our very suffering) that our field must therefore be crucial for the maintenance of the systemic hegemony of this particular quilting point. After all, to say that we feel the pressure to "confess" our allegiance, to "fix" ourselves on the territorial maps that emerge under the auspices of this offstage voice, is to say (simultaneously) that we could play a potentially subversive role in unhinging the opposition and thus loosening up for rearticulation that complex network of words and things that have found their pre-scripted places under its imperial banner.

I know by now that this risk to our imaginary selves – religious or secular – is not one many will venture, as if to find the rhythms of global thought by losing one's identitarian life. But, nevertheless, in the hope that there may yet be some who, like Bartleby, "prefer not" to repeat this compulsive, mechanical either/or, it is worth saying that as a discipline we have some experience in the scrivening activism it would take to throw a monkey wrench into the grinding wheels of this single discursive machine. As a field, we, too, have before uttered the apparently pointless "I prefer not to" of a Bartleby!

Throughout much of the nineteenth century, for example, it was difficult for most New Testament scholars to find space for questions that did not (implicitly at least) contribute to the answering of that imperious, underlying question to which all their research seemed fated to contribute an answer: what is the original difference between Christianity and Judaism? When and how did Jesus, Paul, or early Christianity "break" from Judaism? Or, as I like to put the real political stakes of this interpretive obsession of modern, and largely Christian, scholarship – how can I be sure that I am not Jewish? And yet, somehow, the possibilities for our work – our research, our writing, our teaching – do not now seem to be thus scripted in relation to this imperious and politically loaded question of earlier scholarship – at least not with the same force. And does this example not make clear that it was not more information, but rather a political and social reconfiguration of the generally offstage or paradigmatic demand, that has provided us with this post-nineteenth century potential? My call is, therefore, for biblical studies to take advantage of the compulsive pressure we now feel so acutely in order to configure differently the paradigmatic or offstage demand we hear (ever louder and ever more hysterical of late) to confess, to declare ourselves – and thus to seal up our critical intellectual and social potential – in the discourse of the religious-or-secular.

Without the safety of this orienting distinction, in the midst of ambiguity and risk, we will need to invent new ways of orienting critical thought and situating the critic in biblical criticism. Surely, such a project will need the most brilliant minds and most industrious workers in the field. But, then again, has the time not long since passed for biblical scholars to stop re-presenting pre-fabricated worlds of the religious or the secular and to start tinkering away at the invention of new mixtures – new distinctions – of heaven and earth altogether? Who knows what will yet become of this "religion" or this "secularity", looped as each already is? Forget the pre-scripted demands for confession from the religion-or-secular machine. What we need is to become neither secular nor religious in order to clear an experimental path for scrivening activists of profane illumination. It is out of this exploratory (non) ground from which will arise a critic from biblical criticism.

## Endnotes

\* Ward Blanton is Senior Lecturer in New Testament Studies for the Department of Theology & Religious Studies at the University of Glasgow.

1. I have previously explored the systemic inversion of these two identities, their secret sharings, and their mutually contestatory history in relation to modern New Testament studies (see Blanton, *Displacing Christian Origins: Philosophy, Secularity, and the New Testament*, Chicago, IL: University of Chicago Press, 2007). The programmatic demand of the present essay emerges directly from this larger study.

2. I realize that this statement does not take into account the scholars within the field who would never dream of themselves as translating, let's say, the "Christian theology" of the New Testament into anything else. That is, there are some for whom the fundamental idea of a distinctively *modern* biblical scholarship fails to hold any allure. Even these, however, almost invariably speak in the name of, and with the language of, history, sociology, cultural studies, and so on, and surely this is no mere ruse, or surely it is something that calls for an analysis of the nature of the "modernity" in its own discourse. More fundamentally, perhaps, such are the current limitations of my optimism that I expect so little experimental and groundbreaking thought (for me the goal of biblical studies) from the rear-guard host of neoconservative functionaries that I tend not to include them in my "we" of critical biblical scholarship. The crucial stance to acknowledge is that against all the more or less sophisticated identifications with a "religion" that remains unscathed by modern critique or modern political catastrophe – and there are *many* of these imaginary identifications being peddled today, with great

financial success and many followers – I continue to suspect that modernity (now late, hyper-, or post-) is indeed in the throes of an exhilarating paroxysm in which its categories are being inverted, but that the entry fee for such apocalyptic inversions remains that one has actually *gone through the modern experience.* Again, such are my limitations, the limitations (I might add) that Gianni Vattimo. (See Gianni Vattimo, *Nihilism and Emancipation: Ethics, Politics, and Law* [New York: Columbia University Press, 2004, pp. 31–36]), defines more generally as the aporetic necessity and impossibility of doing metaphysics today, or what Vincent Pecora (see Vincent P. Pecora, *Secularization and Cultural Criticism*, Chicago, IL: University of Chicago Press, 2006, pp. 195–208), has analyzed in relation to postcolonial cultural criticism. To mention only two more recent studies that I find particularly helpful in thinking about the paroxysm or "dialectic of Enlightenment" in which we now find ourselves, see Stathis Gourgouris, *Does Literature Think? Literature as Theory for an Antimythical Era* (Stanford, CT: Stanford University Press, 2003). See also Hent de Vries, *Minimal Theologies: Critiques of Secular Reason in Adorno and Levinas* (Baltimore, WA: Johns Hopkins University Press, 2005). Like my "looped" rendition below, both Gourgouris and de Vries call for an exploration of the *performative self-grounding* of the very distinction between religion and the secular.

3. Believe me, I am not romanticizing the years of scandal. Among other things, the economic threat to radical biblical scholars meant that only the self-sufficiently wealthy (or those who were able to write for a popular book market) could push critical agendas with real zeal. My point is not to romanticize the costs paid to critique but to say that biblical scholarship hardly remains faithful to such a legacy without some risk, today, to itself. More to the point, scholars seem to me in bad faith when they claim faithfulness to such a tradition without assuming a similarly questionable stance in relation to *their own institutional and cultural limits.* Taking up such a risky stance would be a far cry from the usual guild hand-wringing about how *other* institutions, *other* individuals, *other* religions, and so on, are not yet tolerant enough. If such pronouncements are being made from the safety, and with the self-feeding power, of class and institutional status, the result is mere self-congratulatory image without substance. We should therefore add to our initial presentation of the Marxist truism that potential revolutions tend to misrecognize themselves in their predecessors: this is not just a mistake; it can pay to engage in this little ruse!

4. Indeed, following the neo-Weberian Niklas Luhmann, of whom I am very fond, we could trade all the hackneyed narrations and increasing "secularization" of biblical scholarship for a story about the increasing specialization (or complexification) of knowledge about the Bible during this period. Just to give an everyday example, we should not forget the way that it is generally to counteract the *complexity* of the classroom narration of Christian origins that students tend to make use of overt *theologoumena.* God-talk allows them to reduce this complexity dramatically (the four Gospels saying, essentially, the same thing; the historical Jesus being, essentially, the same as his presentation in the Gospels, and so on). We continue to treat such conversations as the great battle between "religion" and "secularity", but aren't we really seeing something much more banal? Isn't it namely, an effort to cope with a proliferation of specialist knowledge with which it is difficult to identify as a living, breathing human (without, of

course, actually becoming a Bible scholar oneself)? One finds the same proliferation of complexity (the *sine qua non* of modern scholarship on any topic) and homespun strategies to reduce *it in any field*, and comparison with these other fields opens up new ways to articulate what is happening in epistemic transformations within our own. Indeed, that we resist doing so in order to privilege the old story of the progressive (historical) overcoming of a prior (religious) prejudice I have analyzed elsewhere as the self-deception of otherwise "secular" renderings of the field (see Blanton, Biblical Studies in the Age of Bio-power: Albert Schweitzer and the Degenerate Physiology of the Historical Jesus, *The Bible and Critical Theory* 2 [no. 1, 2006]: 6.1–6.25).

5.  In terms borrowed from Hegel, that early master of cultural theory in a globalizing age, this is the critical intellectual and political mistake, as our thinking needs for this dualism a distinction between these identities that likewise mediates. We need, in other words, a kind of analysis that makes sense of the fact that this oppositional distinction between religion and the secular plays itself out as a larger agonistic game that we must now consider in its own right. That the "right" of this larger (indeed, global) economy is pressing itself on our awareness all the more as time goes on I take to be implied by the increasingly hysterical efforts of the avowedly secular or religious to convince people to ignore it, to take up the old existential stances without reference to it, to look inside (or to the past) for the essence of the religious or secular identity itself, rather than to allow one's identity to be turned inside out, "looped", by a focus on this more general context. Why is it that the obsession with identity has become an academic mantra during the new age of humanitarian intervention and the inflation of language about "human" rights? That is, why is it at the very moment of new, globalizing transformations that we become so obsessed with identity? Similarly, as should be clear, to speak of an economically agonistic or competitive link between religion and the secular in this way is the farthest thing from the silly versions of "postmodern" pop Nietzscheanism that seem to have sprung up over the past three decades. In such superficial reductions of the conceptual and historical issues at stake, "agonistics" are imagined to be personal, transparent stakes for the individual players involved, and therefore straightforwardly conniving in the obvious sense of attempting to manipulate others. This unfortunate rendering of the "postmodern" frames, for example, at least parts of the rhetorical plea for the dominance of "mainline" "history" against the imagined suspicions of "postmodern" methods of interpretation within John J. Collins (see his *The Bible After Babel: Historical Criticism in a Postmodern Age*, Grand Rapids, MI: Eerdmans, 2005), e.g., chapter 1. What we need to do, rather, is to realize that, increasingly, the designation of the religious or the secular as a significant way to parcel out people, ideas, and places must *itself* be considered as an *economy* with its own tendencies and logics. Turning our thinking around (from the religious and the secular) to analyse what has hitherto been operating behind the identitarian backs of these designations has little to do with the pack of weasels that seems to be envisioned by pop Nietzscheans and their critics alike.

6.  Indeed, in an argument with which my own thinking about the (in)distinction between the religious and the secular is in profound agreement, Gil Anidjar (Secularism, *Critical Enquiry* 33 [2006], pp. 52–77), presses the case that Said

could have recognized this reality even more, to the point that Said would no longer have presented effective cultural critique under the name of the "secular", as if such a name were to refer to an outside of the expansionist regime of colonialism. To believe in the critical force of the secular misses the way the orientalizing, colonizing West expands itself *by way of the distinction between the religion and the secular.*

7. And while my essay tends to remain within the boundary of the religion-versus-secular, it is worth pointing out here that the distinction-making game works just as well when the generalizable, universalizable European contribution is not explicit "secularity" so much as a "universal religion" or even, as Tomoko Masuzawa has pointed out in a fundamental challenge to received narrations of religious studies, "world religion" as a category. See Masuzawa's *The Invention of World Religions: Or, How European Universalism Was Preserved in the Language of Pluralism* (Chicago: University of Chicago Press, 2005). As Pecora (see Vincent P. Pecora, *Secularization and Cultural Criticism* [Chicago, IL: University of Chicago Press, 2006], and I (Ward Blanton, *Displacing Christian Origins: Philosophy, Secularity, and the New Testament* [Chicago: University of Chicago Press, 2007]), are all saying, there is an eventual breakdown between "religion" and the "secular" into the same "globalizing" movement of money, power, and mind that identitarian liberalism cannot comprehend.

8. See Alain Badiou, *Ethics: An Essay on the Understanding of Evil. Wo Es War* (New York: Verso, 2002). See also Giorgio Agamben, *State of Exception* (Chicago, IL: University of Chicago Press, 2005a).

9. See Jacques Derrida, "Faith and Knowledge: the Two Sources of 'Religion' at the Limits of Reason Alone". In Jacques Derrida and Gianni Vattimo (eds), *Religion* (Stanford, CA: Stanford University Press, 1996), pp. 1–76. Derrida ties together in the "faith and knowledge" essay a distinction between religion and the secular with that *self-obstructing* logic of a system struck by an "auto-immune" disorder. This peculiarly aporetic systemic logic he describes at the level of the body, of the expansion of tele-technologies, and of the globalization of capital, religion, and Western notions of humanity. Within this systemic operation, the attempt to exclude, excise, or overcome the religious or the secular simply feeds its capacity for self-organization.

10. For such considerations, described in a conversational manner, see Giovanna Borradori (*Philosophy in a Time of Terror: Dialogues with Jacques Derrida and Jürgen Habermas* [Chicago, IL: University of Chicago Press, 2004]. Precisely because it raises dynamic questions in relation to a multitude of otherwise discrete fields, the study of self-organizing systems has exploded beyond the limits of a quick summary. Here I find particularly helpful the work of Niklas Luhmann (see for e.g. Luhmann's *Social Systems* [Stanford, CA: Stanford University Press, 1996]; and William Rasch's *Niklas Luhmann's Modernity: The Paradoxes of Differentiation* [Stanford, CA: Stanford University Press, 2000]). As mentioned, however, my own thinking on this point is informed above all by my archival investigations of the modern study of the New Testament (set out in Blanton, *Displacing Christian Origins*). In other words, while the global thinking and systemic analyses of a self-limiting or self-organizing system in thinkers Hegel, Heidegger, Luhmann, and Derrida are all very relevant for me, it is worth remembering among biblical scholars that my formalisation (and ultimate

rejection) of religion-and-the-secular arises from my paying attention to the language of religion, theology, and the secular within the history of modern New Testament scholarship. My formulations are an immanent critique if ever there has been one!

11. I do not mean to imply that the issue is one localizable within "postcolonial theory", as is sometimes implied (usually to dismiss the concerns at hand). But those interested in the history of expansionist exportation of tactics of governmentality from the West are, no doubt, in a good position to ask the fundamental question that faces all Western academics (and not just them) today: Why is it that the societies so gripped by visions of liberal multiculturalist tolerance are the most colonial and interventionist? See Wendy Brown, *Regulating Aversion: Tolerance in the Age of Identity and Empire* (Princeton, NJ: Princeton University Press, 2006). See also Aihwa Ong, *Neoliberalism as Exception: Mutations in Citizenship and Sovereignty* (Durham, NC: Duke University Press, 2006).

12. Dipesh Chakrabarty, *Provincializing Europe: Postcolonial Thought and Historical Difference* (Princeton, NJ: Princeton University Press, 2000), pp. 11–16. See also Vincent P. Pecora, *Secularization and Cultural Criticism* (Chicago, IL: University of Chicago Press, 2006), p. 200.

13. Again, Derrida's "Faith and Knowledge" essay is correct to read the global movements and logics of self-organizing and expansionistic systems as involving an elaborate panoply of "tele-technologies", from muskets to telephones to religious broadcasting. Religion and the secular, I am suggesting, are the techniques of a projective mapping that is indistinguishable from an effort to get a grip, literally, on new global territory. In Heideggerian terms of which I am very fond, it is only as we allow this distinction between religion and secularity to collapse into indistinction that we are able to "stay with" a globalizing system that continually draws on these two "identities" as a single "standing reserve" of imperial power.

14. In a similar vein, the entire political oeuvre of Michael Taussig may be read as allowing early ethnographic theories of the magical substantialism of "primitive" societies to reflect back upon the modern ethnographic gaze that produced them. Taussig's work is, in this respect, extremely significant for a rethinking of biblical studies (See Michael Taussig, *The Magic of the State*, London: Routledge, 1996, and also Taussig, *Defacement: Public Secrecy and the Labor of the Negative*, Stanford, CA: Stanford University Press, 1999).

15. That this little trump card continues to operate within academic, and ostensibly critical, biblical studies as that favoured mode of adjudicating competing interpretations is clear. I explore the rhetorical performance of one such instance (from a sea of such instances) in Blanton, "Biblical Studies in the Age of Bio-power."

16. See for e.g. David Chidester, Savage *Systems: Colonialism and Comparative Religion in Southern Africa* (Charlottesville, VA: University of Virginia Press, 1996); Webb Keane, *Christian Moderns: Freedom and Fetish in the Mission Encounter* (Los Angeles, CA: University of California Press, 2007); Wendy Brown, *Regulating Aversion: Tolerance in the Age of Identity and Empire* (Princeton, NJ: Princeton University Press, 2006), pp. 149–205; William E. Connolly, *Why I Am Not a Secularist* (Minneapolis, MN/London: University of Minnesota Press, 1999), p. 77.

17. As I keep repeating, contemporary U.S. foreign policy alone should leave us with no illusions that such distinctions are something we left behind in the naughty nineteenth century. Consider the significance of the U.S. hesitations to recognize the results of democratic elections in Palestine or South America, an irony that has not been missed (for example) in the various ideological critiques of U.S. military presence by Iraqi mullahs. Again, as Giorgio Agamben (see Agamben, *State of Exception*. [Chicago: University of Chicago Press, 2005a]) and David Harvey (see *A Brief History of Neoliberalism* [Oxford: Oxford University Press, 2006], pp. 5–63), have both argued so clearly recently, the paradox is constitutive of the triumph of a neo-liberal ideology of freedom as free markets.

18. One could explore the implications of this collapse into indistinction by considering Alain Badiou's often repeated dictum that capital (like Heidegger's stone) is without a "world". Capital is, in other words, beyond the horizon of the religion and the secular in any phenomenological sense.

19. David Friedrich Strauss, *Das Leben Jesu*. Gessamelte Schriften 3(Bonn: Verlag von Emil Strauss, 1877), p. 6.

20. What irks me above all in such "kinder, gentler" narratives within biblical studies is the good conscience that is implied about oneself in relation to, say, the nineteenth-century German who was part of a systemic anti-Semitism. Is it not increasingly obvious, however, that if the ethical engagement of nineteenth-century biblical scholarship seems judged by its subtle complicities or overt failures to criticize anti-Semitic policies and practices, then early twenty-first century scholars stand judged already by their failure to launch an effective critique against new exclusions and colonizations of the Arab world, many of which operate under the auspices of different categorizations of the religious and secular?

21. The theme is ubiquitous in McLuhan's work, from his records and comic books to his academic lectures. He was clearly touched by this peculiar madness! Along with Niklas Luhmann's descriptions of modernity, McLuhan's "probes" into the cultures or environments of the global remind us of what we tend to forget, that what we usually think of as the theoretical or methodological reflexivity of modern critique is a symptom of a much more general, material emergence of looping or self-feeding systems during this period. Niklas Luhmann (*Observations on Modernity* [Stanford, CA: Stanford University Press, 1999]), for example, sees the rise of sociology as inextricably linked to the rise of mass communications and the appearance of the modern novel, both of which give body to new forms of what is, essentially, the emergence of a global, reflexive ontology. My point here is something which I find myself increasingly wanting to make clear for modern academic biblical studies: modern, reflexive analysis has always – now more than ever – been an operation that is not merely reducible to a specialized European rationality, but which should be read likewise as an indication of globalization itself. It is this insight, and the panoply of political questions it raises for biblical studies, that has led to the inauguration of the Geopolitical Bible Project at the University of Glasgow.

22. Agamben, *The Time that Remains*.

23. See for e.g Giorgio Agamben, *Potentialities: Collected Essays in Philosophy* (Stanford, CA: Stanford University Press, 1999, pp. 243–74).

24. Thus I read Levinas through McLuhan and vice versa, salvaging a reading of the former from a clichéd humanism and the latter from an equally hackneyed linear narrative of the "media" as print, radio, TV, silicon chip, etc. All this I take to be the full post-humanist and non-identitarian implications of McLuhan's well known dictum that the content of any medium is always another medium.

25. In relation to McLuhan's efforts to rethink identity in a globalizing (and therefore increasingly reflexive) environment, it is likewise helpful to take up Giorgio Agamben's notions of a (messianic) potential for identities to be gutted ("as if they were not", in his beloved Pauline lingo from 1 Cor. 7), deployed as *gestures* in a politics that has become looped enough to realize it is pantomime. When we take up religion and the secular through the category of performative gesture, then we are neither religious nor secular. See Giorgio Agamben's, *Potentialities: Collected Essays in Philosophy*, (Stanford, CA: Stanford University Press, 1999, pp. 62–76); *Means Without Ends: Notes on Politics* (Minneapolis, MN: University of Minnesota Press, 2000, pp. 49–59); *State of Exception* (Chicago, IL: University of Chicago Press, 2005a, pp. 33–43).

26. I describe in detail the nineteenth-century aesthetic contexts that made this shift from self-conscious "authors" to unconscious "relaters" such a shock in *Displacing Christian Origins*, published in 2007. See chapter two, "The Mechanics of (Dis)Enchantment: Nietzsche and D. F. Strauss on the Production of Religious Texts in the Age of Industrial Media".

27. The diverse and unpredictable ways in which our disciplinary history is traversed by debates about religion and secularity suggest that it is not simply helpful, but is rather absolutely necessary, to negotiate these identities by way of what William Connolly (see *Why I Am Not a Secularist* [Minneapolis, MN/London: University of Minnesota Press, 1999, pp. 143]), describes, following Foucault and Deleuze, as an experimental micropolitics. Or, to sum up the relevant issues in another way, discussions of religion and secularism must begin to grasp the full implications of what Jean-Luc Nancy (see *The Creation of the World or Globalization* [Albany, NY: State University of New York Press, 2007), has described, in a Heideggerian vein, as the self-grounding of the world, the abandonment of the world to itself, or, simply, its singular existence. That is to say, as I explore consistently in my 2007 work (see *Displacing Christian Origins*), the collapse of onto-theology forces us to throw both religion *and* secularity back onto the same immanent, world-ly sphere of cultural production. Contrary to the essentially conservative and phantasmatically identitarian arguments of both religious and secular today, neither identity is able to serve as the privileged ground from which to explain the other any more than either can escape the world they both repeat and create anew.

28. Jacques Lacan, *The Seminar of Jacques Lacan, Book III: The Psychoses* 1955–1956 (New York/London: Norton, (1993) [1981], p. 268.

29. More accurately, there *are* gauges or models of both sacrality and profanation, but they are models that are performatively grounded. I explore such an understanding of biblical criticism, in keeping with a Heideggerian notion of the "work" of art, elsewhere. Again, without stable ground in the secular or the religious, we need to become increasingly sophisticated in our awareness of the diffuse *performative models* by which this distinction has been fixed over time.

# From Jefferson's Bible to Judge Moore's Ten Commandments Monument: Secularizing the Bible in the USA

*Edgar W. Conrad**

## Note to the Reader

I am a dual citizen of the USA and Australia. Having lived in Australia for thirty years has given me the opportunity to look at the country of my birth, the USA, from a distance. This article, which grows out of research exploring the occurrence of "the Bible" in the news media examines recent events such as those reported in news sources about the Ten Commandments monuments and historical information on the Jefferson Bible in order to suggest some readers' uses of the Bible in contemporary culture. I conclude by calling attention to the potential promise of a focus on readers' uses of the Bible as a component of biblical studies. The article was written before the 2008 presidential election while George W. Bush was President of the United States.

## Welcome to Brooksville

Driving along Highway 67 in Alabama in early 1999, one would have encountered the following friendly greeting sign, "Brooksville Welcomes You". The sign written in red letters on a luminous white background also quoted Mt. 18: 20, "Where two or three are gathered together in my name there am I in the midst of them". Brooksville is one of those small towns about which drivers sometimes joke, "Don't blink or you will miss it". It consists of mobile homes and a few houses with a population of about 600 people. Although quite small, it was covered in national news articles for a short time in 1999. The lead paragraph in a story by Hanna Rosin in the Washington Post on 17 May reads,

> Most people look at this scrubby hilltop in north Alabama and see red mud
> and catfish ponds, a few dozen double-wide trailers streaked with rust,
> overgrown lots choked with insolent weeds. The Rev. James Henderson looked
> up at that same patch of earth and saw a Promised Land, a chance to create a
> shining city on a hill. To make his vision real, Henderson and about 200 of
> his neighbors will submit to an Alabama court next month a petition to
> incorporate the community of Brooksville as an official town run solely on
> Christian principles.

The article goes on to explain how the welcoming town of Brooksville will
operate:

> Their plan is so simple it barely needs writing down: The town charter will be
> the King James Bible, its ordinances the Ten Commandments. 'It is our
> intent to conduct the community's business according to the teachings of
> Jesus Christ', reads the charter, typed in all capitals. The rest of its rules
> follow naturally. For example: Observe the Sabbath day and keep it holy, you
> shall not murder, and you shall not steal.

In a newsletter about the petition, Rev. Henderson, a former army colonel,
at that time a defence contractor and the spokesman for the Brooksville
Incorporation Committee, visualized that the new town will have 'no
property restrictions, no building permits, no paid mayor and council, no
million-dollar town hall, no taxes, no red tape and no secrecy'.[1]

Brooksville never did become an incorporated town based on the King
James Bible as its charter. A probate judge ruled against the petition on
technical grounds; the community failed to lay the proper groundwork
required by state law for an incorporation vote. The petition included too
few signatures and contained no maps showing where exactly the
community would be located. In his verdict the judge did not address the
issue of whether a town could use the Kings James Bible as its legal
framework.

My interest in the Brooksville petition is not with the legal issues nor
with the judge's failure to put forward an opinion concerning the use of
"the Bible" as the officially authorized basis for town law. Rather I am
interested in the vision Rev. Henderson and other members of the
Brooksville Incorporation Committee had of a town based on the King
James Bible, which they thought would restore a lost social order. The
Brooksville committee was contemplating a mythic return to origins before
the world of rapid change they perceived as threatening imminent chaos.

The town of Priceville, the very name of which (though unintentionally)
ironically embodied intruding commercialization, was recognized by the
Incorporation Committee as overtaking Brooksville. Priceville moved ever

closer in 1999 already having developed three subdivisions and incorporated in its boundaries portions of Brooksville. A Burger King and a Dairy Queen along with a number of truck stops had recently been established. Further plans were being made for strip malls, swimming pools and additional subdivisions. This encroaching development was too much for Hubert Porter, a close ally of Henderson. He believed Brooksville as a biblically based town was essential in order to avoid its being swallowed up by Priceville's advancing development. Rosin in a *Washington Post* story reported Porter as saying, "If we fail, Priceville is coming up the hill so fast it will make your head spin". Porter has a peculiar definition of Christianity, which he says is a faith that lets him do whatever he wants:

> 'It's the only religion that allows you to question things', he said, meaning rules, or the need to own things, or to conform'. Porter, a retired aerospace engineer, who also writes short stories recalling his childhood, ends one of the stories with the words, 'Those were the days when the words family, parents, children and home had special meanings'.[2]

Porter's longing for the past reflects Rev. Henderson's nostalgia for former times:

> 'People like me are old enough to know what's been taken away from us', he said recalling his days at Priceville High School when each class began with a Scripture reading, when the students sang hymns before football games, when the Ten Commandments were so common they'd be used as a handwriting sample. 'It was never an issue. It just was', he said one afternoon, resting after a half hour of lugging groceries to a Christian shelter. 'Over the years, the judges have stolen religion from us. And with it they took a sense of community, of neighbors helping each other'.[3]

This longing for the past is not only for the boyhood days of youth but also for a return to what the committee understands to be the youthful days of the USA. Bragg[4] in a news article reports Henderson as saying, "We're not doing this because it's a novel idea. We have strong beliefs about how God should be a part of government... That's the way the founding fathers meant it to be'. Henderson expands on how the founding fathers contribute to his myth of origins in a later *New York Times* article, "What we are trying to do, with this little country crossroads, is bring together the church and state. We want to make life make sense again, for people'.[5]

In attempting to return to a meaningful life, however, Henderson was not simply basing his worldview on the King James Bible. He was also reading from another book that had gained great authority among the political and religious right in the USA, contributing to his myth of origins.

Hanna Rosin[6] in a *Washington Post* article reports that Henderson will show anyone talking with him a page "from his other bible". She is referring to David Barton's influential book, *The Myth of Separation: What Is the Correct Relationship between Church and State?*[7] Barton's book is published by WallBuilders, an organization of which he is founder and president. The group is dedicated to the restoration of what the group refers to as "America's forgotten history and heroes"[8] and wants to restore a closer association between church and State, which it insists was espoused by the founding fathers.

The residents of Brookville share this mythic past with the religious right in America that entwines the King James Bible with the origins of the USA. Indeed, Barton's WallBuilders group (see http://www.wallbuilders.com/aboutus/index.htm) defines itself with an Old Testament image:

> In the Old Testament book of Nehemiah, the nation of Israel rallied together in a grassroots movement to help rebuild the walls of Jerusalem and thus restore stability, safety, and a promising future to that great city. We have chosen this historical concept of 'rebuilding the walls' to represent allegorically the call for citizen involvement in rebuilding our nation's foundations. As Psalm 11:3 reminds us, 'If the foundations be destroyed, what shall the righteous do?'

Barton's highly questionable use of the word "allegory" should alert a reader who views his website to conclude that his academic credentials may be wanting. He holds a BA from Oral Roberts University in religious education, and before he began his crusade to restore America's lost history he was a mathematics and science teacher for eight years in a Christian School founded by his parents. Serious academic scholarship has dismissed his claims. Speaking to a hundred students from Oral Roberts University in the rotunda of the United States Capital Building, Barton pointing to a picture of Benjamin Franklin and Thomas Jefferson on the wall is reported to have said, "Isn't it interesting that we have all been trained to recognize the two least religious founding fathers? And compared to today's secularists these two guys look like a couple of Bible-thumping evangelicals!"[9] To refer to Jefferson and Benjamin as evangelicals is, of course, anachronistic since this term was not used in North America until at least the nineteenth century.

In an article called "Sects, Lies and Videotape", Rob Boston[10] refers to a distortion Barton made concerning Jefferson's comment concerning a wall of separation between Church and State, which is commonly understood to give a clear view of Jefferson's understanding of the First Amendment.

Boston points out that in a video, "America's Godly Heritage", Barton claimed Jefferson used the words, "a wall of separation of Church and State", in a speech in 1801 and that Jefferson also said, "That wall is a one directional wall. It keeps the government from running the church but it makes sure that Christian principles will always stay in government". Barton was wrong about the date – the comment was made in 1802 and not 1801; he was wrong about the source – it was in a letter Jefferson wrote to the Danbury Baptist Association of Connecticut; and he was wrong about attributing to Jefferson the phrase that the "wall is a one directional wall... Christian principles will always stay in government" – such a statement cannot be found in the letter.[11]

This claim about Jefferson's intent funnelled through the thoughts of Barton clearly informs Henderson's myth of origins, which in turn feeds his myth about Brooksville's return to a past. As noted above Henderson says:

1. "What we are trying to do... with this little country crossroads, is bring together the church and state";

2. "We're not doing this because it's a novel idea. We have strong beliefs about how God should be a part of government".

3. "That's the way the founding fathers meant it to be".

The Brooksville Incorporation Committee appears to be nourishing its myth of origins with the religious right's propaganda presenting the founding fathers as evangelical Christians who argued for the close union of Church and State.

### The Jefferson Bible

About the same time as Brooksville's bid to become a town, which was supposedly the way the founding fathers wanted it to be, *The Jefferson Bible* was also making the news. The reissued Bible, published by Beacon Press (2001), was edited with an Introduction by Forrest Church, a Unitarian Minister. Church is the son of the former senator Frank Church, who had received a copy of *The Jefferson Bible* in a packet of material given to him at his inauguration as the senator from Idaho in 1957. Later Sen. Church presented this Bible to his son. *The Jefferson Bible*, originally compiled by Thomas Jefferson, the third President of the United States (1801–1809) and principal author of the Declaration of Independence, has as its sub-title the heading Jefferson originally gave his work: "The Life and Morals of Jesus of Nazareth Extracted Textually from the Gospels" (see http://www.angelfire.com/co/JeffersonBible/).

The inhabitants of Brooksville would have looked in vain for the Ten Commandments. The Jefferson Bible contains no Old Testament; Jefferson deleted that part. Brooksville residents would have also been surprised to discover how Jefferson's Bible begins and ends. At the beginning there is no mention of a virgin birth, of angels, or of shepherds, or of Wise Men following a star. God has no role in Mary's pregnancy. At the end of the story, there is no indication of the resurrection; Jesus remains in the sepulchre where he was laid and those who put him there simply departed. Not only did Jefferson excise the Old Testament, he also got rid of everything outside the Gospels. Even the Gospels were reduced by excising any mention of miracles or the divinity of Jesus (see http://www.angelfire.com/co/JeffersonBible/).

Commencing when he was in the White House and continuing 15 years later at Monticello, Jefferson literally used scissors and paste to cut out and assemble what he thought were essential teachings of Jesus the philosopher while discarding the rest. He arranged his selections from the Greek, Latin, French and English (the King James) in parallel columns. He made Jesus into a moral teacher, a philosopher, while eliminating any reference to Jesus as God. He described his method in a letter to John Adams dated 1813:

> In extracting the pure principles which he [Jesus] taught, we should have to strip off the artificial vestments in which they have been muffled by priests, who have travestied them into various forms, as instruments of riches and power to them... We must reduce our volume to the simple evangelists, select, even from them, the very words only of Jesus, paring off the amphibologisms into which they have been led by forgetting often, or not understanding, what had fallen from him, by giving their own misconceptions as his dicta, and expressing unintelligibly for others what they had not understood themselves. There will be found remaining the most sublime and benevolent code of morals which has ever been offered to man. I have performed this operation for my own use, by cutting verse by verse out of the printed book, and arranging, the matter which is evidently his, andwhich (*sic*) is as easily distinguishable as diamonds in a dunghill. The result is an 8 vo. of 46. pages of pure and unsophisticated doctrines, such as were professed and acted on by the *unlettered* apostles, the Apostolic fathers, and the Christians of the 1st century.[12]

Although Jefferson had created this work for his own private purposes and had no intention of publishing it, Rep. John Lacey, a republican member of the House from Iowa about a century ago, discovered Jefferson's scissors and paste Bible in the archives of the Smithsonian Institution. Lacy thought that the work should be published and in 1904 the Government Printing

Office printed 9000 copies (the English version only), and eventually it came to be known as *The Jefferson Bible*. Because there was a surplus of volumes the Congressional tradition developed of distributing a copy of Jefferson's work to all new members of Congress until the 1950s. This practice explains how Sen. Frank Church received his copy of *The Jefferson Bible*, which he later gave to his eight-year-old son.[13]

Beacon's publication of *The Jefferson Bible* in the present climate is interesting when the religious right is claiming that the founding fathers were evangelicals, providing a biblical foundation to American institutions like the incorporated town envisaged by Brooksville. Thomas Jefferson while he was in the White House and later at his home in Monticello was acting as a nascent do-it-yourself Jesus Seminar, creating Jesus in such a way as to define him as a philosopher devoid of divinity and the miracles that offended Enlightenment rationality. While Henderson claimed to have "strong beliefs about how God should be part of a government", Jefferson, as one of the founding fathers, was not only building a wall of separation between the Church and Government but was also busy distancing Jesus from divinity in order to restore him to full humanity as a great philosopher. It's clear that Jefferson as a founding father would have experienced Brooksville and its myth of origins to be alien.

### Presidents and Philosophers

Jefferson identified the philosophers he admired in a letter to William Short on 31 October 1819 to be Epicurus, Epictetus and Jesus of Nazareth. He writes to Short, "I too am an Epicurian" and goes on to explain that he sees the thought of Jesus to be a supplement to Epicurian philosophy.

> The greatest of all the reformers of the depraved religion of his own country, was Jesus of Nazareth. Abstracting what is really his from the rubbish in which it is buried, easily distinguished by its lustre from the dross of his biographers [i.e. the authors of the Gospels], and as separable from that as the diamond from the dunghill, we have the outlines of a system of the most sublime morality which has ever fallen from the lips of man; outlines which it is lamentable he did not live to fill up. Epictetus and Epicurus give laws for governing ourselves, Jesus a supplement of the duties and charities we owe to others.[14]

He goes on in the letter to say, "I have sometimes thought of translating Epictetus (for he has never been tolerable translated into English) by adding the genuine doctrines of Epicurus...and an abstract from the Evangelists of whatever has the stamp of the eloquence and fine imagination of Jesus".[15]

It is evident here that what has been published as the Jefferson Bible was conceived by Jefferson to be a supplement to a larger whole, Epictetus, the genuine laws of Epicurus and the abstracted gems of Jesus' thought.

It is doubtful that the Incorporation Committee of Brooksville would have wanted a town charter that supplemented the King James Bible with the philosophical thought of Epictetus and Epicurus. Nor do I think that George W. Bush had Jefferson's Jesus in mind when he identified his favorite philosopher. "Asked in December 1999 during a Republican primary debate which 'political philosopher or thinker' he most identified with, then-Gov. Bush replied abruptly, 'Christ – because he changed my heart'".[16]

The language is revealing here. Jefferson's philosopher is Jesus; Bush's philosopher is Christ. Jefferson's philosopher speaks to the head (reason); Bush's philosopher speaks more emotively to the heart. It is widely known that Bush's involvement with bible study aided his recovery from the abuse of alcohol. When he read the Bible and encountered "Christ", he found a philosopher who, consistent with Jefferson's view of Epictetus and Epicurus, gives "laws for governing ourselves". However, when Jefferson read the Bible, he discovered the moral philosopher Jesus who, he understood, summarized "the duties and charities we owe to others".

Jefferson has produced a Bible depicting Jesus for the age of reason – the Enlightenment. Bush's Christ is from a "typical Southern style of Protestantism that focuses on religion of the heart, not the head" and is reflected in the popular bumper sticker, "Jesus: Saving the World One Soul at a Time".[17] President Jefferson's heady Jesus is found in a Bible produced for a different time and place than that of the "touchy feely" Christ of President Bush. George W. Bush, the republican President of the religious right, clearly was not reading from *The Jefferson Bible*, and it is not clear what he would have done with his copy of *The Jefferson Bible* had he ever been elected to Congress. Carl M. Canon sums up the difference between Jefferson and Bush succinctly in his article, "Bush and God",

> Two hundred years before Bush did so, Jefferson also cited Jesus as the most influential political philosopher or thinker. But the Sage of Monticello did so in a way that would render most modern American politicians unelectable to national office. Suggesting that Jesus's teachings were the underpinnings of democracy, Jefferson concluded that the emphasis on Jesus's divinity was a distraction from the teachings of the man whose 'system of morality was the most benevolent and sublime probably that has ever been taught, and consequently more perfect than those of any of the ancient philosophers'.

Jefferson, like other eighteenth-century intellectuals, was a Deist believing in God the Creator, who left the universe alone to run without divine intervention, having given human beings reason and freedom of choice to determine the course of their lives. For the residents of Brooksville to base the ordinances of a town on divinely given laws would have appeared to Jefferson as a failure to use rational judgments about self-determination. In Jefferson's universe, god was detached; he was not an interventionist. Jefferson produced his Bible for a world in which the creator is absent.

It is difficult to know what Bible Bush reads, but Hanna Rosin[18] in a *Washington Post* article on 4 July 2000 suggests it may be *The Living Bible:*

> Late last year, Barbara Bush told Washington Post reporters she used to read to her son from the Bible, and sometimes she caught him reading it on his own. Once, when George was a teenager, she was showing her new house to a visitor. When they got to George's bedroom, both spied a Bible lying open on the bed. In the new third-floor sauna and exercise room, lying near one of the machines, 'there was a Living Bible, looking tattered and worn', she recalled. 'George has always delved into the Bible'.

Bush was not reading a Bible in four languages, including the original Greek, as Jefferson did in order to sort out the thoughts of Jesus, the philosopher from Nazareth. He appears to be reading a contemporary translation in familiar present-day English and encountering Christ who spoke to his heart in the characteristic form of Southern Protestantism.

### On the Road Again

> The Ten Commandments monument banished from Alabama's state judicial building began a national tour on the back of a flatbed truck on Saturday – starting outside the courthouse [Dayton, Tennessee] where the teaching of evolution was put on trial almost 80 years ago.

> Jewell Sneed, 70, snapped photos of her 7-year-old great-grandson, Jacob, standing beside the monument. 'I think it was awful for them to make them move it from the courthouse', Sneed said. 'That is what our country is based on, is God and the Bible. Why we want to take God out I don't know. I think we are headed for big trouble when we take God out of schools and everything'.

> 'I'm glad I didn't carry my gun. I'd probably be in jail right now'. Rocco said. 'I believe in the Ten Commandments, and I don't appreciate what people like him are doing to my country'.

These comments are taken from an Associated News story, "Commandments Start National Tour Alabama Monument's First Stop: Tennessee", on 1 August 2004. The story concerns the 5,280 pound monument that Roy Moore had placed in the lobby of the Judicial Building in Alabama where he had been Chief Justice until he had defied a federal court ban to remove what has become known as "Roy's Rock". It is not clear whether Judge Moore drove his truck along Highway 67 in Alabama and, if he did, whether he noticed Brooksville's welcoming sign. However, with a Ten Commandments monument on his truck, he undoubtedly steered clear of Monticello.

Moore is convinced that the Ten Commandments are the very basis of the United States constitution and system of law and should be prominently displayed in government buildings. He is not alone because all over the USA people are "hanging ten" to use a phrase of Mark Eddington in an article "Battling God's Ouster from Government". In the article Eddington reports,

> Mark and Irene Reichner's monuments are not there for the courts to command. The Provo couple have (*sic*) one set of Ten Commandments rooted in their front yard and another on their garage. It is their way to protest the forced removal of the Decalogue from a courthouse in Alabama and legal action in Utah to oust similar monuments from where they sit in Pleasant Grove and Duchesne...The Reichners are not alone...American Fork resident Rosemarie Taylor's Ten Commandments monument is prominently displayed facing the street. British expatriates Peter and Barbara Leadenham, of St. George, have two in their front-yard garden. 'We have one facing each direction so traffic going both ways [on the street] can see them', Barbara Leadenham says. 'It's a small thing we are doing, but we feel someone must take a stand'.[19]

Judge Moore, also often labelled by his supporters as the "Moses of Alabama", not only identifies himself with the original lawgiver but also with the prophet Daniel.[20] He is convinced that the First Amendment does not ban the moral rules of "God", and by this he means the Judaeo-Christian "God". He claims that no government can tell "God" what to do. According to a *New York Times* article, Moore "places God at the top of a pyramid-like hierarchy, above the church and the state. Perhaps more importantly, Moore said he believes that the Judeo-Christian God is responsible for the system of freedom of religion in the United States".[21] Our government, he claims, is built on "God's" morality summarized succinctly in the Ten Commandments, and they should be made visible in public places.

Judge Moore thinks the commandments that appear on his monument provide absolute and unchangeable standards for humankind. In response to Chris Matthews' question on MSNBC's Hardball[22] about why some people, including other Christians, protest against his stance on the Ten Commandments, he responds,

> Well, they're complaining because they don't like to think that there's a higher
> authority, that there are standards that are immutable and nonchanging.
> And they want that out of their lives. And they've been taught that God has
> no place in public life.

Although Moore, like others from the religious right, claims support from
the founding fathers like Jefferson, he does not appear to be reflective of the
fact that he, like Jefferson, has taken scissors to the biblical text, constructing
on his stone monument an edited list that is limited like Jefferson's modified
version of the "Life and Morals of Jesus of Nazareth".

He does not seem to be aware that in Exodus 20 and Deuteronomy 5, the
texts from which his list of the Ten Commandments are derived, there is
no reference to "the ten commandments". In Exod. 20:1 the laws are referred
to simply as "the words" and in Deut. 5: 5 simply as "the word of the LORD".
The notion of ten commandments (or "ten words"), comes from Exod. 34:
28; Deut. 4: 13 and 10: 4. Furthermore, within the Judaeo-Christian
tradition, to which Moore refers, the Ten Commandments are constructed
in different ways. The Ten Commandments are not simply downloaded
from "the Bible". Moving them from bibles to catechisms, confessional
statements or stone monuments is not a simple matter of transporting the
same cargo. The order of the commandments and what is included in
them is different.

> In Jewish communities the first commandment is 'I am the LORD your god
> who brought you out of the house of bondage' and the second commandment
> is 'You shall have no other gods besides me'. These two taken together form
> the first commandment in Christian lists.
>
> A prohibition against graven images in Protestant versions is not found in
> Catholic or Lutheran versions.
>
> Roman Catholic and Lutheran versions split the commandment on coveting
> into two. The ninth commandment is against coveting a neighbor's wife and
> the tenth commandment is against coveting a neighbor's other possessions.
>
> 'Do not kill' in some commandment lists is 'Do not murder' in others.

Judge Moore does not seem to be aware of these differences in the Judaeo-
Christian tradition. Furthermore these variations highlight the problem
with his assertion to Chris Matthews that the Ten Commandments are
"immutable and nonchanging". Moore does not seem to understand that
the Ten Commandments themselves do not exist as a standard. There is
no set order and there is no agreement on what should be in or out of these
ten divine absolutes. One would expect that the Ten Commandments

conveying god's immutable standards would themselves be regular and unchallengeable.

As suggested above, Moore, however, is perhaps more like Jefferson than he realizes when one considers what he has cut out of the Bible in identifying the immutable Ten Commandments placed on his monument. Judge Moore's Ten Commandments contain 73 words – phrases that he has lifted from Exod. 20: 1–17 and Deut. 5: 6–21 in the King James Bible. The full text, in which Moore's Ten Commandments are embedded, contains 326 words in Exod. 20: 1–17 and 387 words in Deut. 5: 6–21. Are we to assume that these other 253 words in Exodus and 314 words in Deuteronomy are unimportant for understanding the immutable 73? Who decides what should be dropped out of a biblical text when constructing a monument? The means by which the Ten Commandments are unloaded from a Bible and placed on a new conveyance such as a stone monument is not incidental to their meaning. A substantial number of words have been deleted in Moore's 73-word Ten Commandments. Just as Jefferson constructed Jesus as a philosopher by eliminating references to divinity and to miracles, so Moore's condensing of the commandments has altered their meaning.

When read in a fuller context, it is interesting to see what is left out in Moore's monument and the implications these deletions have for meaning:

> The god mentioned is a particular god – the one "which have brought thee out of the land of Egypt, out of the house of bondage". This divine being is a particular god; he has a name, Yahweh. This divine being is not, like Jefferson's Creator, found in Nature or Nature's laws.

> The graven images are not to be like anything in heaven above, the earth beneath or in the water under the earth. Do people in the contemporary world have any idea where these places are, let alone what graven images could exist in any of those places?

Yahweh is mentioned by name again in vs. 7. What does it mean to take a name in vain? Steve Casey, a Chaplain who is posting a commandment a month on billboards in Schreveport Louisiana, cited this commandment in the month of June with the added note that God's last name does not begin with D.[23] This commandment, however, appears not to have so much to do with cursing such as "God Damn" as it does with using the proper name of this god, Yahweh, as if it meant nothing.

The extra words associated with the Sabbath connect its meaning with rest after creation in Exodus. That would be from sunset on Friday to sunset on Saturday according to Old Testament texts and according to practice in Judaism. Christians observe their rest day on Sunday but for a reason associated with the day of resurrection. Is this immutable law different for

Jews and Christians? (In Deuteronomy the reason for resting on the Sabbath is connected with Israel's Exodus from Egypt rather than with creation.)

Honoring fathers and mothers is described as ensuring a long life. There is no consideration that a child sexually molested and physically abused by his or her parents would find it difficult to see the immutable value of this commandment.

The commandment not to covet is a simple blanket statement in Moore's list; in the Old Testament, coveting refers specifically to all the possessions of a neighbor: wife, male slave, female slave, ox, ass or anything else that belongs to a neighbor.

To put Moore's Ten Commandments in a biblical context does not make them the immutable and universal norms for behaviour that Moore and his followers promote. The commandments are not addressed to everyone but to a select few: to the ones who own homes, not the homeless; to slave owners, not to slaves; and to men whose property also includes their wives, not to women. The command to honour father and mother are addressed to the mature – to fathers, rather than to children.

To reduce the Ten Commandments to 73 words out of 326-word or 387-word passages is to alter their meaning considerably. Judge Moore's Monument has reduced and altered the meaning of the words in Exod. 20 and Deut. 5 as radically as Jefferson's reduction of the full Gospels to arrive at the kernel of the morals and teachings of Jesus of Nazareth altered the original.

In closing this section, I want to mention a forgotten reason that there are so many displays of the Ten Commandments across America. Ellen Goodman in *The Cincinnati Post* article "Making Religion Secular' reminds us that ten commandments monuments, like the one on the grounds of the Texan Capitol that was contested in the US Supreme Court in 2005, were placed there nearly half a century ago as part of Cecil B. DeMille's publicity overdrive to promote his movie epic "The Ten Commandments" starring Charlton Heston. Ten Commandment Monuments found in many places in America were not erected as the result of patriotic fervor linking an immutable law code with the foundations of American law. DeMille funded the Fraternity Order of Eagles to place Ten Commandments monuments, like the one in Texas, all over America to promote a film.

## Down the Road

When anyone travels down roads in the USA, whether Highway 67 or some other route, biblical texts may be encountered on billboards, on bumper stickers, in front yards where individuals are "hanging ten" and perhaps even on monuments on the back of pickup trucks. In contemporary America "the Bible" and the authority attributed to it is often sought as a foundation to build, as the WallBuilder David Bardon has done, the basis for an ideology that claims that the USA and its founding fathers built the country on "God" and "the Bible" that contains "God's" words. They do not acknowledge that the idea of "God" and the interpretation of his words are dependent on the readers who construct a Bible's meaning. By constructing the Bible to fit their ideology, then, the residents of Brooksville and Judge Moore are in some ways like the founding father Jefferson. However, the resemblance is one they probably would not recognize. They, like Jefferson, have abstracted from "the Bible" words that support their respective ideologies. Jefferson made Jesus a philosopher to support his rationalist Enlightenment thought confirming "the duties and charities we owe to others". The religious right in the USA has constructed "the Bible" to support right wing ideology/theology promoting the view that Christ confirms their peculiar notions of individual morality.

Motoring down American routes, where ideological road maps point in many different directions of biblical meaning, requires that the traveler remain alert. New roads open quickly, and the complacent tourist can easily become lost in what may deceptively appear as familiar terrain. Clearly, not all evangelical roads veer to the Republican right of Bush's Texas. Although left-leaning evangelicals avoid Priceville, they do not turn right to Brooksville, Alabama. They are taking a lot of left turns and in one sense are beginning to "see red". As Tony Compollo, the spiritual advisor to Bill Clinton, an ordained Baptist minister, and the founder of the "Evangelical Association for the promotion of Education" says:

> The term evangelical has become synonymous with the religious right. While we are evangelical in our theology, we have to turn away from that name. So we're calling ourselves Red Letter Christians, alluding to the red letters in the Bible, which are the words of Jesus. That's very much taking hold in England. They're embarrassed with American evangelicalism.[24]

> The old Bibles always had the words of Jesus printed in red letters. We started calling ourselves 'red letter Christians' (*sic*) the values of Christ, the teachings of Jesus take precedence over everything else. We take seriously the rest of the Bible, but we have to say that we understand the rest of the Bible in light of what Jesus said and did and is. Jesus becomes the lens through which we focus ourselves on the rest of the Scriptures.[25]

While they are more evangelical than Deists like Jefferson, they are making the words of Jesus central. They see the words of Jesus, whom they understand to be a divine being born of a virgin, as the hermeneutical clue for understanding "the Bible" as a whole. Compolo says:

> The big issue in this country is that the religious right has made sexual issues the primary focus of their politics: abortion and homosexuality. We affirm the importance of these issues, but we are pointing out that there are over 2,000 verses of Scripture that call upon people of faith to respond to the needs of the poor. Poverty is the overwhelming issue. Justice for the poor. A voice for the oppressed. Addressing the issues of child slavery around the world. We're very, very committed to the poor because we feel that the Bible is overwhelmingly committed to the poor. We want to put the emphasis where the Bible puts the emphasis.[26]

Red Letter Christians remind us that it is not "the Bible" that is making its readers turn to the right or to the left. Rather "the Bible" is zigzagging from right to left by those who interpret it and steer it in different directions.

As we move down the road of the twenty-first century the study of bibles and their meanings constructed in secular culture should be an important component of critical biblical studies. Bibles have always been in the process of becoming what its readers want them to be. The malleability of "the Bible" enabling it to appear in many different forms with a multitude of meanings has contributed to its enduring tenure as a sacred text. For biblical studies to centre its efforts on the historical-critical pursuit of constructing original meaning, typical of biblical studies during the last century, is to focus attention on a mythical "the Bible" and to overlook the many forms bibles have had in a plurality of cultural *Sitze im Leben*. To concentrate the efforts of biblical studies in arcane pursuits about a quasi-original intention excludes and obscures the meanings attributed to bibles in one or another of their many forms. Readers have adapted bibles as a foundation for theological/ideological (ab)use, and the central role of reception is ignored in the pursuit of what is thought to be the clarity of original meaning. Greater attention needs to be given to the reception of biblical texts in contemporary culture and the way in which the authority of "the Bible" is used to provide a foundation for ideology.

## Endnotes

* Edgar Conrad is retired Reader in Studies in Religion and currently Honorary Research Consultant in History, Philosophy, Religion and Classics at the University of Queensland, Brisbane, Australia.
1. Hanna Rosin, "Community Aims to Incorporate, Operate on Christian Principles", *The Washington Post*, 17 May 1999.
2. See Rosin, "Community Aims to Incorporate, Operate on Christian Principles".

3. See Rosin, "Community Aims to Incorporate, Operate on Christian Principles".
4. Rick Bragg, "Community Residents Want Christian Municipality", *Associated Press Newswires*, 7 December 1998.
5. Bragg, "Community Residents Want Christian Municipality".
6. Hanna Rosin, "'King James' would rule small town Alabama preacher envisions a Promised Land," *The Washington Post*, 21 May 1999.
7. David Barton, *The Myth of Separation: What Is the Correct Relationship Between Church and State* (Aledo, TX: WallBuilder Press, 1989).
8. See the section "About Us". http://www.wallbuilders.com/aboutus/index.htm
9. David D. Kirkpatrick, "Putting God Back into American History", *The New York Times*, 27 February 2005.
10. Rob Boston, "Sects, Lies and Videotape", *Church & State* 46.4 (1993), pp. 8–12.
11. Thomas Jefferson, Messrs. Nehemiah Dodge and Others, a Committee of the Danbury Baptist Association, in the State of Connecticut Nehemiah Dodge and Others, a Committee of the Danbury Baptist Association, in the State of Connecticut January 1 1802. Retrieved on 31 May 2007 from http://etext.virginia.edu/toc/modeng/public/JefAddr.html
12. See Thomas Jefferson, The Code of Jesus – Letter to John Adams, 12 October 1813. Retrieved on 31 May 2007 from http://etext.virginia.edu/toc/modeng/public/JefLett.html
13. Michael E. Grass, "Our First Fifty Years: Genius or Heretic?" *Roll Call*, 24 January 2005.
14. Thomas Jefferson – I too am an Epicurean – Letter to William Short (31 October 1819). Retrieved on 31 May 2007 from http://etext.virginia.edu/toc/modeng/public/JefLett.html
15. Jefferson – I too am an Epicurean, http://etext.virginia.edu/toc/modeng/public/JefLett.html
16. Carl M. Cannon, "Bush and God", *National Journal* 3 (January 2004).
17. Cannon, "Bush and God".
18. Hanna Rosin, Applying Personal Faith to Public Policy; "Changed Man" Advocates Church-Based Programs, *The Washington Post*, 24 July 2000.
19. Mark Eddington, "Battling God's Ouster from Government", *The Salt Lake Tribune*, 29 September 2003.
20. Jeffrey Gettleman, "Alabama's Top Judge Defiant On Commandments' Display", *The New York Times*, 21 August 2003.
21. Manuel Roig-Franzia, "Ten Commandments Display Ordered Out of Courthouse", *The New York Times*, 19 November 2002.
22. Chris Matthews, Interview with Judge Moore on *Hardball*, 3 March 2005.
23. Associated Newswires, "Minister Paying for Ten Commandment Billboards", *Associated Press*, 13 June 2004.
24. Bill Sherman, "Evangelical Left Leader to Speak", *Tulsa World*, 17 March 2007.
25. Jen Waters, "Religion from the Left: Author Hits Hijacking of Evangelism", *The Washington Times*, 3 April 2007.
26. Sherman, "Evangelical Left Leader to Speak".

# FROM RUTH TO FOREIGN WORKERS IN CONTEMPORARY ISRAEL: A CASE STUDY IN THE INTERACTION OF RELIGION, POLITICS AND THE ECONOMY

*Athalya Brenner**

## A Disclaimer

In recent years, one of my chief interests in the Hebrew Bible revolves around how it operates in contemporary cultures. This is why I read it against contemporary issues, viewing both the bible and today's events as reciprocal, bi-directional texts. Moving from the one to the other, their meanings change mutually along the reading process as they reconstruct and deconstruct each other, so to speak, much to my personal perplexity and at times delight.

In the present instance, I shall read the biblical Ruth against the current situation of migrant workers in contemporary Israel, and vice versa. While these two "texts" may refract each other, reading them together also enables reflections upon politics of religion and the economy in two cultural locations: the one a literary location from the past, the other a contemporary geo-political one.

## A Story

*Early one morning.* If, early one morning, you meet a fairly young woman wandering...She's on her own, wearing an evening gown. She seems to be aimlessly walking about. While she is definitely dressed up, her hands and skin seem those of a manual labourer... So you think to yourself, "Not a prostitute, but who knows? And she is obviously foreign", since she cannot speak the language properly, you can hardly understand her although her lingo is similar to your own somehow. You look more closely and she seems disoriented and unstable. Is she drunk perhaps? Or on drugs? Moreover, she mumbles something about "the man, the man". Is she hurt? No, she does not look molested or harmed. You're a good citizen so you have a problem. What to do?

*Yes, you are a responsible citizen.* So you notify the police. The police come. They arrest the woman, who has no ID documents, and threaten her with deportation. Still, she seems not to respond to their interrogations and threats too well. The police must bring in an interpreter, and this is what emerges. She has a story: She is a widow, a foreigner, a farm worker nearby, employed by a rich local farmer. With her work she supports herself and her former mother-in-law. No, she has neither visa nor work permit. But, she claims, her employer is going to marry her.

The cops laugh: such Cinderella stories do not happen so often in our insular society. Rich local farmers do not marry their foreign female workers so easily. But since the woman has made a claim that might affect her personal status and the case, they have to call in a lawyer. The woman may be eventually deported, but no deportation is possible without a court order, even when the facts seem clear. And then the woman has a right to legal defence.

*The lawyer* calls the rich farmer named as employer and future husband, and the alleged mother-in-law. He finds out the woman has told the truth. She is indeed a migrant worker. The farmer has promised to marry her and intends to keep his promise. Alas, nevertheless, she remains an illegal alien, thus a candidate for speedy deportation.

*Court and Happy End.* The matter is brought before the judges. The farmer is passionate in his plea for the woman and their relationship, while the woman keeps quiet. In order to help resolve the legal problem, she hastily converts to Judaism. They marry on the spot. Eventually, as decorum dictates, the woman has a son by the rich farmer.

*And the woman is* **Ruth**, grandmother to King David (Ruth 4.18–22), foremother of Jesus (Mt. 1).

A skit similar to this appeared several years ago, in 2005 if memory serves, in *Ha'aretz* ["*The Land*"], an Israeli newspaper, just before Shavu'ot (Pentecost), when the biblical book is traditionally read in the synagogue. It is worth noting that *Ha'aretz* is a left-of-centre and totally "secular" newspaper. Its general editorial policy is to promote Israeli/Jewish culture, even help to shape it, but bible study is not privileged. The fact that such a skit/article was published witnesses not only the Israeli public's fondness for biblical stories, especially those that belong to the recurrent liturgy, but also that the Ruth story can be read as bearing similarities to the plight of foreign, migrant female workers in the Israel of today. And just to prove the point: on 22 May 2007, two days before Shavu'ot was again celebrated, Avirama Golan published an article in the same paper. Its name, as translated, is "Ruth Would Have Remained a Moabite" – this time, a discussion of the difficulties faced by gentiles wishing to convert to Judaism, especially women, and especially women who wish to join the community and become Jewish citizens of Israel. Although originally from *Ha'aretz*, this article was considered topical enough for a general Internet portal to publish online under its "News" heading.[1]

### *So Why Did Ruth Accompany Naomi to Bethlehem (Ruth 1)?*

Commentators attribute Ruth's decision to accompany her mother-in-law to her love for Naomi, or to her commitment, or other ideals. But I have read it differently for some time.[2] A non-idealizing possibility is that for her, a widow, going to a foreign country with her former mother-in-law is preferable to staying behind in her country of origin. This is as good a reason for her becoming a migrant worker in the fields, for food for her and for her mother-in-law, a reason not stated in the biblical text but supported by her situation as narrated.

This reading, and my publications on it, were reinforced by what I knew of the situation of foreign female workers in Israel from the late 1980s. In turn, the reading itself reinforced my interest in the legal and social situation of those workers. Let me therefore present the case of migrant workers in Israel as a case study, then proceed to gender differentials, and then return to the question of migrant workers' social integration, and to Ruth.

### *Migrant Workers in Contemporary Israel*

My sources for the actual and legal aspects of this presentation are official publications. Summaries are available on the Internet.[3] Especially important for my purpose is the *Israel's Central Bureau of Statistics, 2006 Annual*, again as published on the Internet at the end of 2006.[4] The relevant materials, presented below, come from the document published on the site and released to the Press on 27 November 2006 and called "The Demographic Situation in Israel, 2005: Typical Trends – An Overview".[5] It is worth noting that the official numbers are perforce of legal or formerly legal migrant workers only.

*Entries and Countries of Origin, 2005:* In 2005, 29,000 foreign nationals entered Israel with a work permit/visa. In that same period, 24,000 foreign visa holders were registered as leaving Israel. More than half the workers came from two countries: Thailand (29 percent) and the Philippines (23 percent). [Most of the Thai workers were male; most of the workers from the Philippines were female; this is borne out by the actual situation and by experience, but does not appear in the official statistics.]

*Those Workers Who Stayed, 1990–2005:* In the years 1990–2005, 98,300 foreign nationals entered Israel with a work permit (visa), without record of leaving: which means that they may still be living in Israel. Of these, 30 percent are from Thailand, 24 percent from the Philippines, 15 percent from Romania and 10 percent from China. Two-thirds of these entered Israel in the last four years (2002–2005). At the end of 2005, the number of foreign nationals from developing countries who entered Israel on a tourist visa, and remained in the country after their visa had expired, was 80,000. This number adds to the upper limit for estimating the number of workers without a work permit (visa) currently living in Israel. At the end of 2004 the estimate was 180,000; it is now lower by about 10,000 or so, probably due to a rigorous deportation policy. This policy will be discussed later; however, let us note here that it clearly reverberates through the *Ha'aretz* rendering of/updating neo-midrash on *Ruth*, as paraphrased above.

*Gender and Class:* As can be seen, gender numbers are not supplied (for occupations see further below). However, my impression is that women form about two-thirds of the migrant workers' total. Those women are mostly from disadvantaged urban or rural communities, mostly with no high-tech skills beyond traditional female capabilities, that is, domestic work and health care. However, global economy facilitates their mobility. It allows them to travel, albeit under disadvantaged conditions, and to export money back home.[6] Thus, paradoxically, they and their male counterparts are Global Workers who uphold the fluidity of global economy. Further on gender differentials see below.

*Procedure and Recruitment of Migrant Workers for the Israeli Economy:* In theory, the rules are strict, based on demand, and regularly revised. However, the main beneficiaries of the whole phenomenon are the recruitment, go-between agencies. Outside Israel the workers are recruited by specialized agencies and have to pay those, at times exorbitantly. Inside Israel:

1. Employers must apply for and receive an employment license, having proved compelling need for foreign workers in their field. In that sense, workers are "imported" for a specific type of employment.
2. Agencies arrange red tape and deal with the labour department and social services inside Israel before and after the workers arrive.
3. Fee from employer and employee is paid to the agencies, and this fee is officially regulated and subject to government control.

*Worker and Employee, Rights and Obligations:* Employment of foreign workers in Israel is ostensibly dictated by tough government regulations, designed to protect workers from exploitation. Some of the regulations are:

1. Minimum wage in the specific employment branch must be guaranteed.
2. Change of the originally requested-for employment type for a certain worker, any worker, is not legal.
3. Withholding a passport from an employee, as often done as a means of blackmailing and exploitation, is not legal.
4. Binding of employee to the importing employer (the so called "conditional visa" of the past) is no longer legal (but see further below).
5. Health insurance is mandatory for all workers, at employee's expense, but with special rates.
6. There is a mandatory weekly rest day, which can be exchanged for money or further employment.
7. Issues of pregnancy, maternity and workers' children born in Israel are currently being re-formulated and will be discussed below.

In spite of these safeguards, the possibility of exploitation, especially of live-in [mostly female] workers, is always present. Legal venues for employee complaint, governmental and NGO, are available but their usage is balanced by the worker's fear. Ignorance of rights and local laws and language (at least to start with), deportation if caught without a valid working visa or in the wake of an employer's complaint, criminal charges, and the possibility of legal action through the agencies, are pertinent threats for employees.

*The Official Statistics:* The statistics refer to the portion and salary of migrant workers in the Israeli economy of 1997–2005 (the CBS Statistical Abstract of 2006), with a distinction between migrant workers and Palestinian workers since 2000 (the second *Intifada* = Palestinian uprising, when Palestinian workers' access to Israel proper became restricted; until then, Palestinian workers were considered a special class of "foreign workers"). Even with the change in presentation method in the statistics and the almost total absence of legal Palestinian workers from the Israeli economy since 2000, it is quite clear that according to the official sources, the numbers of migrant and other foreign workers within Israel has diminished considerably over this period.

Even a cursory glance at the statistics reveals that:

1. Until the 9/2000 *Intifada*, Israeli agriculture and building industries could not exist without workers from the Occupied Territories; beyond 2000, the same role is undertaken by other foreign workers.
2. These occupations are traditionally male occupations, in the sense that the majority of workers in the agriculture/construction work sectors are male. Therefore, the statistics do not reflect the occupations undertaken by female foreign/migrant workers, occupations that are subsumed in the first table under "other". For the situation with regard to female workers we therefore have to turn elsewhere.

*Help and Information Agencies:* Help and information agencies for foreign workers are available and active. These may be either governmental or NGOs. Differences between law and law enforcement on the one hand, and legal/social praxis on the other hand, are acknowledged and acted upon, not only by state agencies but also by NGOs such as women's and human rights organizations. Two of the immediate addresses for instances of abuse, fight for rights and personal complaints, are *Kav La-Oved* (Heb: Workers' Line)[7] or the *Hotline for Migrant Workers*.[8] Also available are *Physicians For Human Rights*, for health issues; and *Mesila*, for child education.

## Gender Differentials: Female and Male Workers in Contemporary Israel

*Occupations:* Typical female work sectors, in descending order, are: health care, domestic help, the tourist industry; few work in agriculture. [Illegal] prostitution is a big human problem. It deserves independent and special attention. However, it will be discussed here only briefly, since its practitioners are a minority in the female workers' constituency. Typical male occupations/work sectors, as has been stated, are construction and agriculture work. Working in the health and tourist/catering industry is a minority male occupation.

In general, then, menial and low paying jobs are characteristic for both genders, but there is a clear gender differential between domestic and industrial, so called "productive", occupations. Females mostly work in the care sector.

*Salaries and Conditions* vary according to occupation and vocation, as do living conditions. Complaints about abuse of rights come more from more female workers, perhaps because domestic services, usually with a live-in arrangement, facilitate more possibilities for abuse – although cases of workers abusing their infirm or elderly employees are recorded as well.[9]

*Country of Origin:* There is also a differential as far as place of origin is concerned. Female workers are mostly from the Philippines and Eastern Europe; males from the Far East (Thailand, China) as well as those countries.

*Religion:* Source countries are also indicative of religious affiliations. When Christian, most workers would be either Catholic or Eastern-Orthodox, with a well developed [sub]culture of Christian worship instituted in Israel's large urban centres, and this tends to be the workers' focal place of socialization.[10]

*Age and Marital Status:* From the perspectives of age and marital status there is not much difference: workers may be from their late teens to their mid-fifties.

A tendency to *remain in the country illegally* after the work visa has expired is statistically noted as more female. *Marriage* with local partners is almost negligible. However, when it occurs, it is mostly between local Israeli males and foreign female workers, which is problematic in view of both the State's foundational rules and Halakhic Judaism. There is no civil marriage in Israel; marriage according to Israeli Law is governed by religious rulings, in the case of Jews by the Rabbinate;[11] and since according to Jewish Halakha a child's Jewish status depends on his mother's, unless the foreign mother converts, her children cannot participate fully in Jewish life, even in the largely "secular" Israel.

Hot issues at this time are: quotas of workers allowed into the country; the nature of their licenses and work permits; human trafficking and prostitution (which will not be discussed here); salaries and conditions; and children born in Israel.

*Quotas* are decided upon periodically by government agencies according to need and demand in various economic sectors, with a declared policy aimed at limiting the number of incoming workers and exercising control over their types of employment. The statistics about sectors reflects governmental channelling of the foreign work force, as well as local priorities as recognized.

*Nature of Licenses and Work Permits*: The strict controls over type of work allowed in the work visa, when widely interpreted, may undoubtedly be considered a violation of the worker's human rights, since once the type of employment originally requested and decided upon, cannot be changed. On the other hand, by a recent Supreme Court ruling, binding an employee to a single employer is no more legal: in other words. Certain mobility within an economic sector is allowed.

*Human Trafficking and Prostitution*: Prostitution is practiced mostly by women who are smuggled into the country by air and land. Prostitution is illegal but prevalent. The women mostly come from the European former Eastern bloc. Information for this aspect of female migrant workers in Israel is to be found, for instance, on the Amnesty International website,[12] and can be compared with general information on global human trafficking on the UN website.[13]

*Workers Without a Permit*: Workers without a permit fall into three main classes: those who came into the country on a tourist visa and decided to stay and work, or planned to do this from the very beginning; those whose permit/visa has expired; and those who left their original employer. Such workers are considered illegal and are liable to immediate deportation, as enforced – at times brutally – by an active deportation police (instituted in 2003). Involvement of helping institutions is possible but rarely successful.

*Why is Israel so Tough about Work Permits, or Visas?* Israel still has to decide whether it is a *Jewish State* or a *State for all its Citizens:* it has no constitution but it has Basic Laws. Paramount of these is The Scroll of Independence (14 May1948), which defines Israel as a Jewish state and homeland for Jews worldwide.[14] This foundational text was carefully crafted to advocate Jewish independence in the newly-declared state as historically and politically valid for the international community, while also acceptable to all internal parties. It is as mindful of the Shoah and its legacy as of secular and religious stakes inside the small community of 1948 Palestine/ Israel-to-be. The result is a mixed and self-deconstructive document that delineates an equal-status, secular, Western style democracy which, paradoxically, incorporates strong religious (not only cultural and national) elements:

- The State of Israel will be open for Jewish immigration and for the Ingathering of the Exiles.
- It will foster the development of the country for the benefit of all its inhabitants.
- It will be based on freedom, justice and peace as envisaged by the prophets of Israel.
- It will ensure complete equality of social and political rights to all its inhabitants irrespective of religion, race or sex.
- It will guarantee freedom of religion, conscience, language, education and culture.
- It will safeguard the Holy Places of all religions.
- It will be faithful to the principles of the Charter of the United Nations.[15]

Although various in-voices, from [Arab] citizenry to [Jewish Israeli] post Zionists, would like to advance Israel's character as a state for all its citizens, with equal human and civil rights for all with no difference introduced because of religion, gender, race, nation or other affiliation, at this time the balance is in favour of a Jewish State, with Jewish orthodox-religious principles dictating personal status and the *Law of Return*[16] assuring every Jew in the world of entry and citizenship – unless s/he has a criminal record. This Law then effectively bars legal immigration of non-Jews to Israel unless converted.[17] While the definition of "who is a Jew" has been broadened beyond the Rabbinic one[18] ("whose mother is Jewish") in order to accommodate Russian and Ethiopian Jewry – certainly since the big immigration waves in the early 1990s – it still stands in opposition to the democratic right of immigration for all potentially suitable humans, and Halakhic definitions persist in many areas of Israeli life – for reasons of tradition, certainly, but mainly because of the influence of religious political parties.[19] Therefore, almost the only possibility of becoming a permanent resident or citizen is by a bona fide marriage and/or conversion.[20] Otherwise, extension of a working visa is possible through local agencies and assured employment for a limited work period, but then leaving or deportation is expected and/or enforced; and public outcry about methods of deportation does not always help.

*Salaries and Conditions* are different for live-in jobs (mostly women) and in other sectors. In live-in jobs, higher salaries for veteran workers are the legal norm after a certain period. By law, such salaries should conform at least to the minimum wage requirements although, in practice, they may not. Vacation time and a day's rest are mandatory for [female] domestic workers as well, but this might be at the mercy of employers. Add to these very high transport costs and the previously mentioned commissions to agencies abroad and locally, and the reward for menial and hard work is hardly outstanding in Israeli terms – although it may be and is at times considered as such by the foreign workers themselves.

Potential exploitation by employers is prosecuted by the State; employees may receive [free] legal aid from the relevant government and NGOs.

*Children Born to Foreign Workers in Israel* are covered by the country's general [obligatory] education laws. However, they are subject to deportation with their parents if circumstances so dictate. For comparison, let us remember that in most democratic countries you automatically become a citizen once you are born in that country. This rejection of what has become a global norm is, once again, the result of Israel's basic paradox: if it is to be a Jewish homeland, and a democracy with a Jewish majority that would insure its character as such, it cannot be a state where all its citizens, including non-Jews, are equal; and it has to uphold its Jewish demographic supremacy. This situation is conceived of as a necessity, an unwilling cautious response to the Shoah and the security concerns that have accompanied Israel since its inception but, of course, undermines the country's continuation as the only democracy in the Middle East.

A solution for such children, whose language and culture is Hebrew/Israeli and who might have had no other culture all their lives, has recently been suggested. A recent Supreme Court decision allows permanent resident status to children of migrant workers/foreigners born in Israel before 2001, that is, children who fit into the "culturally integrated" category. This is largely a welcome measure; however, several borderline cases are still pending at this time.

## Summary: Why, Then?

The stay of *legal* **migrant**/foreign workers in Israel is, at least theoretically, regulated by state law, which means that they have basic labour and human rights. However, their sojourn in Israel is limited in duration and options, not least by the nature of the Israeli State as well as Israeli society's insularity and xenophobia. Lack of social integration is in fact expected, a given factor conditioned by law, society and religion. A foreigner on a menial job, be that job important for the economy as it may, will always remain a foreigner and will finally have to leave at the end of her/his contract.

Why, then, do these workers – foreign hence migrant in Israeli terms, and this is why I've used foreign/migrant here almost interchangeably – and especially women, many of them with children back home, try to remain in Israel, a dangerous place to live in at any time, beyond their visa validity? The answer can only be, because what awaits them back home is far, far worse. In other words: staying seems to them the best of two evils; in their subjective considerations, they do not really have a choice if they wish to support their families back home, educate their children, have a kind of life, see a bit of the world, and so forth.

### And This Leads Us Back to the Biblical Ruth

Ruth has been romanticized freely, in confession as well as in scholarship. In Judaism, her words to Naomi, "I shall go where you go…" (Ruth 1.17), were understood and used in post-biblical times as a voluntary conversion formula. In scholarship, her words and behaviour were variously interpreted as signifying loyalty, love, legal obligation towards Naomi and/or her family. But what we can also assume, and with as much if not more validity than anything else for Ruth's actions, and in light of the female workers' behaviour patterns, is that Ruth might have had no choice, at least in "her" view. She might have felt that remaining in her source community, as the widow of a foreigner and with his family gone, she would have no chance of survival; and that in his source community, with his mother, she might have more opportunities for finding work, that is, for surviving. And yet, even though Ruth goes voluntarily, she remains throughout "The Moabite", that is, a foreigner. Even in her exemplary case, ethnic – and also class – considerations do not disappear, even though she is a positive literary character.

Ruth works in the fields (Ruth 2). Against all the odds, the landlord notices her and favours her (Ruth 2). Still, to take it further, a little female trickery must be devised (Ruth 3). Ruth marries the local, rich landlord, thus altering her civic status; and has a son, thus altering her social status.

And yet, at the end, she disappears from her own story; hence, even after marrying and having a son, she is not "integrated" into the target community. At best one can say she is "assimilated", "swallowed" by her target society. And Jewish tradition insistently requires her to have converted, although the biblical text contains no hint of that beyond her declaration to Naomi early on, "Your people is my people and your god is my god" (Ruth 1:16).

Ruth is a mother in Israel, one of several "foreign" women whom the Bible (Hebrew Bible and New Testament) cites as important matriarchs (Rahab, Bathsheba, Tamar...), not to mention Hagar and others. Such foreign women may save the people, refresh the line, take social risks to advance the collective cause. And yet, biblical attitudes concerning those Other women, of different ethnicity often coupled with low-class or suspected sexual morality issues, remain ambivalent.

And today? Israel, because of its basic constitutional issue (Jewish State!), is indeed a special case. Its insularity, the fissures in its aspirations for democracy, the basic paradox between aspired Jewishness and equality that is inherent in its being so far insoluble, the political pressure of orthodox/ religious parties to make Israel a Halakha state (while claiming all this time that it is losing its "Jewish" character) – all these factors are perhaps more present today than they were almost sixty years ago, when the Scroll of Independence was written and Israel was declared a state. The memory of the Shoah, the fear that it could happen again, the security threats, are at times exploited as propaganda but are simultaneously genuine. The problematics of being Jewish – Is Judaism a religion? A nation? A culture? A "race"? A combination of those, or several of those? – has been pondered etically and emically ever since the European Enlightenment. Israel and "secular" Zionism's position in this existential debate is complex. This lack of clarity invades every facet of life in Israel. It is also expressed, among other things, in the employment of foreign workers under limiting and strenuous conditions. But is this exploitation, is this so unique when seen against similar phenomena in other countries, when compared to cultures that are older and more confident of themselves? In other words: Is Israel unique in its treatment of migrant foreigners, especially lower-class unskilled foreigners, for these or other, economic and xenophobic reasons? This is a rhetorical question. Migrant workers do not fare much better in other countries, where the extra "Jewish" factor doesn't feature but the class factor may perhaps weigh as much as the xenophobic element.

In this age of globalized migration, the unskilled workforce, especially women, hold up the global economy where and when it's needed. Such workers are regularly victimized, self-victimized or in turn declared victims by human rights and other activists. Exploitation is of course prevalent and abhorrent and should be fought against. However, not recognizing the potentially elective nature of becoming a migrant worker, the choice between the evil-from and the evil-to, is unfair as well. And in order to understand that, a fresh look at the biblical Ruth might be instructive, especially if romanticizing[21] this widow-turned-matriarch is given up.

## Endnotes

* Athalya Brenner is Professor Emeritus at the University of Amsterdam, The Netherlands, and at Tel Aviv University, Israel.

1. A. Golan, "Ruth Would Have Remained a Moabite", (http://news.walla.co.il/?w=/1110743). http://news.walla.co.il/?w=//1110743

2. Athalya Brenner, "Ruth as a Foreign Worker and the Politics of Exogamy", in Brenner (ed.), *A Feminist Companion to Ruth and Esther* (Second Series, Sheffield: Sheffield Academic Press 1999a), pp. 158–62; Athalya Brenner, "Wat, wenn ich Rut bin?" *Bibel und Kirche* 54.3 (1999b), pp. 117–22; Athalya Brenner, *I Am: Biblical Women Tell Their Own Story* (Minneapolis, MN: Fortress Press, 2005); and (http://news.walla.co.il/?w=/1110743). http://news.walla.co.il/?w=//1110743

3. For instance on the official Israel Government site, http://www.gov.il/FirstGov/NewsEng/News_GuideMigrantWorkers.htm.

4. http://www1.cbs.gov.il/reader/

5. The material is translated from the Hebrew version of the Overview, as it appears on http://www1.cbs.gov.il/reader/newhodaot/hodaa_template.html?hodaa= 200601252. Materials are from November 2006; see particularly Tables 12.33 and 12.34 online, reproduced from the printed edition of the *CBS, Statistical Abstract of Israel 2006*.

6. For instance: import of money from migrant work income is one of the mainstays of Philippine economy.

7. http://www.kavlaoved.org.il/media.asp

8. http://www.hotline.org.il/english/index.htm

9. The Ma'ariv (http://www.nrg.co.il) website of 2 May 2007 records a court case about a [male] worker who consistently physically abused his helpless employer, with a prison sentence meted out.

10. No official statistics are necessary to notice how foreign workers have invigorated Christian communities in Israel, in addition to creating their own religious communities and places of worship. Also, that female piety is noticeably greater that that of males.

11. Although, in the last two decades, other possibilities do exist, and the marital status of partners thus wed must be officially registered as such by the Ministry of the Interior.

12. http://web.amnesty.org/library/Index/engMDE150172000

13. http://www.unodc.org/unodc/en/trafficking_human_beings.html

14. For the official English translation see http://www.knesset.gov.il/docs/eng/megilat_eng.htm.

15. On the website of the Israel Ministry of Foreign Affairs, http://www.mfa.gov.il/ MFA/Peace%20Process/Guide%20to%20the%20Peace%20Process/ Declaration%20of%20Establishment%20of%20State% 20of%20Israel.

16. The official version of the Law of Return, 05/07/1950, from Israel's Ministry of Foreign Affairs site: http://www.israel-mfa.gov.il/MFA/MFAArchive/1950_1959/ Law percent20of percent20Return percent205710-1950.

17. Traditionally conversion to Judaism is difficult, and this is upheld by [ultra]orthodox Judaism with enthusiasm – not only to the point of not recognizing non-orthodox conversions, but also to the point of not-recognizing

some orthodox ones. This policy is upheld by the Israel Chief Rabbinate and the Conversion Authority it runs, and one of the reasons given is to prevent convenience conversions, that is, conversions aimed at acquiring citizenship. Golan's cited article of 22/05/2007 deals with such problematics, while accepting without question the traditional Jewish view of Ruth as a convert as valid for the biblical story.

18. Originally accepted de-facto as binding by the State in the Law of Return but later (1970 and onwards) contested on marital and other grounds again and again, with the involvement of non-Orthodox and human rights organizations.

19. About 20 percent of Israel's Knesset (Parliament) members belong to Zionist and non-Zionist religious parties. These parties then exercise, together and separately, the kind of political clout that can not be ignored – and are, more often then not, run by Rabbis rather than by the politicians that are ostensibly their leaders or representatives in the legislature.

20. Non-Jewish refugees and fugitives, from Asia as well as Africa, have been accepted in the past and are still accepted as such. Another category is that of Arabs who collaborate with the Israeli security forces. However, the number of people in these two categories is insignificant by comparison to other foreigners, and they do not belong to the "foreign/migrant" workers' category.

21. I here re-adapt further Naomi Steinberg's concept as expressed in her article: Naomi Steinberg, "Romancing the Widow: The Economic Distinctions between the `ALMANÂ, the `SSÂ-`ALMANÂ, and the `EŠET-HAMMET", in *God's Word for Our World* ed. by J. Harold Ellens (JSOT Supp: New York, 2004), 327–46.

THE SAMARITANS: BIBLICAL CONSIDERATIONS IN THE
SOLUTION OF A POLITICAL PROBLEM

*Yairah Amit**

This article concerns not only the Bible's positions on the Samaritans and how they have been interpreted. It also deals with the role of the Bible in the changing attitude towards the Samaritans in modern Israelite society – that is, in the State of Israel.

Therefore the discussion is divided into two parts: in the first, I describe and analyze the ancient sources; and in the second, I describe the modern problem, how it was solved and which sources were the most influential and why.

## The Bible's Positions

### 2 Kings 17: 24–41

The main text that depicts the attitude of the Bible towards the Samaritans is, of course, 2 Kgs 17: 24–41. This text suggests that the Samaritans were descendants of nations, exiled from their countries by the King of Assyria, who settled them in the cities of Samaria. There they replaced the Israelite inhabitants, who had been exiled to other lands in the Assyrian Empire (v. 24). Although this description reflects the Assyrian policy of exchanging parts of the populations by means of two-directional deportations,[1] it gives the impression that the land was emptied of its Israelite population and filled with immigrants from other countries.[2]

It should be noted that the term "השמרנים" (= the people of Samaria who are the Samarians or the Samaritans)[3] – which appears only here in the Bible (2 Kgs 17: 29) – applies to the original Israelite inhabitants of the country, not to the new population which was brought in by the Assyrians.[4] The word "Samaritans", which would later become the usual designation of the inhabitants of the north,[5] and which I use throughout this article, was taken from the name of the kingdom and its capital Samaria. Nevertheless, Samaritan tradition interprets it as deriving from the verb *sh-m-r* – that is, to keep or preserve – indicating that they were the original preservers of the Torah.[6] No wonder, then, that in this polemic the Sages avoided the term Samaritans, and gave them epithets that expressed their negative attitude, based on the text in 2 Kings 17: "Cuthites" (v. 24), "Lion proselytes" (vv. 25–26), and "heretics" (vv. 29–41).[7]

This text of 2 Kings 17 assumes that after the Assyrian conquest of Samaria in 720 BCE, the country was left empty of its Israelite population, as it is written in 2 Kgs 17: 6 and 23b: "In the ninth year of Hoshea, the king of Assyria captured Samaria, He deported the Israelites to Assyria and settled them in Halah, at the [River] Habor, at the River Gozan, and in the towns of Media [...] So the Israelites were deported from their land to Assyria, as is still the case".[8] In the place of the Israelites "the king of Assyria brought [exiles] from Babylon, Cuthah Avva, Hamath, and Sepharvaim, and he settled them in the towns of Samaria in place of the Israelite; they took possession of Samaria and dwelt in its towns" (2 Kgs 17: 24). This text goes on to say that "When they first settled there", these newcomers "did not worship the Lord", and only after being attacked by lions they asked to learn "the rules of the God of the land". Then the King of Assyria ordered an Israelite priest to be brought back from exile to teach the new settlers "how to worship the Lord" (2 Kgs 17: 25–28). The result was a syncretism of faith and cult "They worshiped the Lord, while serving their own gods according to the practices of the nation from which they had been deported" – which means that they did not worship the Lord in the proper manner (vv. 29–33). The text emphasizes that not only "To this day they follow their former practices (v. 34), but that "To this day their children and their children's children do as their ancestors did" (v. 41).[9]

The central question is whether the northern population of Samaria was composed of only immigrants or of immigrants and remaining Israelites. In other words, are they appropriate to participate in the Jerusalem temple.

Many scholars are convinced that this text was not only composed and added as a deuteronomistic polemic against the northern population, but that it was edited by later redactors reflecting the Judahite position in the historical debate during the Persian Period.[10] This debate concerns the northerners' right, or to be more exact – lack of right, to take part in the Jerusalem cult, which was renewed by the exiled Judahites who had returned from Babylon.[11] It is possible that there were social and political reasons for the northern population's wish to join the Jerusalem cult, but these are not mentioned. The reader is impressed from the texts in 2 Kgs 17: 29–41 and in Ezra 4 by the desire of the writers, who reflect the atmosphere of the returning exiles, to maintain their religious distinction, probably after their experiences in the Babylonian exile.

## *Ezra 4: 1–5 and 6–23*

The second text, in the book of Ezra, although it is not identical to the one in 2 Kings 17, it offers a complementary and supporting view of the northern population as a mixed alien group, brought into the country by the Assyrian Empire. This group adopted the religion of the Israelite God, but was differentiated from the Judahites and Benjamites who returned from the Babylonian exile. The first text in Ezra (4:1–5) calls the Samaritans "the adversaries of Judah and Benjamin", as opposed to the "returned exiles" (v. 1) and describes them as those who wish to take part in building the temple in Jerusalem, arguing "since we too worship your God, having offered sacrifices to Him since the time of King Esarhaddon of Assyria, who brought us here" (v. 2). But the " returned exiles", led by Zerubbabel and the priest Jeshua and the chiefs of the clans, rejected the Samaritans' offer, saying: "It is not for you and us to build a House to our God" (v. 3). The result of this conflict was that the building of the Jerusalem temple was delayed until the reign of Darius.

A similar dispute concerned the fortification of Jerusalem in the reigns of the Persian kings Ahasuerus and Artaxerxes. This dispute gave rise to a malicious letter to Artaxerxes, described in Ezra 4: 6–23. This letter also indicates that those who opposed the residents of Jerusalem and Judah are identified with the descendants of the immigrants from the Assyrian Empire, who had been brought over by Osnappar, who is Assur-banipal (vv. 9–10).

## *The Book of Chronicles*

There is another biblical source on this subject, our third text, which not all scholars mention, and it is the book of Chronicles.[12]

*The exile of the Northern Kingdom:* the Chronicler gives a different description of the fate of the northern Israelite kingdom. It avoids an explicit description of the fall of the northern kingdom and the deportation of its inhabitants. The fall and deportation are referred to partially and marginally in the genealogy that opens the book (1 Chron. 5: 23–26), but not in the historical sequence and not in the correct chronological place.[13] Only the genealogical lists mention the exiling of the northern tribes, but of only the two-and-a half eastern tribes – the Reubenite, the Gadite and half of Manasseh. According to this description, the deportation was carried out by Pul and by Tilgath-pilneser, kings of Assyria.[14]

On the other hand, the Chronicler's historical sequence shows that during the reigns of the Judahite kings Hezekiah and Josiah not only were most of the inhabitants of the western northern kingdom still living in their land, but that the religious reforms carried out by these kings included all of Israel. Under Hezekiah the call to come and keep the Passover for the Lord God of Israel in Jerusalem encompassed "all Israel and Judah... from Beer-sheba to Dan...the remnant of you [Israel] who escaped from the hand of the kings of Assyria...the couriers passed from town to town in the land of *Ephraim and Manasseh till they reached Zebulun...Some of the people of Asher and Manasseh and Zebulun*, however, were contrite, and came to Jerusalem" (2 Chron. 30: 1–11). Under Josiah too the reform encompassed not only Judah and Jerusalem, but "the towns of *Manasseh and Ephraim and Simeon, as far as Naphtali*...throughout the land of Israel". Moreover, the silver which was then brought (in the days of Josiah) to repair the house of God was collected "from *Manasseh and Ephraim and from all the remnant of Israel* and from all Judah and Benjamin and the inhabitants of Jerusalem" (2 Chron. 34: 3–9, see also v. 23, 33; 35:18; all the emphases are mine).

*The Interpretations:* this description of the Chronicler, which does not match those in the second book of Kings and Ezra 4, prompted two different, even contradictory, interpretations.

The first was pioneered at the start of the twentieth century by Torrey in his *Ezra Studies*[15] and continued most prominently by Noth in his *Überlieferungsgeschichliche Studien* (1943).[16] According to them the aim of the entire book of Chronicles, was to present an anti-Samaritan position, to emphasize the divine election and legitimacy of Judah, of the House of David and of the temple in Jerusalem, and thus reject the legitimacy of the Samaritans.

The second interpretation, which was proposed in 1969 by Grintz in his Hebrew book titled (translation of the Hebrew): *The Origins of Generations*,[17] and whose leading proponent is Japhet in her doctoral thesis titled *The Ideology of the Book of Chronicles and Its Place in Biblical Thought*, which was submitted in 1973 and was published in Hebrew as a book in 1977.[18] These scholars suggest that the description was intended to present the Samaritans as descendants of the tribes of Western Israel, who most of them were never exiled, and thus the brothers of the Judahites and an integral part of the Israelite nation.

The interpretation suggested by Torrey and Noth and their followers continues and completes the attitude of the books of Kings and Ezra, which expressed hostility and superiority towards the people of the north.[19] Whereas, the interpretation of Grintz and Japhet and their followers suggests an attitude of conciliation and tolerance, a call to end hostility and superiority and to unite the whole western Israelite nation around the worship of the Lord in the Jerusalem temple, under the leadership of the House of David.[20]

*The Assyrian Information Regarding the Scope of the Exile:* it seems to me that the decisive factor in preferring one of these two interpretations of the attitude of the book of Chronicles is the information we learn from the Assyrian inscriptions that describe the scope of the Israelite deportation. These inscriptions tell us more than once that the number of inhabitants exiled from Samaria by Sargon the second was 27,290.[21]

The Assyrian monarchs were not known for their modesty; therefore, if they were satisfied with this number, we have no reason to question it. However, we can deduce from this number that not all the inhabitants of Israel were deported, and many remained living in their land. Moreover, those who remained continued to pay taxes, which fed the Assyrian war machine. This conclusion agrees with the Assyrian policy of deportation, which was to transfer the social elites and those individuals with skills needed by the empire, and to leave the humble masses in their countries.[22] It also agrees with the Babylonian policy, which followed in some extent that of their Assyrian predecessors, and left in Judah "the poorest people in the land", "to be vinedressers and field hands" (2 Kgs 24:14–16, 25:12, 22–24).[23]

Although the Assyrian evidence has its own literary and ideological aims, it also warns us to regard the different biblical texts I have quoted as tendentious sources which exaggerate whatever suits their purposes, and colour the historical record accordingly. In other words, it strengthens the argument that the description in 2 Kings 17 and its supplements in Ezra 4 – both of which imply a comprehensive mass deportation – was a polemical one. Its purpose was to depict the Samaritans as aliens, as people who could not claim to be genetically part of Israel, and did not deserve to be included. At the same time, the Assyrian evidence sheds a positive light on the text in Chronicles, which is usually criticized as historically unreliable,[24] about the "remnant of Israel" that stayed on its land in the north, suggesting that in this case it is trustworthy evidence that hints at the identity of the northern people.

The Assyrian evidence, in fact, supports the second interpretation – namely, that the Chronicler did not seek to alienate the northern population, the Samaritans, but, on the contrary, wanted to bring them closer, because he thought that they were part of all Israel. The Chronicler is doing this not by declarative means, but by using indirect means in order to achieve his purpose – a historical depiction that emphasizes the continuity of the people of Israel, who are Jacob's descendants, in their land, the Land of Israel.[25] Therefore:

- He ignores the depiction of Kings and Ezra.
- While on the other hand – he enables us to know that he knows about the exile of the North by the genealogical list in 1 Chron. 5: 23–26, and by using the phrasing "the remnant of you who escaped from the hand of the kings of Assyria" in 2 Chron. 30: 6. Thus, he reduces the scope of the exile into two and a half tribes, and he limits it to the eastern part of the Jordan.
- He presents the northern inhabitants in the reigns of Hezekiah and Josiah as descendants of the ten tribes.

While on the other hand he is certainly aware of an alien population in the reign of Hezekiah (2 Chron. 30: 25), but he views it as proselytes, who come from around the country to take part in the Passover sacrifice in Jerusalem.

### Conclusion

An attempt to reconstruct the history underlying this issue demands that we consider all the data, both within and external to the Bible, with their limitations and agendas. Having considered the different sources, with their reliable and unreliable elements, it seems reasonable that in reality the northern population was mixed, containing both Israelites and alien deportees who had been brought in. However, we don't know the exact ratio, and can not determine exactly what percentage of the population were the 27,290 who were exiled, and how many exiles from elsewhere were brought in the reigns of Esarhaddon and Osnappar (Ezra 4:1, 10). This doubtful picture is a good reason for creating different versions of histories and for interpreting them according to the circumstances, needs and Ideologies of their different authors and interpreters.

## The Bible's Positions in the service of Politics

A rather similar debate, probably also not free from bias, took place in our time, in reference to the status of the Samaritans who came to live in the State of Israel.

### After the Establishment of the State

Before the establishment of the State, the person who studied the Samaritans and wrote favorably about them was Yitzhak Ben-Zvi, who would become Israel's second President.[26] Thanks to him, the Israeli government determined in 1949 that the Samaritans, who had left Nablus, then under Jordanian rule, and come to live in Israel, had the same status as any Jew who immigrated to Israel from one of the Arab states.[27]

This meant that the Samaritans were covered by the 1950 Law of Return (חוק השבות), which states that every Jew is entitled to come to Israel, and those who wish to remain become new citizens entitled to what are known as "Immigrant Absorption Benefits". Thus the Samaritans who settled in the State of Israel were given immigrant rights and were classified in the population register as "Samaritan Jews".

*1992.* In 1992, following an amendment to the Law of Return of 1970 (Clause 4B), the government changed its position, declaring that the Samaritans were not like people born to a Jewish mother, and were in reality members of a different religion, which meant that in the future, Samaritans would not be entitled to immigrant rights. The Samaritans petitioned the High Court of Justice, arguing that their descent from the tribes of Ephraim and Manasseh, as their tradition asserts, means that they belong to the Israelite nation, even though they do not descend from the tribe of Judah. Furthermore, while they do not follow the rabbinical tradition, they are like the Karaites and like them should not be excluded from the Israelite entity. The Court sought the advice of an expert and applied to Prof. Shemaryahu Talmon, a biblical scholar of the Hebrew University in Jerusalem. His documented opinion, which was given in 1994 highlighted the link between the Samaritans and the remnants of the tribes of Israel, primarily by discounting the historical validity of the text in 2 Kgs 17: 24–41.[28]

*1994: Talmon's Document.* Talmon quoted first the Samaritans' own position about being descendants of the House of Joseph and the contradictory position in the book of Kings, which describes them as the descendants of foreigners. Here he adds, "Some new commentators regard this tradition as historical evidence." But then he dismisses the statement in the book of Kings, quoting other commentators, and in effect agrees with them. These others, Talmon argues, maintain that the narrative in the book of Kings "is not historical evidence, but a tale of marvels, in which lions act as agents of the Almighty – a repeated motif in the prophetic stories, such as in 1 Kgs 13: 20, 20: 35–36, and so forth." Not only does Talmon question the historicity of the source in Kings by including it among the "tales of marvels", he even emphasizes the link between 2 Kings 17 and Ezra 4 and notes "the polemical tone of the tradition given in 2 Kings 17", with the three repetitions that it is all true "to this day" (vv. 23, 34 and 41). From all these he concludes that "the tradition in 2 Kings 17 reflected the conflict between the returned exiles and the inhabitants who had not been exiled, namely, the 'adversaries of Judah and Benjamin', mentioned in the book of Ezra." Talmon also suggested in the same documented opinion that the author of Ezra 4 amended the story in the book of Kings "so as to depict the people who remained in northern Eretz Israel after its fall, after the fall of Samaria, as not being Children of Israel." To show that the northern inhabitants worshipped the Lord, he stressed that neither the author of the story in Kings nor of the one in Ezra accused the northerners of following "another religion".[29]

*Is Talmon Objective?* Talmon's opinion may not be an objective analysis either. While the text in Ezra does describe the Samaritans as worshipping the Lord, that is not the case in the book of Kings. There the people that the Assyrians deported to the kingdom of Israel are described as continuing to worship the gods they had brought with them, and as creating a new syncretic religion, which means: a different religion. However, Talmon preferred to ignore this evidence. Moreover, his cherry-picked statements from the Sages, which display only positive attitude towards the Cuthites, enabled him to conclude that "the Sages did not regard the Samaritans as being of a different religion, but as a branch of the nation of Israel."[30]

Interestingly, Talmon, on the one hand, was one of the scholars to discuss widely the importance of the Assyrian evidence to the complexity of the Samaritan origins in biblical literature,[31] but on the other hand he ignored the evidence of the book of Chronicles. He did this in his early article *"Biblical Traditions on the Beginning of the Samaritan's History"* from 1973. However, after more than 30 years, in his expert opinion, Talmon neither used the evidence of the book of Chronicles, nor the numerical information of the Assyrian inscriptions.

Perhaps he preferred not to base his argument on more materials that might be described as unreliable, such as the Assyrian annals and display inscriptions, or the book of Chronicles generally discounted as historically valid. Moreover, Perhaps Talmon did not base his expert opinion on the Assyrian evidence, because while it shows that most of the population was not deported but remained in their country, it also indicates the genetic problem, because an alien population was brought in under Assyrian policy, and he knew the likely reaction of some politicians and anti-Samaritans in 1992. It seems to me that Talmon did not want to give them any support regarding the possibility that the Samaritans are not "pure" Israelites. Therefore, he preferred to emphasize that the known and accepted testimonies of 2 Kgs 17 and Ezra 4 are unreliable, and thus gave the impression that the positive position of the Sages was the decisive element in this case.[32] Given that the Sages decided that the Cuthites were not foreigners, Talmon advised the court to follow in their footsteps.

*Political Statement.* There is no doubt that his choice of sources from the Bible and from the Sages' literature and his interpretation in his expert opinion lead to a political rather than a scholarly opinion – showing that the Samaritans are part of the community of Israel. In this, Talmon was following the approach of Izhak Ben-Zvi and the Israeli government of the early days of the State, who applied to the Samaritans the Law of Return and categorized them as Jews. In so doing he opposed the political motivation of an extremist political group which suddenly, in 1992, tried to deny the Samaritans these rights.

As a result of Talmon's expert opinion, the Israeli government's policy of applying the Right of Return to the Samaritans adheres to the interpretation outlined in the book of Chronicles, namely, to regard the Samaritan community as an integral part of the nation of Israel.

Today there are in the State of Israel some 600 Samaritans, representing the majority of the Samaritan community. Their integration in Israel and its modern way of life threatens the Samaritan's community with assimilation and loss of its unique identity, preserved in incredibly difficult conditions through more than two thousand years. On the other hand, integration fulfils the purpose of the Chronicler in his pro-Samaritan tendency, which was to depict the Samaritans as having been part of the people of Israel since time immemorial.

## Endnotes

* Yairah Amit is a Professor of Biblical Studies at the Department of Hebrew Culture Studies of Tel Aviv University, Israel.

1. On the Assyrian policy, see B. Oded, *Mass Deportations and Deportees in the Neo-Assyrian Empire: Justifications for War in Assyrian Royal Inscriptions* (Wiesbaden: Dr. Ludwig Reichert Verlag, 1979).

2. See B. Oded, "Where Is the 'Myth of the Empty Land' To Be Found? History versus Myth," in O. Lipschits and J. Blenkinsopp (eds), *Judah and the Judeans in the Neo-Babylonian Period* (Winona Lake, IN: Eisenbrauns, 2003). See especially p. 59.

3. There is a great confusion in the translation of this term, but I'll not discuss it here.

4. M. Cogan, and H. Tadmor, *II Kings* (AB) (Garden City, NY: Doubleday & Company, Inc., 1988), p. 211. References to the term "Samarian(s)" in Assyrian documents see I. Eph'al, "The 'Samaritan(s)' in the Assyrian Sources," in M. Cogan and I. Eph'al (eds), *Ah Assyria...Studies in Assyrian History and Ancient Near Eastern Historiography Presented to H. Tadmor* (Scripta Hierosolymitana v. 33, Jerusalem: The Magnes Press, The Hebrew University, 1991), pp. 36–45. For a revised and updated Hebrew version of this article see I. Eph'al, "The 'Samaritans' in the Assyrian Sources," in E. Stern and H. Eshel (eds), *The Samaritans* (Jerusalem: Yad Ben-Zvi Press, Israel Antiquities Authority, Staff officer for Archaeology Civil Administration for Judea and Samaria, 2002), pp. 34–44 (Hebrew).

5. In addition to what is mentioned above the term appears only in post-biblical materials as for example: Josephus (Antiq. XI: 297–347; XII: 257–64), the New Testament (Mt. 10: 5; Lk 9: 52), Ben Sira (50: 37–38), the Sages (b. Berakot 47b; b. Snhedrin 63b). For additional occurrences see also Shemaryahu Talmon, "Biblical Traditions on Samaritan History" in E. Stern and H. Eshel (eds), *The Samaritans* (Jerusalem: Yad Ben-Zvi Press, Israel Antiquities Authority, Staff officer for Archaeology Civil Administration for Judea and Samaria, 2002), pp. 7–27 (Hebrew).

6. On the Samaritans' tradition, see Talmon, "Biblical Traditions on Samaritan History", p. 9; M. Gaster, *The Samaritans: Their History, Doctrines and Literature* (London: H. Milford, Oxford University Press, 1925), pp. 7–12.

7. On the names used by the Sages, see also b. Qiddushin 75b.

8. Compare with 2 Kgs 18:11. All citations are taken from the new JPS Translation (1985).

9. On the place of the editor in this unit see Y. Amit, *The Book of Judges: The Art of Editing* (Leiden: Brill, 1999), p. 9 note 13 (Hebrew version: 1992). See also Talmon, "Biblical Traditions on Samaritan History", p. 12, note 22.

10. For example see J. Gray, *I & II Kings: A Commentary* (London: SCM Press, 1970, 2nd rev. edn; first published: 1964), pp. 651–56. According to Talmon, "Biblical Traditions on Samaritan History", pp. 23–27, this unit reflects one of the latest stages in the editing of the book of Kings, namely after the return to Zion.

11. See Ezra 1–6 and p. 195 below.

12. But see M. Cogan, "The Early Biblical Polemic concerning the Residents of Samaria," in Stern and Eshel (eds), *The Samaritans* (Jerusalem: Yad Ben-Zvi

Press, 2002), pp. 28–33 note 10, p. 30 (Hebrew). Also see, M. Cogan, "For we, like you. Worship your God: Three Biblical Portrayals of Samaritan Origins," *VT* 38 (1988), pp. 286–92.

13. For this convincing theory, see S. Japhet, *The Ideology of the Book of Chronicles and Its Place in Biblical Thought* (Frankfurt am Main: Verlag Peter Lang GmbH, 1989, 1ˢᵗ edn in Hebrew 1977), pp. 308–34.

14. See S. Japhet, *I & II Chronicles*: A Commentary (OTL), (Louisville, KY: Westminster/John Knox Press, 1993), p. 142. Japhet thinks that the chronicler uses the two names of one king. G.N. Knoppers, *I Chronicles 1–9* (AB), (New York: Doubleday, 2004), p. 381, thinks too that the *ww* is explicatory, but he does not deny the possibility of two different people.

15. C.C. Torrey, *Ezra Studies* (New York: Ktav Publishing House, 1970; 1ˢᵗ edn 1910), pp. 154–55; 208–13.

16. M. Noth, *The Chronicler's History*, JSOTS Sup 50 (Sheffield: Sheffield Academic Press, 1987, 1ˢᵗ edn published in German, 1943), pp. 100–106. But see the criticism of Williamson: "During the central decades of this century, the Chronicler's contribution to this debate was misunderstood. He was portrayed as adopting an anti-Samaritan stance…This misunderstanding has been dramatically reversed during the past decade, however." See also the bibliography he mentions. H.G.M. Williamson, *1 and 2 Chronicles* (NCBC) (Grand Rapids, MI: Wm. B. Eerdmans Publ. Co.; London: Marshall, Morgan & Scott Publ. Ltd, 1982), p. 24.

17. Y.M. Grintz, *Studies in Early Biblical Ethnology and History* (Jerusalem: Hakibbutz Hameuchad Publishing House, 1969, pp. 275–77 (Hebrew).

18. Japhet, *The Ideology of the Book of Chronicles and Its Place in Biblical Thought*, pp. 325–34.

19. An example for a later follower is M. Garsiel, "The Book of Chronicles as a Hidden Polemic with the Samaritans," *Beit Mikra 151* (1997), pp. 293–314 (Hebrew).

20. An example for a later follower is Cogan, "For we, like you. Worship your God, pp. 286–92. See also Cogan, "The Early Biblical Polemic Concerning the Residents of Samaria", in Stern and Eshel (eds), *The Samaritans*, pp. 28–33 (Hebrew).

21. J.B. Pritchard (ed.), *Ancient Near Eastern Texts Relating to the Old Testament* (Princeton, NJ: Princeton University Press, 1955), 284–85. M. Cogan and H. Tadmor, II Kings, p. 200 and see the bibliography there.

22. Oded, *Mass Deportations and Deportees in the Neo-Assyrian Empire*.

23. D. Vanderhooft, "Babylonian Strategies of Imperial Control in the West: Royal Practice and Rhetoric," in O. Lipschits and J. Blenkinsopp (eds), *Judah and the Judeans in the Neo-Babylonian Period* (Winona Lake, IN: Eisenbrauns, 2003), pp. 235–62.

24. See S. Japhet, "The Reliability of the Book of Chronicles – The History of the Problem and Its Significance within Biblical Studies," in A. Rofé and Y. Zakovitch, *Isac Leo Seeligmann Volume: Essays on the Bible and the Ancient World*, Volume I (Jerusalem: E. Rubinstein's House, 1983), pp. 327–46, (Hebrew). See also S. Japhet, "The Book of Chronicles: A History," in S. Japhet (ed.), *Shnaton – An Annual for Biblical and Ancient Near Eastern Studies XIV* (Jerusalem: The Hebrew University Magness Press, 2004), pp. 101–17 (Hebrew).

25. On the pro-Samaritans hidden polemic in the book of Chronicles, see Y. Amit, *Hidden Polemics in Biblical Narrative* (Tel Aviv: Miskal Publishing House, 2003, Hebrew), pp. 210–16.

26. I. Ben-Zvi, *The Book of the Samaritans* (Jerusalem: Yad Izhak Ben-Zvi, 1970, Hebrew; rev edn; first published 1935). See especially the editor's preface, pp. v–vi.

27. M. Corinaldi, *The Enigma of Jewish Identity – The Law of Return: Theory and Practice* (Israel: Nevo Publishing House, 2001, Hebrew), 132–35.

28. Talmon's document is included in Corinaldi, *The Enigma of Jewish Identity*, pp. 235–37, which is supplement 8.

29. See Talmon in Corinaldi, *The Enigma of Jewish Identity*, especially p. 236.

30. See Talmon in Corinaldi, *The Enigma of Jewish Identity*, p. 237.

31. Shemaryahu Talmon, "Biblical Traditions on the Beginning of the Samaritans' History," *Eretz Shomron, The thirtieth Arcaeological Convention, September 1972* (Jerusalem: The Israel Exploration Society, 1973, Hebrew), pp. 19–33, and see there pp. 27–28.

32. On different opinions of the Sages and through history, see Allon, "The Origin of the Samaritans in Halachic Tradition", pp. 146–56 (Hebrew); Corinaldi, *The Enigma of Jewish Identity*, pp. 127–31. But see Talmon, in Corinaldi, *The Enigma of Jewish Identity*, p. 237.

# The Biblical Roots of Secularism

*Philip Davies**

## Secularism

Secularism is defined by the Shorter Oxford English Dictionary[1] as "The doctrine that morality should be based solely on regard to the well-being of mankind in the present life, to the exclusion of all considerations drawn from belief in God or in a future state". Had the phrase been "public morality" the definition might have been acceptable. As it stands, it is a definition of utilitarianism. I prefer a tighter definition, such as The Chambers Dictionary:[2] "the belief that the state, morals, education, etc. should be independent of religion". The definition provided by France, which established itself as a secular state in 1905, puts it even better: "the neutrality of the State, local government and all public services in matters relating to one or more religions or to one or more creeds".[3] As the self-definition of an officially secular state, this has, for me, the greatest authority.

Other modern states are more or less secular, though they do not define themselves officially as such and do not consistently follow secular principles. In the United States, the First Amendment to the Constitution is that "Congress shall make no law respecting an establishment of religion, or prohibiting the free exercise thereof". This is a qualified expression of neutrality. But the words "one nation under God" contained in the Pledge of Allegiance arguably reflect more accurately the sentiments of American citizens, and pressure to institutionalize prayer (not to mention public displays of the Ten Commandments) betray a popular view that American public morality is seen as "biblical".[4] Secularism, then, is not, as both supporters and opponents of secularism sometimes assert or imply, anti-religious; it is non-religious. But at least one major US politician has eloquently defended secularism as follows:

What our deliberative, pluralistic democracy demands is that the religiously motivated translate their concerns into universal [!] values. It requires that their proposals must be subject to argument and amenable to reason. If I am opposed to abortion for religious reasons and seek to pass a law banning the practice, I cannot simply point to the teachings of my church or invoke God's will and expect that argument to carry the day. If I want others to listen to me, then I have to explain why abortion violates some principle that is accessible to people of all faiths, including those with no faith at all.

– Barack Obama[5]

Obama avoids the word "secular" (he was at the time an American Presidential hopeful) and his phrase "deliberative, pluralistic democracy" is reminiscent of the distinction made by another American, Jeffrey Stout. In his *Democracy and Tradition*,[6] he distinguishes between three social regimes: *secularism*, the public disavowal of religion, *liberal democracy*, the encouragement of religious virtues and *new traditionalism*, in which the community shares the same theological values. Of the three, Stout commends liberal democracy, on the grounds that a healthy democracy should benefit from the insights of religion. I am not certain that his distinction is absolutely clear here, for secularism does not proscribe the expression of religion or even discourage it; the essential point is that religion is given no political *status*.

Democracy is an important element in modern secularism. It is opposed to *theocracy*, effectively the position taken by "new traditionalism". For deities cannot have votes unless they are on the electoral register and submit the ballot papers properly (even monarchs and their families are ineligible to vote in democratic monarchies). The possibility remains (and is very close to reality in some parts of the world) that a democratic election may install a party dedicated to institute religious law; but as long as there remain free elections, it remains a democracy, though not a *liberal* one, since such a policy would be contrary to the Universal Declaration of Human Rights. However, democracy is not *essential* to secularism. Whether or not Soviet Russia under Stalin was either democratic or secular (rather than totalitarian and atheist, atheism in this case functioning as a state religion), I shall presently be arguing for secularism in the Bible. I cannot possibly argue that the Bible is democratic. It is totalitarian, throughout. I will argue, nevertheless, that a large part of the Bible asserts that religious belief should play no role in politics. Yes, secularism is biblical.

## New Testament

I shall begin with the New Testament, since here one finds unanimity. There is neither a prescription in the New Testament for Christian political action nor interest in political administration. The writers of the New Testament mostly ignore the whole question of political action, but where they do address it, they encourage obedience to the existing order. Thus, Jesus is made to utter the impeccably secular comment: "give to Caesar what is Caesar's and to God what is God's" (Mt. 22:21; Mk 12:17; Lk 20:25). The statement can, of course, be exegeted in many ways so as to demarcate the wall between the imperial and the divine realm, but taxation is perhaps the clearest symbol of political control and submission (as the Boston Tea Party exemplifies). Again, the statement "my kingdom is not of this world" (Jn 18:36) expresses another secularist principle; that the realms of religion and the state do not intersect. The statement "Do not think that I have come to bring peace to the earth; I have not come to bring peace, but a sword" (Mt. 10:34) probably does not signify violence on the part of Jesus' followers but either violence against them or (as the context rather suggests) discord among them.

Here is what the most famous letter of Paul of Tarsus (Rom. 13:1–7) has to say, more directly, on this subject:

> Let everyone be subject to the governing authorities; for there is no authority except from God, and those authorities that exist have been instituted by God. Therefore anyone resisting authority resists what God has appointed, and those who resist will incur judgment. For rulers are not a terror to good conduct, but to bad. Do you wish to have no fear of the authority? Then do what is good, and you will receive its approval; for it is God's servant for your good. But if you do what is wrong, you should be afraid, for the authority does not bear the sword in vain! It is the servant of God to execute punishment on the wrongdoer. Therefore one must be subject, not only because of [this] punishment but also as a matter of conscience. For the same reason you also pay taxes, for the authorities are God's servants, busy with this very thing. Pay to all what is due them – taxes to whom taxes are due, revenue to whom revenue is due, respect to whom respect is due, honour to whom honour is due.

The theory here is quite clear: human authority is endorsed by God and should be obeyed. It is a curious kind of secularist theory, but secularist it is nonetheless: there is no divine political authority except as vested in secular authority. In the first century CE that authority was Caesar's; but had the Republic been a true democracy, then Paul's statement could be summed up in the phrase *vox populi vox dei*. Since I shall not discuss it later, I should observe here that this theory is also found in Daniel (2:37), who addresses the king: "You, O king, the king of kings – to whom the God of heaven has given the kingdom, the power, the might, and the glory". This is not to exclude the possibility of kings obstructing the divine will, but when they do so, the remedy lies with the deity and not in any human action. All the religious believer can do is suffer and wait for the miracle to happen.[7]

The viewpoint expressed in Col. 1:15–20 is only slightly different, but no less irenic: everything, including "thrones, dominions, rulers and powers", has been made through and for Christ. The statement excludes the possibility of any protest in the name of Christ (*ergo*, of religion) against political authority. One may interpret 1 Pet. 3:22 in the same way: all power, including political power on earth, is subjected to Christ.

Other NT texts, however, suggest that the world is not in divine control:

> For our struggle is not against enemies of blood and flesh, but against the rulers, against the authorities, against the cosmic powers of this present darkness, against the spiritual forces of evil in the heavenly places (Eph. 6:12)

The writer, however, makes no mention of political struggle: the "evil one" is to be resisted by prayer and moral steadfastness. The belief that the world is in the control, not of God but of a wicked power, is most fully expressed in Revelation. The dream of a theocratic order, of the punishment of Satan, the fall of Rome and the submission of all to the sovereignty of the Lamb is colourfully expressed in the traditional language and imagery of Jewish apocalyptic literature; but precisely because "the time is near" (Rev. 22:10) there is no question of political engagement let alone intervention on the part of the believer. Like Daniel, the role of the believer is to suffer and hope.

There are several obvious reasons for this stance. The present age was not expected to last for much longer. Human history (and thus politics) was in any case in the hands of the deity who would bring it to its predestined goal. Another reason is that to proclaim any Christian political agenda would attract the unwelcome attention of Rome and alienate those who were content with its rule, having no notion of what might be better.

But it should not be forgotten that political action in the name of religions was neither inconceivable nor impossible. The numerous Jewish uprisings against Rome, both in Palestine and elsewhere, and the major Jewish revolt against Rome of 66–73 CE, which cast a shadow over the Christian gospels, were a violent expression of religiously motivated political action, just as the resistance against the Seleucid king Antiochus IV had been in the mid-second century BCE. Belief in the divine control of history and in the imminent *eschaton* do not necessarily prevent political action from religious motives. I am not suggesting that Christians did not engage in political resistance; only that the New Testament itself does not provide any basis for such activity and actually forbids it.

## Hebrew Bible/Old Testament

Here the picture is more complex. If the New Testament articulates a personal and small-group religion with little or not interest in politics (for various reasons), the Hebrew Bible/Old Testament reflects an ideology of national religion. For ancient Israel and Judah, as for all ancient Near Eastern states, various deities and various kinds of religion were venerated: household, tribal, urban and royal.[8] But the canonized literature, disregarding the odd hint of a different state of affairs, presents fairly uniformly the religion of "Israel" as exclusively that of one deity. He appears in various guises and with various names: Yhwh, El, Elohim, Elyon (plus various epithets) and with features that match various well-known types: war god, weather god, ancestral god, city god, sky god, sun god, and high god.[9] But the governing profile combines the features of a national god with those of a universal high god: the god of all, but also of Israel.[10] In a large portion of the scriptures, "Israel" in whatever form – as kingdom, as province, as temple-community, as *ethnos* – exists as the people of this one god. There can be no question of secularism in these writings. A communal indifference to religion and the absence of religion from public affairs is inconceivable to the Deuteronomistic literature. This was also the common view of ancient societies. In practice, Athenian democracy came closest to secularism, and it might be argued that what we would now call "civic religion" better characterizes its public cults. But Athenians accepted that the gods did, or might, intervene in history and that they should be consulted in certain matters of public policy.[11]

In view of the almost universal cultural belief in the necessity of divine consultation over almost everything, it is perhaps surprising (at least to the non-specialist) to be confronted with the notion that the Bible does not universally subscribe to the notion that Israel is the "people of God" (as theologians still like to express it).[12] But here it also reflects a wider (sub-)cultural phenomenon: the professional politicians. The clash between this view and the prevailing one was the topic of William McKane's 1965 monograph *Prophets and Wise Men*, which examined the role of wisdom in statecraft. In 1965 it was still uncommon for biblical scholars to make no distinction between "Old Testament" and "ancient Israel", and this book follows that convention. But in this case the distinction is not important; we are dealing with biblical ideas, not ancient history.

McKane's[13] starting point is 2 Sam. 16:23:

> And the advice of Ahithophel which he gave in those days was as if one should ask concerning the word of God. Thus was all the advice which Ahithophel gave both to David and Absalom.

He is concerned especially with the distinction between עצה and דבר, as referring respectively to "wisdom" and "prophecy". McKane is here referring to what he calls "old wisdom", which he distinguishes from "new wisdom" in being empirical and rational rather than subordinating all such human knowledge and activity to Torah piety.[14] In McKane's[15] view, this old wisdom "has no commitment to ethical values". (I shall later challenge this opinion). By so characterizing it, however, McKane[16] wishes to compare it with the shrewd calculation that characterizes statecraft: he also calls it "hard-headed". He identifies the practitioners of this craft with "scribes" (סופרים), "counsellors" (יועצים) and "wise" (חכמים). Having analyzed the terminology of these ancient Near Eastern wisdom practitioners, he concludes as follows: Their ideals are thus intellectual honesty, rigour and probity and they are convinced that it is such a disciplined empiricism which qualifies a man to administer and govern a state.

This intellectual reserve of the Israelite *sôpᵉrîm* or *hakmîm* and the absence of ethical commitment which we have noticed in the vocabulary of old wisdom do not indicate that these men were necessarily hostile to religious belief and morality, but only that they were persuaded that the world in which they had to operate and take decisions was not amenable to the assumptions of religious belief.[17]

Von Rad had assessed this kind of wisdom in similar terms, but concluded that עצה was not understood to contradict the דבר of Yhwh; on the contrary, he asserted that "the starting point of this education is knowledge of God"[18] McKane,[19] on the other hand, suggests that conflict could arise between the claims of each kind of knowledge. Indeed, the "wise" counsellors

> thought it right to challenge the encroachment of religious authority on their sphere of responsibility, for they argued that they had to reckon realistically with political existence and to deal faithfully with the world as it was and not as it ought to be.

This is actually a rather bold assertion for a biblical scholar: to imply that the "word of Yhwh" does not correspond to the "world as it was"! If he is

correct, however, the biblical wisdom tradition – or rather, a particular
strand of it – maintains a strongly secularist position. McKane's
disagreement with von Rad stems partly from his understanding of the
sphere of activity of these "wise men"; in his view theirs is a wisdom of
statecraft not just (or even mainly) of everyday ethics. He does not deny
(see below) that the biblical wisdom tradition became strongly influenced
by piety but regards this as a later development. We may indeed reasonably
deduce that with the disappearance of independent statehood in Israel
and Judah the tradition of political counsel did attach itself rather to the
temple which represented the only sphere in which such influence could
be exercised. This is the explanation also adopted by Blenkinsopp,[20] who
writes regarding this original ("old") form of wisdom:

> There was nothing particularly religious about it, and so it is not surprising
> that the political pragmatism and rationality of officials trained in this way
> inevitably came into conflict with the claims and demands of those prophets
> who, like Isaiah and Jeremiah, were deeply involved in the political affairs of
> the nation.

As McKane[21] argues, such conflict seems to be acknowledged in the narrative
itself. He points in particular to 2 Sam. 17:14:

> Absalom and all the men of Israel said, "The advice of Hushai the Archite is
> better than Ahithophel's". For Yhwh had commanded (צוה) to defeat the good
> counsel of Ahithophel, so that Yhwh might bring ruin on Absalom.

But as he also points out,[22] the "command" does not eventuate in any
miraculous action, but in what he calls a "lack of intellectual discrimination"
on the part of Absalom's entourage. The reader is supposed to accept that
the advice of Ahithophel was good and that its rejection was a mistake; the
consequences themselves bear this out.

Other passages cited by McKane in which עצה and דבר are apparently
opposed are 2 Sam. 14:17, 20 and 19: 28 [EV 27], where David's judgment
is said to be "as an angel/messenger of god" – in other words, as good as a
divine oracle. There is, then, in his view, a clear conflict expressed in the
text between the two modes of political advice, what I would characterize
as the secularist and the theocractic.

The remainder of McKane's book is a demonstration of how this
empirical, rational wisdom came under attack by those for whom the "word
of Yhwh" was to be paramount in politics as everything else. In the books of
Isaiah, Jeremiah and Ezekiel: the "wise" are attacked for their false
knowledge, and Yhwh is presented as the only true "counsellor". The political
advice offered by both Isaiah and Jeremiah to their monarchs defies the

rationality of conventional statecraft and thus represents the victory of one kind of knowledge over another – at least within this section of the biblical canon, the Latter Prophets.

What attracts me to McKane's treatment is that he does not – as biblical theologians generally tend to do – either try to minimize the conflict between these two ways of political decision-making nor to come to terms with one as against the other. He concludes[23] simply that

> For myself I do not see how the statesman can concede the prophetic demand and continue to be a statesman. If he were to conduct the business of a state on the assumption that the *locus* of power is outside historical existence and is concentrated in God, this would amount to an abdication from political power and responsibility.

By contrast, he writes:

> The prophet believes that faith or confidence has a creative potential and can transform a situation. If we had faith in God and loved our neighbour and were prepared to take the absolute risk for the sake of Christ, the world would cease to be an armed camp.[24]

This second comment needs some updating from forty years ago. There are modern "prophets" who believe that if politicians adhered to the commandments of God as written in the Bible, the woes of the world would vanish, with or without the intervention of a Second Coming. These represent an extreme version of the view that what one takes to be the will of God (be he Yhwh, Allah or whomever) should be obeyed in matters of politics regardless of the usual forms of calculation. In many cases, nevertheless, the secularist observer may entertain the suspicion that religious motivation is a convenient cloak for non-religious calculation. But this generally applies to the statements and actions of politicians themselves and not to others. Moreover, while the principle occasionally extends to foreign politics, it is more often felt in domestic and social issues such as abortion, capital punishment, the rights of homosexuals and women.

The view that these issues should be determined by the word of God as believed to reside in scripture will nearly always claim the Bible itself for support. Indeed, even if an alternative viewpoint can be detected, McKane's treatment may further the impression that, after all, within the Old Testament/Hebrew Bible canon it was דבר that triumphed over עצה, even though McKane himself does not sympathize with that view. His own conclusions show that for him the canon presents both views, and that they are irreconcilable. The Bible, if we like to put it this way, agrees that theocracy and secularism are incompatible. But the Old Testament/Hebrew Bible doesn't univocally support theocracy while, I have argued, the New Testament supports secularism.

There is just one respect in which I want to disagree with McKane (and Blenkinsopp): their characterization of עצה as being unconcerned with ethics. In such an evaluation I detect a prejudice (whether or not intentional) of a kind I myself encountered during a semester's teaching in the USA fifteen years ago. I was confronted by a polite but puzzled student, who, on discovering that her "Bible professor" was not a religious believer, wondered not just what I was doing teaching the subject but where I got my moral system from. The latter part of her question had never occurred to me before, but some years later, in conversation with Tony Benn, the left-wing British MP, he told me what he has repeated many times in public: that whether or not religion was true, it undeniably contained great moral teaching without which we would be lost. (Had he not been a politician, I might have been able to conduct a fruitful argument with him.)

Such an opinion is, I suspect, widespread and undergirds the frequent claim that in matters of ethics religious leaders have a right to be consulted, presumably as "specialists", as if they or their leaders had some special knowledge or insight in this matter (there is no evidence that all religious leaders personally stand out as exemplars of morality). Clearly, the view is quite widely held that morals derive from religion, and hence, at least in those where ethical questions are concerned, a religious input is desirable.

This is both a wrong and a pernicious view. The three "Abrahamic" religions that still dominate Western societies all derive their distinctive ethical beliefs from scripture. Their ethical argumentation therefore has to be exegetical: if one departs from that, the conclusions cannot be sustained as divine in origin. But biblical (like Quranic) ethics is not based on a set of principles but on an authoritative divine declaration that such and such is the case. There is no moral *reasoning* in these writings. What is right is right because the deity says so. This formulation will cause a shudder to many theologians for its crudity: but sometimes crudity is the only way to make the point clearly. Religions do not offer ethical *systems*.

But part of the Bible forms an exception, and it is that part that I am calling "secularist". The book of Proverbs is mostly what McKane calls "old wisdom". It argues (in its own way) that the created order has a moral system built into it.[25] That system is not given but deduced. The deity who is credited with it is a creator deity, but has no special dealings with Israel and has given no special revelations. What is good and profitable must be learned (wisdom is to be *sought*): and because God created the world, what works is what he intended to work when it was created (It is a kind of Cartesian universe.) It is a pragmatic theological argument, but one in which it would not be easy to dispense with God, since the existence of one god is the guarantee of order and justice on which any plausible ethical system depends. But it does not entail communication with or from this god who is, of course, a universal deity to whose system Israelites are no more or less subject than anyone else. The view that God does not subsequently intervene in the world (and might even have died on the eighth day) has an echo in Qoheleth, though this writer does not offer any comparable system of morality. As I pointed out earlier, the secularist may or may not believe in god(s): the issue is their role in society or in the state. On this issue Proverbs offers a fully secularist system.

This is not the place to explain in detail this system, which is not always completely consistent and has a strong element of class interest about it (it is the rich who are blessed rather than the poor). But the spine of this system is the doctrine of retribution. Retribution is also its weakness. The lack of belief in an afterlife might otherwise have made the system potentially virtuous: good done because it is good. But this could not be accomplished, because in order for a deed to be shown to be good it must, according to the system in Proverbs, be shown to deliver benefit. Hence it must in some ultimate sense be utilitarian. Hard work leads to wealth, justice and honesty enhance reputation. It is therefore morally bad to be poor – but it is also morally bad to take advantage of the poor. On the other hand, to help the poor can bring credit to the helper (generosity = prestige). That it brings benefit to the poor is incidental, for the poor should cease to be poor not through charity but through hard work.[26]

But retribution is also the weakness of the system. It is demonstrably the case, as other biblical writers point out, that retribution does not in fact occur regularly enough to validate the theory, even allowing for cognitive dissonance. Yet, in principle individual retribution, which old wisdom endorses, is fairer than some of the biblical alternatives, such as punishing cities for the crimes of some of the inhabitants, nations for the crimes of kings and children for the crimes of their parents.

My point is that this is a moral *system*, not simply a set of commands. It is also closer to a modern secularist one than to a religious one, for although it maintains belief in a creator, it does not entail any consultation of this deity's will in the conduct of life. It is the ethics of the "wise" that McKane described. It is rational and empirical. What is good is what is seen to work. What works must be found out and will not be revealed from above. If it does not offer much discussion about the nature of the good, about means and ends, about motivation and knowledge, it is still as near as we get to ethical discourse in the Bible.

A final remark about religion. "Religion" is often used in popular discourse to mean belief in God, and this belief in turn is often narrowed down to divine creation of the world. But neither of these is a religious question. The creation of the world is a metaphysical problem that should be solved, if at all, by examining the history of the universe. The hypothesis that there was an ultimate cause, a Prime Mover or Intelligent (or even Stupid) Designer still does not in any case provide grounds for religious belief or activity. Ethics is not a religious question, either, but a philosophical problem. Religion – as we understand it in the West – is the belief that relations should be established with superhuman powers; that these can exercise a control over human affairs which can be negotiated by human response. In the case of the "Abrahamic" religions, that negotiation also includes the communication to humans by the deity in a definitive written form. Insofar as this belief encompasses individual negotiation or consensual group behaviour, it should neither be approved nor disapproved. Whether this form of activity should be extended to human politics is what divides secularism from theocracy. The view that it has no place in public life except as the expression of an individual opinion or as a lobby group, is not a modern invention; it does not even begin with the Greeks. It's in the Bible.

## Endnotes

\*   Philip Davies is Emeritus Professor in Biblical Studies at the University of Sheffield, UK.

1.  *The Shorter Oxford English Dictionary on Historical Principles* (1973). Prepared by William Little, H.W. Fowler and Jessie Coulson. Revised and edited by C.T. Onions, Volume 2. (Oxford: Clarendon Press, 1973, 3rd edn [1926]).

2.  See *The Chambers Dictionary* (Edinburgh: Chambers Harrap, 2003), p. 1371.

3.  See the website http://www.diplomatie.gouv.fr/label_france/DUDH/english/glossaire.html.

4.  Yvonne Sherwood, "Bush's Bible as a Liberal Bible (Strange Though that Might Seem)", *Postscripts* 2.1 (2006), pp. 47–58.

5.  Barack Obama, *The Audacity of Hope* (New York: Crown, 2006).

6.  See Jeffrey Stout, *Democracy and Tradition* (Princeton, NJ: Princeton University Press, 2003); Barack Obama, "The Spirit of Democracy and the Rhetoric of Excess". *Journal of Religious Ethics* 35 (2007), pp. 3–21.

7.  For divine punishment, see Dan. 4:25.

8.  Cf. R. Albertz, *A History of Israelite Religion in the Old Testament Period* (London: SCM Press, 1994). Albertz distinguishes especially domestic and civil;

and Zevit (see Z. Zevit, *The Religions of Ancient Israel: a Synthesis of Paratactic Approaches,* London: Continuum, 2001), who surveys a broader range.

9. For a useful description see J. Day, *Yahweh and the Gods and Goddesses of Canaan* (Sheffield: Sheffield Academic Press, 2002).

10. See for e.g. D.V. Edelman (ed.), *The Triumph of Elohim: from Yahwisms to Judaisms* (Kampen: Kok Pharos, 1995).

11. On Greek religion generally, see Walter Burkert, *Greek Religion: Archaic and Classical* (Oxford: Oxford University Press, 1985; German original *Griechische Religion der archaischen und klassischen Epoche,* Stuttgart: Kohlhammer, 1977). On "polis religion" as exemplified in Athens, see Walter Burkert, "Athenian Cults and Festivals", in *The Cambridge Ancient History: The Fifth Century B.C.,* (Cambridge: Cambridge University Press, 1992, 2nd edn), pp. 256–62.

12. The phrase itself occurs only four times in the Bible: Judg. 20:2; 2 Sam. 14:13; Heb. 4:9, 11:25.

13. William McKane, *Prophets and Wise Men* (London: SCM Press, 1965), p. 13.

14. See William McKane, *Proverbs: A New Approach* (London: SCM Press, 1979).

15. See McKane, *Proverbs: A New Approach,* p. 15.

16. McKane, *Proverbs: A New Approach,* p. 16.

17. McKane, *Proverbs: A New Approach,* pp. 46–47.

18. See G. von Rad, *Old Testament Theology. Vol. 1.* (London: SCM Press, 1962), p. 433.

19. McKane, *Proverbs: A New Approach,* p. 47.

20. Joseph Blenkinsopp, *Wisdom and Law in the Old Testament: The Ordering of Life in Israel and Early Judaism* (Oxford: Oxford University Press, 1995), p. 16.

21. McKane, *Proverbs: A New Approach,* pp. 55–62.

22. McKane, *Proverbs: A New Approach,* p. 58.

23. McKane, *Proverbs: A New Approach,* p. 130.

24. McKane, *Proverbs: A New Approach,* p. 129.

25. This is the meaning of the claim that the world was created through Wisdom: Prov. 8:22–31.

26. To be fair to Proverbs, the writers had a limited understanding of the laws of economics, and could probably not understand (though they would not have wanted to understand) that distribution of wealth was a structural and not a moral matter. The poor were either poor through indolence or because God made them so (this is also the New Testament view, as far as I can see). Even that great champion of social justice, Amos, has nothing to offer the poor but the punishment of the rich.

# Index of Biblical References

# INDEX OF SUBJECTS

Breinigsville, PA USA
20 November 2010
249680BV00004B/10/P